DIVINE DISCLOSURE

DIVINE DISCLOSURE

*Meditations on Godly Matters
or
Licorice from the Box of God*

ROBERT PAUL ROTH

Resource *Publications*
An imprint of *Wipf and Stock Publishers*
199 West 8th Avenue • Eugene OR 97401

DIVINE DISCLOSURE
Meditations on Godly Matters or Licorice from the Box of God

Copyright ©2006 Robert Paul Roth. All rights reserved. Except for brief quotations in critical publications or reviews, no part of this book may be reproduced in any manner without prior written permission from the publisher. Write: Permissions, Wipf & Stock, 199 W. 8th Avenue, Eugene, OR 97401.

Resource Publications
an imprint of Wipf & Stock Publishers

ISBN: 1-59752-831-5

Cataloging-in-Publication Data:

Roth, Robert Paul
    Divine disclosure: meditations on godly matters or licorice from the box of God / Robert Paul Roth.

x + 242 p.; 23 cm.

ISBN: 1-59752-831-5

BV4501.3 R65 2006

Manufactured in the U.S.A

*So hallowed is the place,
so graced the time*

CONTENTS

Foreword / ix

1. Sounds and Silence, Colors, Touch, Taste, and Fragrance / 1
    Genesis 1:1—2:3; Psalm 8; Psalm 14 / 3
    Creation / 9
    Revelation / 13
    *Revelation through Points of Contact
            and Contrast In Nature and History / 24*
    Freedom, Time, and Change / 30

2. The Sinking Sadness of Death / 35
    Genesis 3:1-24; Matthew 26:14-29; Revelation 12:1-9 / 37
    The Fall / 43
    Death / 49

3. Power and Pain / 53
    Psalm 51; Romans 7;15-25; Romans 5:1-20 / 55
    Sacraments / 61
    Confession and Absolution / 65

4. Time For, Place Where / 73
    Isaiah 9:2-7; Isaiah 53:1-12; Luke 2:1-20 / 75
    Prophecy / 80
    Apocalypse / 86
    Birth and Baptism / 90
    The Real Presence in Baptism / 92

5. And Gladly Wolde He Lerne, and Gladly Teche / 99
    Matthew 5:3-10; Luke 7:36-50; Luke 10:25-37;
            Luke 11:1-4; John 9:1-39 / 101
    Teaching—the Didache / 108
    Parables / 112
    Miracles / 116

6 Paradox and Contradiction / 121
>Mark 15:33-38; Mark 16:1—8; 1 Corinthians 15:35-58 / 123
>Crucifixion / 128
>Resurrection / 132

7 A Water Droplet Yearning / 139
>Isaiah 40:1-8; Psalm 46; Psalm 130; Matthew 11:28-30; Luke 12:22-34; John 3:1-8; Acts 2:1-36 / 141
>The Confirming Fruit of the Holy Spirit / 150
>Spiritual Comfort in Healing and Counseling / 156
>Art as the Revelation of the Holy Spirit / 165

8 Two Loves / 177
>Song of Songs 2:3-13; 1 Corinthians 13; Ephesians 5:8-33 / 179
>Love and Marriage / 183

9 God Calling Yet / 195
>Psalm 23; Isaiah 6:1-10; Amos 5:4-15; Matthew 16:13-19; Mark 1:1-14; John 17:1-26; Romans 12:1-8 / 197
>Vocation / 206

10 Ad Futurum et Mysterium / 217
>Daniel 7:1-14; John 6:28-40; Revelation 7:9-17 / 219
>The Real Presence in Holy Communion / 224
>Eucharist and Eschaton / 232
>Revelation and Eschatology / 235
>A Eucharistic Prayer / 239

Foreword

THESE ESSAYS are about revelation. They weave together the warp of God's creation and the woof of our redemption. God gives us a seamless garment woven with the continuing thread of his boundless grace.

Here are Scripture and meditations to provoke thought and give shape to faith. These words have the ambience of nature and the ambiguity of humankind. The caption on the dedication page, an expanded verse from Shakespeare's *Tragedy of Hamlet*, says that the celebration of creation is without constraint. But this is only because of the Creator. And he is different from what he has made. Also there is an adversary. Subtle but profound recognition of the devastation done by the demonic penetrates every phrase. The goodness of places and times has been shattered. We are surprised by an awareness of the shameful pain that comes from defiance. The story of reality has both protagonist and antagonist.

Something of God's glory is his difference. Our refusal to recognize the difference, whether through religious mysticism, philosophical monism, or arrogant moralism, is the sin that produces death. Yet into this condition of rebellion and victimization comes laughing renewal. In the midst of ambience and ambiguity flow mystifying certainty and the thrusting holiness of grace.

Movement from primeval silence and primordial dread brings screams of agony and whispers of anguish. Then after expulsion and mortal separation come reprieve and faith through forgiveness. With no return to innocence we advance to repentance and new birth and the challenge of service and sacrifice. Hope in the future world is secured by the singing, sacramental mystery of liturgy. The saga of the race is the story of every child, woman, and man. We are each and all children of grace, receivers of the resurrection splendor of Christ.

The rhythm of Scripture and essays sounds the beat of creation, life, fall, death, repentance, redemption, birth, love, fruit of the Spirit, and eschaton. Interlaced contrapuntally are the sacramental themes of confession, baptism, confirmation, healing, marriage, vocation, and eucharist.

The essays presuppose that reality is a story. Both nature and history, two components of reality, are narrative. This is not to say that reality is ultimately illusory as stories are fictional. Hindus say this when they speak of the nature of the universe as *maya*, illusion. The concept of *maya* precludes the notion of story because in it there is no room for freedom, time, or change. Philosophers also eschew story. They find reality to be abstract. Story is particular, the way we experience it. Philosophical abstractions, whether monistic, dualistic, or pluralistic, fail to convey reality as it is experienced. Plato's ideal form, Aristotle's substance, Leibniz's monad, Descartes' matter and mind, Hume's impression, Whitehead's experient occasion are all analogues intended to be irreducible and universally applicable, but they do not say anything about the mysteries of conflict and compassion in the story of reality. Whitehead alone comes close when he speaks of ideas as adventures and of occasions as experienced, but he has no notion of plot with climax and conclusion.

Story, unlike both philosophical and scientific endeavors, does not try to find a single, simple formula to explain everything. It does not do so because there is no such thing. Attempts to do so destroy reality in order to explain it. The truth is that reality is multifarious; it contains many realms, some empirical and some not, some historical and some not. Moreover, there is a conflict that runs through all reality which is conquered through suffering. Thus the nature of reality is dramatic.

Story is not an elemental analogue. It has component parts like scientific models, but scientific models are limited to spheres of observation without claim to be universal. Atomic structure, to be sure, is applied to all observed matter, but it says nothing about the shape and destinies of families and cultures. The human DNA may determine nature but does not include nurture. Story, on the other hand, can speak about the behavior of DNA molecules as they reach their climax as well as the conflict between Christ and Satan. Nature, history, heaven, and hell can all be conceived in terms of a dramatic struggle for reconciliation.

Some Scripture passages are my own translation and versification. For both I am indebted to *The Modern Phrased Version of the King James text of the Washburn College Bible*, published by the Easton Press, and to the *New International Version of the Bible*, for which I was a translator and editor. The text of Scripture tells the story of our life with God and his creatures with beauty and holiness. Perhaps the words will teach; at least they may provoke strange and wonderful thoughts and actions, for they are meant to be not fences that circumscribe but windows that open to new vistas. If these essays preach it is because they are art which tells through sounds and silence, colors, touch, taste, and fragrance the wonders of the story of creation and redemption.

The Lake House of the Golden Dragon, Easter 2006

1

Sounds and Silence, Colors, Touch, Taste, and Fragrance

Genesis 1:1—2:3

*In the beginning
God created
the heavens and the earth.
The earth was without form
and empty.
Darkness was on the face of the deep,
and the Spirit of God
hovered over the waters.*

*And God said,
"Let there be light!"
And there was light.
God saw the light, that it was good.
And God divided the light from the darkness.
God called the light Day,
and the darkness he called Night.*

*Evening came, and morning.
It was the first day.*

*And God said,
"Let there be an expansive space
between the waters
to separate water from water."
So God made space
and separated the water under the space
from the water above it.
And it was so.
God called the space Sky.*

*Evening came, and morning.
It was the second day.*

*And God said,
"Let the waters under the sky
be gathered to one place,
and let dry ground appear."*

*And it was so.
God called the dry ground Land,
and the gathered waters he called Seas.
God saw that it was good.
Then God said,
"Let the land bring forth vegetation:
seed-bearing plants and trees
that bear fruit with seed in it
according to their various kinds."
And it was so.
The land produced vegetation:
plants bearing seed
according to their kinds
and trees bearing fruit with seed in it
according to their kinds.
And God saw that it was good.*

*Evening came, and morning.
It was the third day.*

*And God said,
"Let there be lights
in the expanse of the sky
to divide the day from the night,
and let them be signs
to mark seasons and days and years.
And let them be lights in the sky
to brighten the earth."
And it was so.
God made two great lights—
the greater light to rule the day
and the lesser light to rule the night.
He also made the stars.
God set them in the space of the sky
to give light on earth,
to rule over day and night,
and to separate light from darkness.
And God saw that it was good.*

*Evening came, and morning.
It was the fourth day.*

And God said,
"Let the waters teem with living creatures,
and let birds fly above the earth
across the expanse of the sky."
So God created the great whales of the sea
and everything that lives and moves in the water
according to their kinds,
and every winged bird
according to its kind.
And God saw that it was good.
God blessed them and said,
"Be fruitful and multiply
and fill the water in the seas,
and let the birds increase on the earth."

Evening came, and morning.
It was the fifth day.

And God said,
"Let the land produce living creatures
according to their kinds:
livestock and creeping things and wild beasts
each according to its kind."
And it was so.
God made the wild beasts
according to their kinds,
the livestock according to their kinds,
and all the creatures that creep on the earth
according to their kinds.
And God saw that it was good.

Then God said
"Let us make earthlings—
people in our image,
after our own likeness.
And let them have a royal responsibility
for the fish of the sea
and the birds of the air,
for the wild beasts
and for the creeping things on the land."
So God created people in his own image,

in his likeness he created them.
And he created them male and female.
God blessed them and said to them,
"Be fruitful and multiply;
fill the earth and reign over it.
Care for the fish of the sea
and the birds of the air,
and for every living creature
that moves on the earth."
Then God said,
"I give you every seed-bearing plant
on the face of the whole earth,
and every tree that has fruit
with seed in it.
They will be yours for food.
And to all the beasts of the earth
and all the birds of the air
and all creatures that move on the ground—
everything that has the breath of life in it—
I give every green plant for food."
And it was so.
God saw all that he had made,
and it was very good.

Evening came, and morning.
It was the sixth day.

Thus the heavens were finished
in all their vast array.
On the seventh day
God had completed
the work he had been doing.
On the seventh day he rested from all his work.
And God blessed the seventh day
and made it holy
because on it he rested
from all the work of creating
that he had done.

Sounds and Silence, Colors, Touch, Taste, and Fragrance

Psalm 8

O Lord, our Lord,
how majestic is your name in all the earth!

You have set your glory
   above the heavens.
From the lips of children and infants
   you have ordained praise
because of your enemies,
   to silence the foe and the avenger.

When I consider your heavens,
   the work of your fingers,
the moon and the stars,
   which you have set in place,
What is a man and a woman
   that you are mindful of them,
and little children
   that you care for them?
You made humans a little lower than the angels
   and crowned them with glory and honor.

You made them rulers over the works of your hands;
   you put everything under their feet:
all flocks and herds,
   and the beasts of the field,
the birds of the air,
   and the fish of the sea,
all that swim the paths of the seas.

O Lord, our Lord,
   how majestic is your name in all the earth!

Psalm 148

Praise the Lord.

Praise the Lord from the heavens,
   praise him in the heights above.

Divine Disclosure

Praise him, all his angels,
  praise him, all his heavenly hosts.
Praise him sun and moon,
  praise him, all you shining stars.
Praise him, you highest heavens
  and you waters above the skies.
Let them praise the name of the Lord,
  for he commanded and they were created.
He set them in place forever and ever;
  he gave a decree that will never pass away.

Praise the Lord from the earth,
  you great sea creatures and all ocean depths,
lightning and hail, snow and clouds,
  stormy winds that do his bidding,
you mountains and all hills,
  fruit trees and all cedars,
wild animals and all cattle,
  small creatures and flying birds,
kings of the earth and all nations,
  you princes and all rulers on earth,
young men and maidens,
  old men and children.

Let them praise the name of the Lord,
  for his name alone is exalted;
    his splendor is above the earth and the heavens.
He has raised up for his people a king,
  the praise of all his saints,
    of Israel, the people close to his heart.

Praise the Lord.

Creation

ALL THAT is, except God himself, is the product of his imagination. Out of his infinite aloneness God sings out. In the plangent words of Gerard Manley Hopkins, he "fathers forth." Hence reality is not one but two: God and his creatures. The world has many universes; all are different from God in that they have not emanated from his substance nor are they one with his being. They have all come happily from the sound of his divine locution.

For this reason we cannot know God by extrapolating from the creature, nor by any analogy, positive or negative. God is not man writ large. The medieval theological method of *analogia entis*, both *via eminentia* and *via negativa*, is false. The way to God is not from us to him. Neither empirical experience nor rational logic can tell us about God. They can tell us only about what we perceive and conceive but not about God. By these means we can know something about nature, even something about history, although it will always be warped and partially wrong. Not senses, reason, intuition, nor any human capacity can tell us about God, who he is, and therefore who we are. Revelation is needed. Revelation is God's mysterious speech to his creatures. Neither correspondence nor coherence are sufficient epistemologies. We know God only by revelation through faith, and not the faith that humans beget, but the faith that God gives. Neither senses nor reason, neither science nor philosophy, give us knowledge of God. Always they produce an idol. The Jews thought they knew God because they knew their father Abraham, but Jesus said, "Before Abraham was born, I am" (John 8:58). Since we are in God's image and God is not in ours we must start with God as he first speaks to us.

Notice the biblical story says God said, not God caused. The Bible says nothing about first cause, efficient cause, formal cause, material cause, or final cause. These are Aristotelian concepts, helpful more or less in understanding this world, but our relationship to God is not helped by the category of causality. God did not efficiently bring order out of chaos, nor did he hatch a primordial egg or give birth from a womb or emanate from divine substance or manufacture from raw material. Nor is the world God's body. It is his speech. God spoke his mind. He created from no thing, bringing into being that which was not before, what was not there before and what was nothing before. Hence there is both a before and an after, nothing and a thing. Evening came and morning, and God divided the waters—time and space. The metaphor is speech, not causality. If God were Cause he would be part of the process and all would be God, or in God, and freedom would be lost.

The beginning was not the big bang astrophysicists talk about. The bang was expulsion from the Garden of Eden. Because of the enormity of our sin, which is our greed to become God, God blew us out of Eden to embark on our journey through this universe with its long and arduous evolution and its ultimate decay. This universe to which we have been expelled is the belly of the whale that saves us from the tempter's power. It is the Forest of Arden where we play and sorrow for a time in preparation for our permanent home. It is Prospero's island where we are schooled and disciplined as individuals and as a race for our return to the mainland. Here the descendants of Cain build great and glorious cities in a land of exquisite beauty where the cities crumble and the beauty destroys. Rome burns by the folly of Nero and earthquakes raise the magnificent Matterhorn bringing destruction to everything within their range. From quarks to quasars we have a cosmos, not a chaos, in the vast heap of our universe; but it is doomed to decay because it was meant to be only a temporary learning place. And when the earthy whale spews us forth on the white sands of Paradise we die to this world.

The truth about original creation must be told in story form, not in the literal language of science or the abstractions of philosophy. The revealed story has many chapters about many places. "In my Father's house are many rooms," (John 14:2) and also many times. So we have Heaven and Eden, Earth, and the realm of the dead, Paradise, and the kingdom of God. We have the time of beginnings, the present age of nature and history, the coming age which began with Jesus, and the time after the Eschaton. And who knows what else has come, and will come, from the imagination of God?

We know about God and his creation not from our gathered experience in this place of exile. We are distanced from God. This is our death. But in a surprising novelty God reveals himself to us in this world, in the midst of our experience, through the trembling elements that in his merriment he makes. In all this we come to know that he is different from this world. He alone is holy, good, just, loving, almighty, all knowing, free, unlimited. He is not like any of the things we experience, but if we experience love it is because he first loved us, and if we experience justice it is because he judges the good and evil in nature and history. Nature itself knows no justice. It is only because there is God that there is wrath and mercy.

The semantics of revelation involves a death of our words, and a new birth of God's Word. The Bible speaks of God as Father, a human word, but not because he resembles any human father. God is not seminal source of anyone. He is Father because he is Father and this word and name becomes absolutely unique. The true meaning of human fatherhood is revealed to us only when we heuristically see the filial relationship of Jesus to his Father in heaven. Before Jesus came, however, Christ was the Word spoken in creation, so the Son of the Father was from the beginning.

And also from the beginning the Spirit was the giver of life breathed into the human creature. This Trinitarian God—Father, Son, and Holy Spirit—acted and suffered in creating the world with its many universes and times. The language of Father and Son does not refer literally to a seminal production. Unlike pagan gods and goddesses there is no consort to the biblical Father, no mother of the Son. At first the revelation does not speak of Son, but only of speech, the Word spoken. Later when the Son becomes incarnate the metaphor of Son is used, and it is recognized that the Son was eternal, "begotten, not made, being of one substance with the Father." Although the theological construction of Trinitarian doctrine was not formulated until after the coming of Jesus, it is important to recognize that the revelation was already in place at creation.

God saw that what he had created was very good. It all fit together with a beauty and purpose for everything, "the greater light to rule the day and the lesser light to rule the night." We can see the necessity of interconnectedness without revelation and our awareness may motivate care for the creature, but we do not really know it as creature unless we acknowledge the Creator. Without God all is nature. Indeed in our fear and loneliness, as beings who are both part and product of nature and apart from and rulers of nature, we invariably have made gods out of the forces of nature and "exchanged the truth of God for a lie, and worshipped and served created things rather than the Creator" (Romans 1:25). God is not one with nature, not Primordial Nature nor Consequent Nature, as Whitehead would have it. God is Creator and nature is his creature. The awesomeness we feel before the forces of nature is nothing compared to the awesomeness of God.

Two things more must be said about creation. God created us in his image and God created us male and female. These are not the same thing. Many creatures are male and female but not images of God. Only human beings have that image, and so we have both the glory and the awesomeness of God in us. The God who is imaged in us is Trinitarian. We have that too. As Father he is unique; there are no other gods like him. As Son he is the Word who communicates with intelligence and thereby makes possible community. As Holy Spirit he is free and therefore full of creative novelty, surprise, humor, and mystery. As creatures in God's image we share all these wonders. Because we are unique and free we are not a mirror image or echo, however, but we are responsible for our own lines as we take up the roles God has given us in the holy play he has written for us. Because God speaks to us we can speak and therefore enter into loving relationships. Because we are free we become clods and clones only when we choose. We act not on instinct but by learning through experience. So great is this image that although we were made a little lower than the angels (Psalm 8:5) we are destined also to judge them (1 Corinthians 6:3).

And because God is unique he made us male and female. It is a wonderful paradox that one cannot be unique alone. One must be unique in relationship. God made multitudinous creatures because his uniqueness finds its glory in the midst of variety. Woe to anyone who is the cause of the extinction of any of God's beloved creatures. God made for himself and for us companions in the birds and beasts but they did not have God's image and so they did not suffice. God then took from Adam's rib and made woman, who was both flesh of Adam's flesh and unique in God's image. We are male and female not because God is male and female, for indeed he is neither, but because being unique we must have others with whom we can be united in a loving relationship which also has its uniqueness.

The paradox of being both unique and in God's image makes it possible for us to be both subjects and objects. It is this paradox that beautifully generates males and females not only to establish families but to produce societies which have economies, governments, and cultures. These orders are an advance over nature and they share in the awesome blessings of God's heavenly kingdom, but because of sin they invariably become perverted when we damage our uniqueness by confusing subjects and objects. There is a difference between subjects and objects and we must relate to them differently. To love an object as a subject may lead to idolatry; yet not to respect an object is not love but lust and selfish exploitation. We know many things objectively through our senses and through the ideas we formulate in our minds, but the subject who sees and thinks knows oneself neither by seeing nor thinking. This awareness of self comes by making decisions subjectively about values, meanings, feelings, existence.

Now the real question arises whether this subjective existence with its encounter and connection with the objective realities of nature is all there is. Are we alone with the dust of the earth, or is there Another who is not of this world?

Revelation is the ontological shock that tells us we are not alone. The encounter with the One who is both transcendent to and immanent in this world gives us an understanding of ourselves as creatures of a Creator. We are not caught in causal connections; we are freely created to speak our lines subjectively on the stage of a divine destiny. Creation cannot be translated into the "category" of causality, because causality is not a universal category. It is only a helpful but limited tool in the selective method of scientific investigation. That objectivity is good but it is not everything. There is much more to reality than what science describes and measures. "There are more things in heaven and earth, Horatio, than are dreamt of in your philosophy" (*Hamlet*, Act I, scene 5, line 166). This more brings us our subjectivity and God. And who is God? He is the author of our being, the one who speaks and acts to make us who we are and to give us our tomorrow in the cosmic story of times and places over which he is Lord.

The revelation story tells us of the fall of Adam and also of the fall of Judas. The fall of Adam is the story of Adam's rejection of God as creator. The fall of Judas is the story of Judas' rejection of God as redeemer. We all share in both falls. We defiantly try to live without God's care and welfare for us, choosing to rely on our own creativity and thus abusing the progress we make with an idolatrous obsession with technology and human productivity. This is evident in both political and economic exploitation in which we use the earth and its bounty as if it were an object of our possession rather than a gift for our stewardship. If the earth is a temporary learning place where we are being prepared for heaven we had better not show contempt for our teacher by trashing our school.

The story of Jesus reveals the complicity of all human beings in the rejection of our redemption. The historical account tells of the Sanhedrin, Pilate, the disciples, Judas, Jews, and Romans all participating in the scandal of Jesus' crucifixion. Just as we arrogantly want to make our own world, so we defiantly want to save our own souls. God's grace is abhorrent to us. It robs us of our independence, and so we choose to be alone, death; rather than receive communion with Christ, life.

Revelation

God is not everything. There is something that comes from his divine speech that is not God. The awesome wonder of reality is the "thereness" of both God and what he has made. What God has made does not reveal God to us, but God is revealed to us in what he has made. We do not come to know God from the creature; we can know something about the creature from the creature, but not God. Yet God does make himself known through the creature; and he makes himself known both as creator and redeemer, as creator through all the things we know as the stuff of the universe, and as redeemer through the historic person of Jesus of Nazareth.

Religion, philosophy, and science all seek a reason, or reasons, for what we experience. Religion says God is the reason for what he has made. Philosophy says everything has an antecedent cause which stems from a First Cause. Science looks for a sufficient cause in every sequence of events but does not presume first cause. Whenever causality is invoked to provide rationality the result is determinism. The principle of sufficient reason has come to mean that for every effect there is a cause. Finding a cause and changing it makes for control of both nature and human relationships. Both science and morality are processes of manipulation. We work in laboratories to change things; we go to temples and churches to pray for changes for our betterment. We assume a chain of causation, whether it be determinism as in Western thought or karma as in Eastern thought, but we also assume the freedom to manipulate the chain according to our desires. Or we assume that God may intercept the sequence.

But at this point our thinking becomes something less than pellucid. Freedom and determinism clash. The principle of causality, to avoid infinite regression, affirms a First Cause or Prime Mover. We get caught in a deterministic progression in which God is finally the cause of everything. Now it makes no difference whether you call God Yahweh, Allah, or Brahma; all is determined by the divine will. Science really says nothing about this because science limits itself to observed facts. Even the big bang of scientific theory respects these limits since the theory is based upon calculations derived from human perceptions. We naturally ask, however, what caused the big bang, and some would happily compare it to creation from nothing as revealed in the Bible, but the scientific theory does not say the big bang was from nothing (one cannot observe nothing). It says the big bang came from compressed matter and energy miniscule in size.

But in religion we assume God to be the cause of everything and so we piously say God takes us to himself when we die. This produces resentment and anger until we submit to the power of God and lose our independent free spirits in religious devotion. Thus freedom is denied in favor of divine determinism. But Jesus taught the opposite: "You shall know the truth, and the truth shall make you free." The Christian revelation says that God is all powerful, all just, and all loving; yet he never robs us of the freedom with which we were created. As he is a free Spirit so we are free in his image. Death then is not God's doing; it is something done to him and to us. In this free world God is not the only actor, though he may be the only author. The devil's authorship is abortive, ours is ambiguous.

The patterns we perceive in nature which science describes may have unbroken lines of causality, but we cannot infer universal determinism therefrom. If God is the author of the story of reality, then he is related to what happens through his speech, which is a category of relationship different altogether from the category of causality. Speech is freely given and freely received with the possibility of various responses. And since speech necessarily involves the passage of time God can say different things at different times without contradicting himself. In time something or someone may intervene and make it necessary for God to change his text as he did, for example, with Noah after the flood or with Abraham and Isaac on the mountain in the region of Moriah.

The principle of sufficient reason says there is a cause for every effect. This could mean that there is an infinite series of causes and effects. Every cause is an effect of a previous cause. What is perceived to be a free choice, a cause perceived to be without any previous causes, is really the result of previous conditioning, either genetic or social. There is no freedom in a universe of determinism and sufficient reason. The "choice" to manipulate genes or social behavior is itself determined.

But such determinism seems to us to be absurd even though vast numbers of people in various cultures bow to what they call fate, kismet, karma, predestination. If we live, however, in a universe that has a place for freedom of choice and action, although there are limits, both small and significant, change can be made to alter the course of events without previous cause. We can prevent polio with a vaccine. We can turn our planet into ashes with a bomb. Although prayer cannot manipulate God it can result in a new relationship with God and our fellows. We can interject into the passage of natural occasions a new relationship which produces new causal connections. As we have this freedom of choice and action so God freely interjects changes in the pattern of events which he has previously set in motion. Humans have observed what we call the law of entropy which describes the cooling of energy into a static state, reducing the entire universe into cold ashes. This determinism, however, is contradicted by the interception of a source of energy which is the life force that we perceive to be at work in evolution. There may be various interceptions from the free speech of God. He spoke with wrath in the flood. When he saw what he had done he repented with a rainbow.

Shakespeare's *The Tempest* reflects the revelation that God and his creation fundamentally move in freedom in which decisions and actions are made with only a future aim. Prospero is the rightful Duke of Milan but he is bereft of his kingdom because the lords of Italy are in rebellion against him. He acts at first like the Old Testament God of the imprecatory psalms, or like the prophet Amos with scathing, unrelenting judgment. But suddenly in the last act Prospero changes, giving freedom to Caliban and Ariel, and forgiveness to Miranda and Ferdinand. It seems the change comes by the free prompting of Ariel who describes the sorry condition of the shipwrecked lords and suggests that Prospero's feeling for them would become tender if he beheld them as a human. Prospero chooses this moment to break his wand, to set free his captives, to forgive his enemies. No more will he use magic, miracle, and might to manipulate others. Now he chooses mercy, forgiveness, and the renewal of relationships. Shakespeare's play tells the story of the Bible, the story of the change that has come through the intercession of Christ who became human and thus could plead for human need. Ariel is the Christ figure in Shakespeare's drama. And Prospero is the God figure who, instead of intervening with miracles, lets the world come of age, in Bonhoeffer's phrase. But this freely given grace is costly, not only for us but also for God. There is no forgiveness without the thankful response of *worship*. The freedom we share with God in worship brings a new bondage. We are yoked with God in liberating creativity. Paradoxically God's grand design to free us will not work unless the heavens ring with the doxology of prayer. "Gentle breath of yours my sails must fill." In our worship, which is God coming to us in the grace of baptism, confession, and eucharist, God binds himself to us, and because he is free Spirit, this bondage liberates us to share in his creativity. This is what the Lutheran Confessions call sanctification, and what Eastern Orthodoxy calls theosis.

Gradually from these musings the substance and meaning of revelation should begin to come into focus. Revelation has two poles: God's speech and human hearing (Romans 10:14). Revelation is radically different from mere human knowing and perceiving, both of which are centered in the human mind. Knowing concepts are shaped by the mind from the percepts that are given in experience. This process is the product of the evolutionary development of the human brain. It may be described within the natural pattern of causal sequences. Revelation comes from God, a disclosure hidden in mystery beyond any natural pattern conceived or perceived. When the disclosure enters human consciousness it is grasped by the mind much as any concepts are comprehended, but the mystery of its origin is never solved and the original surprise is never dulled. True revelation is always unanticipated and yet after it is received it becomes evident that it has had a long history in which preparation for its deliverance was made.

Just as true knowledge must be distinguished from false knowledge and genuine perceptions must be distinguished from misperceptions, so likewise genuine revelation must be distinguished from false revelation. While revelation is always a personal matter it is never private. True revelation always comes to a shared community. Private visions occur, but they originate in human individuals and must not be confused with revelation. Visions may be edifying, some are hallucinatory and can be utterly destructive. The visions of people like Gautama, Mohammed, Joseph Smith have had great power to influence many people, and as all religious quests, they have been ambiguously good, but these visions are not to be confused with revelation.

True revelation is described by St. Paul in 1 Corinthians 11:23: "For I received from the Lord what I also passed on to you." And in 1 Corinthians 11:2: "I praise you for remembering me in everything and for holding to the traditions, just as I passed them on to you." Clearly two things characterize genuine revelation: it must come from the Lord, not from a human vision, and it must be shared in a common tradition which can provide scrutiny to distinguish its genuineness.

Revelation comes from God bringing, not the disclosure of esoteric information, but a new and unique relationship which makes possible a new view of reality, God, and oneself and the creation. Paul did not claim a special, hitherto unknown knowledge of God because of his Damascus experience. What he received from the Lord was in the context of the Christian community with its tradition of teachings rooted in the Old Testament Scriptures. Jesus was set in a living tradition that was handed from one to another. He was not simply the historical person remembered by the community but the living presence of the risen Christ who by his Spirit guided the community into all truth (John 16:13). "And the Lord worked with them and confirmed his word by the signs that accompanied it" (Mark 16:20).

The distinction between general and special revelation has been made. It certainly is unthinkable that the God who created and redeemed us all should have revealed himself to and guided one tribe of his creatures to the neglect of the rest. Rather than designating the history of Israel as the holy history of God's chosen people we should speak of the one God providing both creative and redemptive revelation to all his creatures in their various cultures through the guidance of his Holy Spirit. This guidance may be found within all the great religious quests. The remarkable thing about them all is the patience of God in dealing with the horrendous behavior of religionists throughout human history. And the glorious surprise is that in Jesus God has opened himself to us in a unique and gracious way which no other story about God has ever done.

Instead of speaking of general and special revelation we should speak of revelation that comes to us through creation, revelation that comes to us through history, and revelation that comes to us through the unique disclosure of Jesus of Nazareth. This will allow for a reception of God's grace and guidance for every tribe and nation throughout history. It will also allow for a recognition of the preparatory work in the history of Israel for the coming of Jesus. The Old Testament is thus not really "old." It is God's promise to Israel for the world fulfilled in Jesus.

We usually think of general revelation as the disclosure of God to us in nature and apart from the Word of God in Scripture, especially apart from the promise and fulfillment of that Word in Jesus Christ. But an honest appraisal of non-Christian religions will acknowledge that their devotees live by the hope of some kind of redemption through the activity of a divine power, however this is conceived. Leni Lenape American Indians, Muslims, Buddhists, African animists, and ancient Hebrews all solicit the help of God in their prayers.

Such general anticipation does not in the least discount the uniqueness of Jesus. The yearning for redemption is universal, but the deliverance God gives is totally different from what we want or expect. We think we can get our salvation by bargaining with God and earning the merit to deserve deliverance. This method of religion is universal, always contrived out of our sinful desire to get God back after we have rebelled against him, but God's revelation is always a surprise beyond human imagination. This is why we can speak of Jesus as revelation and not religion.

The promise of our redemption by God's grace is revealed alongside the religious quest in the books of both Testaments. The Bible is therefore a source of revelation but an ambiguous one. God certainly has inspired its production throughout, but since God is not a writer, and since all the words of the Bible were written by sinful human beings, the biblical record is an earthen vessel requiring interpretation that is guided by the Holy Spirit. Literalism of Scripture and the notion of inerrancy confuse the distinction between God's Word to us and our words about God. The problem, therefore is always how to know what is God's Word as distinct from merely human words.

We are tempted to separate some words from others according to an enterprise in the name of scholarship. In modern times a gargantuan effort has been made to construct what is called scientific criticism. Our contemporary obsession is historicity. We select what we perceive to be genuinely historical utterances of Jesus and separate them from later community embellishments. The original history is preferred over the later "corruptions," and it is assumed that true Christianity can be derived from attachment to the "original" Jesus.

While such "scientific" criticism has a contemporary credence among scholars, it does not allow for the work of the Holy Spirit in distinguishing between religion and revelation. How can we know when the Holy Spirit is guiding us to truth? Revelation is genuine when it is received by the believing community and is recognized by the fruits of the Spirit as they build a new, growing, living relationship with God through Jesus Christ. Historical studies may be interesting and satisfying to our curiosity, but they do not provide a basis for our faith. We do not believe the good news of grace because we know that a source of Luke's Gospel was the Gospel of Mark. We believe the good news of God's grace because we find ourselves in a community that lives by this incredible story. As Luther said, what drives Christ to the heart is the Gospel, and it is the Holy Spirit who calls, gathers, enlightens and sanctifies the Christian Church.

Just as God did not neglect his care for non-Jews in his story of salvation, so likewise God has not stopped revealing himself after the cannon has been closed. The Spirit is continually active in guiding us to truth. The Spirit helps us in every generation to interpret the Scriptures for our needs.

The history of the Church shows this edifying, healing, uniting work of the Holy Spirit in various crises that have divided the Church. Such was the case in the development of the Apostles', the Nicene, and the Athanasian creeds. When dissension arose appeal was made to the principle that truth may be ascertained when an issue is believed everywhere and always by all. If this could not be achieved a general council of the Church was called and the issues were decided by appeal to the great teachers of the Church: Irenaeus, Athanasius, Gregory of Nazianzen, and Chrysostom in the East; and Jerome, Ambrose, Augustine, and Pope Gregory the Great in the West. Where agreement was found among these teachers the Church found guidance. Of course, the process did not always succeed, but the evidence of the groaning of the Spirit is incontrovertible. And the present ecumenical movement for unity throughout Christendom fairly shouts the good news of the Spirit's healing power.

Therefore the Bible must be read in its entirety with the awareness that it is a two-edged sword. Depending on how its revelation is received it will be either edifying or a stumbling block. Thus, for example, the Bible may be read literally to endorse slavery, but we no longer interpret it that way. Paul wrote to the Corinthians saying that women should keep silent in the churches, and the author of First Timothy required women to "learn in quietness and full submission." Quite bluntly he says, "I do not permit a woman to teach or have authority over a man; she must be silent." Today many Churches ordain women, some have women bishops, and all Churches have women teachers.

The laws relating to holiness in the seventeenth through the twenty-sixth chapters of Leviticus are declared to be revelation from the Lord to Moses: "The Lord said to Moses . . ." Matters of sexual conduct, treatment of the poor, restrictions on the priesthood, dietary laws, observance of festivals, hair style and the shaping of one's beard, breeding of cattle, and the weaving of cloth are all listed as equally regulated with the authority of the Lord. But today the vast majority of Christians recognize that the Levitical code was fashioned with political concern for establishing a stable nation after the Exodus in the newly conquered land of Canaan. This law of the Old Testament is not binding on Christians, however, because the revelation of the New Testament says that "Christ redeemed us from the curse of the law" (Galatians 3:13).

The admonition: "Do not lie with a man as one lies with a woman" is followed by the judgment; "They must be put to death." Do literalists today really advocate capital punishment for homosexuals? Leviticus says: "Do not wear clothing of two kinds of material." Today we would consider the sartorial proscription not only trivial but absurd. At the time it was proscribed, however, it was probably considered necessary to protect the sheep-herding Israelites from competition with the cotton-raising Canaanites and Egyptians. Sexual practices were also guarded to preserve the identity of the Israelites against the customs of their neighbors.

The Old Testament may be read selectively to proscribe homosexuality, but a careful reading of the passages on homosexuality in the New Testament specifically forbid only those practices which are not consensual or are exploitative (1 Corinthians 6:9-10) or are perversely practiced by heterosexuals (Romans 1:26-27). Committed same-sex relations as we know them today are not dealt with in Scripture at all. Although Sodom became a by-word for sexual perversion, and indeed all manner of wickedness (Jude 7; Revelation 11:8; Deuteronomy 23:17, 32:32; Isaiah 1:9, 13:19, Lamentations 4:6), Jesus interpreted the sin of Sodom not as sexual perversion but as inhospitality (Matthew 10:15; Mark 6:11).

Obviously, as with the case of slavery, it will take time for the Church to discover the true guidance of the Holy Spirit with regard to sexual relationships and gender vocations. At present we are divided and division seems to indicate the absence of the Spirit, but again, as with slavery, our struggling may be the indication of the groaning of the Spirit as a new revelation, or a new understanding of revelation, is coming to birth. Clearly the guidance of the Holy Spirit is relevant to the conditions and context of times and places. Laws, customs, and traditions vary and change, and the changes may be good or bad, but the Christian always looks to the Holy Spirit for instruction that edifies and unites us in the body of Christ. If we have hostility now we must seek healing through the intercession of Christ.

Without the inspiring work of the Spirit and the healing work of the living Christ we are left with a dead letter in Scripture and a law that kills. What kind of God do the literalists present to us if we must read at face value passages in Scripture like Deuteronomy 21:18-21: "If a man has a stubborn and rebellious son . . . his father and mother shall take hold of him and bring him to the elders at the gate of his town . . . Then all the men of his town shall stone him to death"? If we read all of Scripture we will quickly see that "time makes ancient good uncouth." Much of Old Testament law is repudiated, certainly all of its legalism, as Jesus said: "You have heard it said of old time, but I say unto you . . ." And Paul said: "Now that faith has come, we are no longer under the supervision of the law." By law Paul meant the books of Leviticus and Deuteronomy, indeed the Torah, and this should be understood by devout Christians who constantly declare that the Bible says this or that.

It must be recognized that the Bible is an earthen vessel written by sinful human beings over a long period of changing times. Yet we also claim it has the inspiration of the Holy Spirit and it leads us to truth. How can we separate the religious quest that is warped by sin which the Bible presents from the revelation that breaks through in the story from beginning to end? If the Bible is read as narrative it is clear that God is its protagonist throughout, and this living person of the drama goes through development. In the beginning God is creator, and as the drama unfolds he becomes a destroyer in the flood, and then a warrior God in the formation of his chosen nation Israel. When his plan for the destiny of his creatures with Israel as a light to the Gentiles fails, God becomes a judging God through the exile. This too fails and finally God takes the onslaught of the Devil upon himself and redeems the world through incarnate suffering. This story is the revelation that must be distinguished from all the human interjections in the tale. It relates a character that unfolded in a drama, and we find ourselves participating in a tale that is not yet finished. Indeed, "No eye has seen, no ear has heard, no mind has conceived what God has prepared for those who love him."

It should become evident that we are distinguishing between religion and revelation. Karl Barth said that Christianity is a revelation, not a religion. Religions are human endeavors to reach God; revelation is God's attempt to reach humans. Conventional wisdom says that all religions ultimately bring us to the one God who is above all gods; they differ only in the forms and methods of approaching God. This is false and wrongheaded. All religions lead us in the end to an idol, a false god created by our sinful, human imagination. Thus we must say that Christianity is not a religion but Christendom is the religion that we have made out of God's revelation.

Furthermore it is not true that all religions equally bring us to God only in different ways. The differences are significantly great and not by any means equal. Some religions are demonstrably more destructive than others. Hinduism has produced a culture that stagnates because of the belief in *karma* and *maya*, determinism and illusion. Buddhism in practice among the masses promotes both of these debilitating doctrines but also has produced architectural and literary masterpieces that edify its devotees. Submission in Islam (the name of the religion translates as submission) has produced a culture of hierarchical tyranny both in society and in the family; but Islam has also produced the Alhambra and the Taj Mahal. By contrast the Christian revelation sets us free for service and creative transformation. We are not fatefully determined. The creation is not a deceitful illusion. God saw all that he had made and declared it to be good. Our destiny is not reincarnation but resurrection. We are free by grace, not subservient through works. The tragic reality, however, is the warping we have done with that revelation. But the Spirit does not weary with well doing, and hope springs eternal. And how else but as fruits of the Spirit can one explain the music of Bach and the glories of the great cathedrals? In the midst of our sinful religious quests the Spirit bequeaths his fruits, and we are sustained through all our tribulations.

One final comment about creation. Today a hot discussion ensues over the question of the scientific theory of evolution versus creationism and the more recent claim for intelligent design. Proponents of creationism think that the theory of evolution precludes a creator, but even Darwin affirms the reality of a creator. Scientific theory is rational explanation based on observed facts. It cannot and does not pretend to speak about a Creator, but also it does not deny the reality of a Creator. Science tries to describe the way things happen in our experience. Revelation tells us who makes events outside our control happen. There can be no conflict between these two approaches to reality.

No Christian will deny intelligent design as the major factor in the destiny of all creation. But no Christian can or should claim this design as a scientific theory in competition with evolution. God's design is not scientific theory. Indeed God's design is undoubtedly more far-reaching and dependable than any scientific theory, because all scientific theories are subject to revision and even replacement as the Ptolemaic Almagest was replaced by Copernicus. But for the present the theory of evolution, like the geological theory of tectonic migration of continents, is the best explanation of the origin of species based on the facts that we know. We can expect refinements and possibly replacements of this theory in the future. We will not get a replacement of the revelation of the incarnation, although we will see as we are seen in the Eschaton.

The scientific view of the universe in modern times has replaced ancient mythologies. It was wrong from the beginning for Christians to try to interpret the revelation of the Christian Gospel in terms of either primitive mythology or modern science. The mythological Gnosticism that was current in the early centuries of Christianity was thoroughly repudiated by Irenaeus in his five volumes *Against Heresies*. The ancient Gnostics talked about revelation too, but for them it was esoteric knowledge accessible only to the elite and it comprised a concoction of multiple subdeities including the Creator, Christ, and the Holy Spirit generated from the Archon by a defect. Today we have a revival of the Gnostic search for truth accompanied by the republication of such texts as the Nag Hammadi manuscripts, the Gospel of Thomas and the Gospel of Judas, none of which can be substantiated as genuine revelation. These mythologies became philosophies, and Origen turned the Christian revelation into Platonism, Thomas turned it into Aristotelianism, Schliermacher turned it into idealism, Paul Van Buren turned it into logical empiricism, Bultmann turned it into existentialism. And the attempt to marry the Gospel with modern science is equally abortive. The Christian revelation is not myth, philosophy, nor science. It is the story God tells us through nature and history and especially through the incarnation of Jesus about our creation and redemption and our everlasting destiny.

Revelation through Points of Contact and Contrast in Nature and History

Stories told around the world often deal with morality and religion. They provide points of contact as well as points of contrast for God's revelation. Parallels in Chinese, East Indian, Classical Greek, and Nordic folk tales are quite remarkable. In narrative form we find mythical explanations for origins, for the celebration of mystery in the supernatural, for the quest or yearning for justice in the face of oppression, and for the extolling of moral virtues such as courage, compassion, fidelity, and perseverance.

Mythopoetic stories signal the struggle of the ancient Chinese people against forces of nature, just as do the myths of Prometheus among the Greeks, Noah among the Hebrews, and Beowulf among Nordic people.

The ancient Chinese pictured the earth as a disc with the vault of heaven supported by pillars along the four borders of the earth. Trouble came when these pillars were broken. There were conflagrations in some parts and great floods in others. Wild animals played havoc with the people. Out of this chaos emerged a great heroine named Nüwa. She melted down stones of five colors to repair the vault of heaven. She cut off the legs of the great Tortoise to make new pillars to support the sky. She put out the fires, subdued the floods, and killed the wild beasts. She was the wise Word that brought order out of chaos. In another version of the story she marries her brother Fu Xi and becomes the mother of the human race.

Nüwa is an example of the personification of courage and wisdom, showing the aspiration of ancient people to control the elements of nature. It is interesting that in China, as in ancient Greece, wisdom is personified as female. In Greece Athene is the goddess of wisdom and the hearth. So likewise the Hebrews personified wisdom as the first born of all creatures with at least feminine gender in grammar, although gender in grammar has no relation to sex.

Later in Chinese mythology another disaster shook the earth, and Gonggon, the god of water and thunder, in a fit of anger broke the pillars again so that heaven tilted to the northwest and earth sank to the southeast, causing a great flood. Once more misery visited the people, but a man named Gün tried to stop the flood by stealing ground from God to block up the water with a giant dam. He failed in this and God executed him for his offense, but after his death a son was born to him from his stomach. His name was Yü. He carried on his father's task, but, learning from his father's mistake, he subdued the flood by channeling and dredging. Instead of fighting the water he directed it so that it flowed away. Yü is the personification of wisdom, perseverance, and selfless devotion. The story of this Chinese Noah is told in the *Shu Ching*, edited by Confucious. Of Yü it was said, "How great was the achievement of Yü. But for Yü we should all have been fishes." The Chinese character for Yü makes a pun with fishes.

The Hindus also teach that the gods come to earth to deliver people from evils that assail them. Their foremost holiday celebrates the victory of Krishna over his adversary Narakasura. On the festival of Diwali the homes and shops of devout Hindus are brightened by candles and oil lamps to mark the light that illuminated India when an evil darkness was dispelled.

This is the story that is told on the feast of Diwali. Many, many years ago, out of the never, never land of heroes and giants and gods and goddesses, there lived a monster called Narakasura. He came from the desert lands like a marauding tiger, seizing and devouring people and cattle alike. His appetite could not be satisfied and with increasing brutality this terrible ogre of the western desert invaded one village after another, claiming his prize and eating the victim before the eyes of the terrified villagers. Soon his debaucheries raised such a loud wail of lament that the gods on top of the Himalaya mountains were aroused from their slumber. Krishna, an avatar of Vishnu, was moved to take unto himself human form and do battle with the evil giant for the sake of the people.

Krishna was a Beowulf, a Prometheus, and a St. George all rolled into one gigantic hero. He is believed by most Hindus to be the greatest of the gods. The dimensions of this colossus may be measured by the fact that he has 16,000 wives, but when he went into the desert to do battle with Narakasura he took with him only one of his wives, the shy and demure little Satyabhama, whose eyes were full and round like the petals of a lotus blossom. With his wife he took a great scimitar and a bow with one arrow. On the desert plain, where the silence spoke loudly of death, Krishna met Narakasura; and for fourteen days and fourteen nights they fought with fire in their eyes and fury in their hearts. They kicked up so much dust with the intensity of the battle that they blotted out the light of the sun and the light of the moon.

The anger of Narakasura was like the thunder in the mountains that plays over the black monsoon clouds. With relentless cruelty he lashed at Krishna with his sword until the great god fell in a swoon on the hot sand. But Satyabhama quickly took up her husband's sword and worried the surprised giant just long enough for Krishna to regain his strength and string his bow and send an arrow straight to the heart of Narakasura.

Now since the light of the sun and the light of the moon had been blotted out, darkness filled the hearts of the people with fear; but Krishna built a great funeral pyre and the light of the flames brightened the heavens and the earth more gloriously than the sun and the moon. And to this day thankful people brighten their homes and their shops with tiny lamps to burn away the darkness and the brutality of evil.

This story seems to have similarities with the Christian Gospel which provide points of contact for dialogue: the Word becoming flesh, the divine intercession, conflict with evil, and final victory. Yet there is something different, something lacking. The Holy Spirit seems to be present like a muse inspiring the tale as far as human imagination can go, and therefore millions of people for centuries have been sustained by its comfort, but there are points of contrast which distinguish the Gospel as revelation and not human religion. Krishna is like mythical and legendary figures of the past. Myths do not explain truth; they are just lacy cobwebs that help us accept mysteries. And legends arise to embellish the exploits of ancient heroes, but they do not reveal truth either. History shows that people everywhere elevate their heroes to divinity or invent mythical heroes to enlighten their darkness. Heroes become legends and some legendary heroes become gods. Jesus was neither a myth nor a legend.

Jesus was definitely not a mythical figure since he lived in remembered and recorded history, unlike Krishna or any of the gods of world religions. He was not just an ordinary man, however, because he was the incarnation of God. Incarnation, not avatar! The mystery of his incarnation is not something one can prove by empirical evidence or the logic of right reason. It is something every Christian acknowledges by faith, and that is the gift of the Spirit. The contrast revealed in the story of Jesus is that God is loving as well as powerful, and his love is expressed by sacrificing himself. Krishna defeated his opponent with a sword and an arrow; Jesus conquered the devil with sacrificial love. If he had not willingly suffered on the cross, he would have fallen in his last temptation, the temptation for God not to be fully incarnate. If Jesus had not used suffering love he would have used evil to overcome evil, and in so doing he would have become another devil.

In spite of similarities a basic difference distinguishes Chinese, East Indian, and classical Greek stories on the one hand and Christian biblical stories on the other. Christian stories, after the expulsion from the Garden of Eden, have a historical ring. They do not personify. Instead of abstract ideas being given personal shape and narrative form, with ultimate reality resting in the abstractions, Christian revelation says that reality itself is the story of persons. The animism of Oriental and Greek myths may at first appear to be highly personal, but it is really only the contrived personification of impersonal forces of nature or abstract ideas of the mind.

Gonggong is the Chinese Poseidon or Neptune; Nüwa is Athene; Krishna is Prometheus. Such personifications are symbols that point to impersonal forces or ideas as if the personifications were mere accommodations and were basically unreal while behind them stand the invisible, unchanging realities. Platonism and Buddhism are basically one here in sharp contrast to the Christian revelation of reality as the goodness of creation by the speech of a benevolent and suffering God. Judeo-Christian revelation does not personify, does not make personal pictures out of abstractions. It deals with real persons in the form of story. A living God speaks to living creatures, and the conversation works into a drama that passes through a climax to a denouement. A real God becomes a real man who triumphs through tragedy.

Another story that is told universally is the triumph of love over death. Here again we find similarities and contrasts with Christian revelation. Two Chinese stories provide examples of the natural human quest for life beyond death: *The Tears of Lady Meng* and the medieval opera *Liang Shanbo and Zhu Yingtai*.

The story of Lady Meng is a protest against tyranny, but it has a deeper religious dimension. This is a story of love, not only the natural love between men and women but also the suffering love of grace. The time was during the reign of the wicked emperor Qin Xi Huang, the tyrant who joined the segments of the Great Wall. He was afraid that the Mongols would break into his country from the north, so he built the wall as a defense. But no sooner was one section of the wall built than another fell down. The wall made no progress. Then a wise priest said: "A wall like this, which is ten thousand *li* long, can be built only if you immure a human being in every *li* of the wall. Then each *li* will have its guardian."

It was easy for the emperor to follow this priestly advice. He regarded his subjects as so much grass and weeds, but all the people trembled. Plans were made for the great human sacrifice, but at the last minute an ingenious scholar said: "We do not need ten thousand men; we need only one man whose name is Wan, because in Chinese Wan means ten thousand." So they found a man named Wan who happened to be with his bride at their wedding feast. He was carried off, and his bride, Lady Meng, was left in tears. Dutifully she went across the mountains to the wall to get her husband's bones and give them a proper burial, but she did not know how to find them since they were inside the wall. There was nothing to be done. She sat down and wept. But her tears dissolved the mortar between the stones and the wall collapsed and gave up the bones of her husband.

News of this came to the emperor and he commanded that she be brought to him. When he saw her he was smitten by her great beauty and he determined to make her his empress. She finally consented under three conditions: that forty-nine days be set aside in the realm to honor her husband, that the emperor and all his officials come to the burial, and that a tower forty-nine feet high be built beside a river where she could make a sacrifice for her husband. Quickly the emperor agreed. When the tower was built she climbed to the top and jumped to her death. In a rage the emperor commanded his soldiers to cut her body into tiny pieces and grind her bones into powder and throw them into the river. When this was done the little pieces each became a silver fish in which the soul of the faithful Lady Meng lives forever.

This is a fascinating story. Notice how the wall kept tumbling down. The more the emperor sought national security the less he found it. This is the judgment of God in history. The more we spend to make ourselves strong and safe the more dangerous and insecure our life becomes. The emperor regarded his subjects as so much grass and weeds. Sacrifices must be made for national defense. People must expect to be trampled upon. The government cares not for them, only for its own survival. There was nothing to be done. Lady Meng wept. But tears are stronger than walls and weapons. Is it not irony that one of the greatest of human achievements is a wall designed to divide people? But tears dissolved the wall. Through suffering love came triumph. In this story we have not only the *via dolorosa* that begins with the watery tears of baptism but also the triumph of resurrection in the life of the faithful wife who lives in the fish. Moreover this is the story of Bathsheba whose husband was killed so she could become David's queen. The story has poignant, personal significance and powerful political implications, but most of all it is the story of the severity of divine love, and because it is beyond human comprehension it has intimations of revelation. But, of course, the contrast between continuing life in tiny silver fish and the resurrection of Jesus is also quite obvious.

The medieval opera *Liang Shanbo and Zhu Yingtai* is another story of the triumph of love. It is popularly called the "Butterfly Lovers." A young girl named Yingtai decided she wanted to go to school. In those dark days no females went to school. She pled with her father, who was very indulgent. She said she would dress like a boy and no one would know the difference. Finally her father relented and she was packed off to boarding school. The incongruities which followed made for hilarious humor on the Chinese stage, just as they did for Shakespeare in *As You Like It*.

Yingtai had a roommate, Shanbo, with whom she promptly fell in love, but he could not reciprocate because he thought she was a boy. She tried every ruse to attract him without revealing her secret, but, of course, to no avail. Finally she invited him to visit her "twin sister" during a holiday. When he came he discovered that his roommate was indeed a girl and naturally he fell in love with her. But tragically Yingtai's father had arranged a marriage according to custom with a rich playboy whom Yingtai despised. Shanbo was devastated and he pined away until he died of consumption. Yingtai now had no choice, but she consented to marry the playboy on the condition that she be allowed to visit her lover's grave on the way to her wedding. She was dressed in a beautiful red wedding garment and carried in a splendid sedan chair. When the procession came to the cemetery Yingtai walked to Shanbo's grave and took off her wedding dress revealing underneath a white mourning cloak. Suddenly the grave opened wide in the stage performance, and as the lights went out Yingtai jumped into the grave. Then just as suddenly the lights returned and from the closed grave two large butterflies emerged. They danced happily to joyful music as all the graves gave up their dead in the form of dancing butterflies.

The story of Yingtai tells how "love is a many-splendored thing" that "covers a multitude of sins." Parental love, romantic love, fidelity love, and finally divine love overcome legalism, the subjection of women, and at last the separation of death.

Story-telling may take form in media other than words. Music, dancing, painting, sculpture, architecture all have been used by various cultures to relate human fears and hopes and laments and aspirations. Especially powerful is the stone sculpture of the Shona people of Zimbabwe. Their carving is not imitative or representational. It is expressionist and narrative. The stones speak. They tell stories inspired by Shona traditional religion. One of the most expressive stories is about the Water Spirit. Water flows and the suggestion of movement in stone as hard as serpentine is a prodigious achievement. The Shona sculptors masterfully express deep emotion which arises from their spirituality. The Water Spirit is half human and half fish. Its face seeks air while water cascades off its back. The Water Spirit benevolently takes a victim of drowning in order to restore the victim to the community. The belief is that if the family members of the victim do not cry and grieve unduly, if they remain calm in the crisis, the Water Spirit will return the loved one after he or she has been instructed in the healing arts and prophecy. The family and the community are thus reassured in the midst of their sorrow that their loved one will return with gifts that will be a benefit to everyone. Once more, this time in stone sculpture, the human story of triumph over death is told.

There is in all human beings a recognition, however reluctant, of our complicity with the evil we suffer. Christians openly confess their sin, but even non-Christians who think of their lives as being determined by some kind of karmic fate feel remorse over what they have done to deserve that fate. Yet in the midst of these stories that tell of our adversities there is a persistent hope that somehow in the end goodness will prevail and wrongs will be righted. In addition to this hope there is the trust that goodness is stronger than evil. As I have indicated, along with these points of contact between cultures there are significant points of contrast. I am not referring to superficial differences in form. Those differences occur and they are a delight. I am referring to the contrast between all these stories of human fabrication and the story of revelation that comes from God speaking to his creatures in both creation and redemption. The human love we sing about, in both our joy and sorrow, must be contrasted with the love God gives us in his nurture of creation and in his gracious sacrifice in redemption. The evil we lament in our human experience must be contrasted with the revelation to us that we are sinners in rebellion against the God we seek. Our human hope must be contrasted with the divinely inspired hope the Spirit gives us when he intercedes on our behalf. Our quest for justice and holiness must be contrasted with the eschatological mystery that God promises through the revelation of the cross and the resurrection of Jesus. The contacts are a delight but the contrasts are totally transforming. They lift us into a new world which no human imagination has ever envisioned. Thanks be to God!

Freedom, Time, and Change

Because there is time there can be freedom. If no time, then no freedom; but all things in time are not free. We perceive the determinateness of nature and so we can predict future natural events by extrapolating from past trends. The indeterminacy in the theory of quantum mechanics, however, does not pertain to the freedom of choice and action in God and humans. The unpredictability of subatomic particles is not because of their choice. Also the predictability of statistical opinion polls is not because of the lack of choice. Although a fair sample of a great mass of people may successfully, within a margin of error, predict the outcome of an election, no one can predict how an individual will choose to vote. Free choice in God and humans entails a fresh understanding of time.

Revelation tells us that God is a free-willing and free-acting person, and humans are free-willing and free-acting persons in God's image. In time some things can be otherwise. The past is determinate and cannot be changed. The present, however, is open for a variety of possibilities, but the present is actual, not potential. It is too late for potentialities. There is an openness to possibilities but the time has come in the present to move to a realization or actualization of one possibility. The future, on the other hand, is not actual; it is only potential. It would seem that the reality of time, with the determinateness of the past, the actuality of the present, and the potentiality of the future, is the same for God and for his creatures. We cannot know this for sure but it would seem so because our experience of freedom reveals this and if our freedom is in God's image then it follows, at least in some respects, that we share with God this reality of time. It does not preclude the mystery that for God there is more to time than what we experience.

Freedom means change. Heraclitus was closer to the truth than Parmenides. All things move and change—mountains, stones, water, air, butterflies, fish, birds, caribou, people, God. Constancy occurs but does not mean changelessness nor timelessness. A person remains the same person from moment to moment, but the sameness does not preclude difference. We become changed by external influences and internal choices, but we retain our identity in the midst of the change. Prospero was Prospero both before and after he broke his wand. God is God before and after the Cross.

To be free means to live, but all living things are not free. To be free and living means to be responsible. Living beings who have the free image of God act not exclusively on instinct or genetic programming. There is also in their being the possibility for free choice and free action. One must accept responsibility for consequences. What one decides to do now will later be manifest. Time will tell.

And time cannot be reversed. One cannot undo in the future what one decided to make actual in the present. Life in time is not as simple as a word processor. We can repent of what we do in the present, and then our past can be forgiven and forgotten, but we cannot change the past. There is a strange combination of change and changelessness in time. Because there is freedom time can bring change in the future; and because there is responsibility time can bring permanence which resides in the past.

Ancient and modern philosophers have conceived a reality other than time, a timelessness which is called eternity. In the philosophers' eternity there is no change. Do they mean then that in eternity there is no freedom?

Eternity is also the word often used to designate heaven, where God is, where we go after death. In this usage, unlike the philosophers' usage, eternal is interchanged with everlasting, both words meaning infinite duration. This meaning is the biblical meaning. It has its setting in the span of time. This meaning is in contrast to the philosophers' eternity which is outside of time. Plato's metaphor of the idols of the cave claims reality for changelessness in being and values. This seems attractive because it holds on to truth, goodness, and beauty in the face of their loss in time. It does not, however, allow for a living growth in truth, goodness, and beauty. Here we can speak of everlastingness, which is a continuing reality in time, as distinguished from eternity, which is permanence outside of time. Christian revelation promises everlasting life continuing in a future kingdom, not eternal life in a static timelessness. The changelessness of eternity is boring and dull. It has no story. The risks of freedom are preferred in revelation.

Many myths of the past tell of the yearning of the gods for the excitement and sensuality of mortals. Zeus constantly praises his mortal paramours to the consternation of the goddesses Hera and Alcmena. The amorous adventures of Zeus express the belief that mortal women are more attractive than goddesses because all goddesses, in their perfection, look alike. The immortal nymph Calypso is attracted to the highly vulnerable Odysseus. She keeps him in her cave, hoping to lure him away from his beloved Penelope, but Odysseus finally chooses to return to his mortal wife rather than remain with an immortal woman who does not change.

The people of the Celebes tell a story about a stone and a banana. In the beginning the Creator brought the sky near the earth and sent down gifts to people at the end of a rope. One of his gifts was a stone. The first parents of people were disappointed. What could they do with a stone? They said to their Maker, "Give us something else." So the Creator hauled up the stone and then sent down on the rope a banana. This was received gladly because it was good to eat. The Creator then said to them, "You have chosen the banana. Your life will be like the banana. Its stem dies when the fruit is grown, so shall you die when your children replace you. Had you chosen the stone you would be changeless and immortal like a stone."

These stories and myths all presuppose the reality of opposition between a temporal realm of freedom, change, and time and an eternal realm of determinateness, changelessness, and timelessness. Biblical revelation presents no such opposition. The Bible speaks of the time of the end but not the end of time. Nor does the Bible speak of the timelessness of God, just his different perception of it. When the Bible speaks of the changelessness of God it refers to his constancy in love and the continuation of his living identity, not the ossified changelessness of a being outside of time. If God is living and free he is growing and changing from glory to glory. And we share this growth and freedom. "Now the Lord is the Spirit, and where the Spirit of the Lord is, there is freedom. And we, who with unveiled faces all reflect the Lord's glory, are being transformed into his likeness with ever-increasing glory, which comes from the Lord, who is the Spirit" (2 Corinthians 3:17-18).

The time of the past has flown, the time of the present is fleeting, and the time of the future is coming. To speak of the future as coming, however, is somewhat misleading. It falsely suggests that the future is something. It suggests that there is a reality that is already there which we receive when the time is right. But if that were so the future would not be future. It would be something already done that is withheld from us until after the present moment has passed. If such were the case freedom would be lost.

The truth about the future is that it is not actual. The future is only potential, and its possibilities are many. This is why the future cannot be precisely predicted. And again, if freedom is real for God, the future is not actual for him either. He may know all the possibilities and what he intends to do, but he cannot be said to know what is not actual, i.e., we cannot talk about God knowing what is not. It is absurd to say God can know what is nothing. Hence we must say the future is not something for God to know or not know. God does not know the future any more than we do because freedom always intercedes with the possibility of change. Such is the portentous, exciting, perilous, rewarding significance of freedom. Actualization of events in the future depends greatly upon the free choice of the Holy Spirit, but also, in our creaturely way, upon the free choice of earthlings in God's image.

The significance of freedom and the potentiality of the future are awesome. Here we find power in the promise of Jesus' blessings and woes. This is why Jesus warned against building on sand or storing up the wealth of this world rather than treasures for heaven. The parable of the rich man and Lazarus, the story of the pearl of great price, the admonition about being anxious for the morrow—the Gospel is abounding with portent for the future.

2

The Sinking Sadness of Death

Genesis 3:1-24

*Now the serpent was more crafty
than any of the wild beasts
which the Lord had made.
He said to the woman,
"Did God really say.
'You must not eat
from any tree in the garden?'"
And the woman said to the serpent,
"We may eat fruit
from the trees in the garden,
but God did say
'You must not eat fruit from the tree
in the middle of the garden.
You must not even touch it,
or you will die.'"
and the serpent said to the woman,
"Surely you will not die.
God knows
that when you eat of it your eyes will be opened
and you will be like God,
knowing good and evil."*

*When the woman saw
that the tree was good for food,
and pleasing to the eye,
and desirable for wisdom,
she took the fruit and ate it.
She also gave some to her husband
who was with her,
and he ate.*

*Then the eyes of both were opened,
and they realized they were naked.
they sewed fig leaves together
and made aprons for themselves.*

Divine Disclosure

When they heard the voice of the Lord God,
as he walked in the garden
in the cool of the day,
Adam and his wife hid themselves from the presence of the lord
among the trees of the garden.
But the lord God called to Adam
and said to him,
"Where are you?"
And Adam answered,
"I heard your voice in the garden
and I was afraid
because I was naked,
so I hid myself."
God said,
"Who told you that you were naked?
Have you eaten from the tree from which I told you not to eat?"
The man said,
"The woman you gave to me,
she offered me the fruit,
and I ate."
Then the Lord God said to the woman,
"What have you done?"
The woman said,
"The serpent beguiled me,
and I ate."

So the Lord God said to the serpent,
"Because you have done this,
cursed are you
above all livestock
and all wild animals!
You will crawl on your belly
and you will eat dust
all the days of your life.
And I will put enmity
between you and the woman,
and between your offspring and hers.
He will crush your head,
and you will strike his heel."
To the woman he said,
"I will greatly increase your sorrow;

with painful toil
you will give birth to children.
Your desire will be for your husband,
and he will rule over you."

To Adam he said,
"Because you listened to your wife
and ate from the tree
about which I commanded you,
'You must not eat of it,'
cursed is the ground because of you;
through painful toil
you will eat of it
all the days of your life.
It will produce thorns and thistles for you,
and you will eat
the plants of the field.
By the sweat of your brow
you will eat your food
until you return to the ground
from which you were taken,
for dust you are
and to dust you will return."

Adam named his wife Eve,
because she would become the mother of all living people.
The Lord God made garments of skin for Adam and his wife,
and clothed them.
And the Lord God said,
"The earthlings have now become
like one of us,
knowing good and evil.
They must not be allowed
to reach out their hands
and take also from the tree of life
and eat and live forever."

So the Lord God banished them
from the Garden of Eden
to work the ground
from which they had been taken.

After he drove the earthlings out
he placed on the east side
of the Garden of Eden
cherubim and a flaming sword
flashing back and forth
to guard the way
to the tree of life.

Matthew 26:14-29

Then one of the twelve—the one called Judas Iscariot—
went to the chief priests and asked,
"What are you willing to give me
if I hand him over to you?"
So they counted out for him thirty coins.
From then on Judas watched for an opportunity
to hand him over.

On the first day of the Feast of Unleavened Bread,
the disciples came and asked,
"Where do you want us to make preparations
for you to eat the Passover?"
He replied, "Go into the city to a certain man,
and tell him, 'The Teacher says his appointed time is near.
He is going to celebrate the Passover
with his disciples in your house.'"
So the disciples did as Jesus had directed them
and prepared the Passover.

When evening came,
Jesus was reclining at the table with the twelve.
And while they were eating, he said,
"Truly, one of you will betray me."
They were very sad
and began to say to him one after the other,
"Surely not I, Lord?"
Jesus replied, "The one who has dipped his hand
into the bowl with me will betray me.
The Son of Man will go just as it is written about him.

But woe to that man who betrays the Son of Man!
It would be better for him if he had not been born."
Then Judas, the one who would betray him said,
"Surely not I, Rabbi?"
Jesus answered, "Yes, it is you."

While they were eating, Jesus took bread,
gave thanks and broke it,
and gave it to his disciples, saying,
"Take and eat; this is my body."
Then he took the cup,
gave thanks, and offered it to them, saying,
"Drink from it, all of you.
This is my blood of the new covenant,
which is poured out for many for the forgiveness of sins.
I tell you I will not drink of this fruit of the vine
from now until that day when I drink it anew
with you in my Father's kingdom."

Revelation 12:1-9

A great and wondrous sign appeared in heaven:
a woman clothed with the sun,
with the moon under her feet
and a crown of twelve stars on her head.
She was pregnant and cried out in pain
as she was about to give birth.
Then another sign appeared in heaven:
an enormous red dragon
with seven heads and ten horns
and seven crowns on his heads.
His tail swept a third of the stars out of the sky
and flung them to the earth.
The dragon stood in front of the woman
who was about to give birth,
so that he might devour her child
the moment it was born.

She gave birth to a son, a male child,
who will rule all the nations with an iron scepter.
And her child was snatched up to God
and to his throne.
The woman fled into the wilderness
to a place prepared for her by God,
where she could be nourished
for one thousand two hundred and sixty days.

And there was war in heaven.
Michael and his angels fought against the dragon,
and the dragon and his angels fought back.
But they were defeated
and they lost their place in heaven.
the great dragon was hurled down—
that ancient serpent called the devil, or Satan,
who leads the whole world astray.
He was cast down to the earth
and his angels with him.

The Fall

ALREADY IN the beginning in the Garden of Eden an adversary appears and brings conflict into the story of God and his creatures. The Bible is a story, a great cosmic tale, and not a scientific treatise with literal descriptions of observed events. Science selects from experience to provide meaning for natural sequences, and so it tells *how* things happen, really only how they appear to us to happen. Science cannot speak of origins or destinies. It tells us only about natural patterns of determined behavior. Revelation tells us *who* makes things happen and *why*. When we speak of who and why we are in the kingdom of story with characters in conflict and community moving toward a denouement which we celebrate because it satisfies. "God saw all that he had made, and it was very good."

The grand saga of the Bible includes myths about characters outside history, legends about historical figures, short stories about fictional characters, and historical records about persons who have dates and places. Examples respectively are Adam, Abraham, Jonah, and Jesus. Included also in the stories are legal prescriptions and epistolary instruction for moral, ritual, and social behavior; prophetic visions of warning and hope; poetic hymns and psalms of praise, lament, petition, intercession, and thanksgiving.

These various tales and texts provide different kinds of truth, but the claim of faith for revelation is that they are all real. There is a real person who masquerades as a serpent and who lied to Eve. He is not an abstract representation for the notion of the demonic. He is the archdemon. There was a real Adam who ate forbidden fruit and defied God. He is not just the representative of the race in illustration of a message or moral. He is a real character in a realm and era who was expelled by the judgment of God to work out his destiny in toil on earth, and whose sin brings the separation of death. The toil of the earthling involves all our pain, fatigue, and frustration in defeat. The death is not, as Tillich would have us believe, the threat of falling from being to nothing. It is the far more serious and devastating reality of separation from God, from one another, and from ourselves. Death is the ongoing existence of loneliness which we chose when we believed Satan's lie rather than God.

The biblical story says that Adam is the father of the whole human race, and because of his sin the world is cursed so that all who come after him suffer for his sin. Paul says, "For just as through the disobedience of the one man many were made sinners, so also through the obedience of the one man many will be made righteous" (Romans 5:19). Here are two difficult claims: all human beings derive from one person, Adam; and all are sinners through him. Why should children be held responsible for their father's disobedience? Paul does not say they are responsible; he says they suffer it. With Paul's insight into the revelation we see that Adam's sin has dire consequences because Adam is both himself and the whole human race. That is, Adam as earthling refers by name to an individual character in the story of original creation and also to the body of humankind which is an organic unity that suffers all the pain of its parts as well as the joy of its promise. If an individual comes late to school and spoils the record of the class the whole class bears the shame of it. If a president is assassinated the whole nation suffers not only the pain of his loss but also the feeling of guilt for having been dishonored. It is a disgrace to us all when such a thing happens.

Also it is a mistake to think of Adam as a prehistoric ancestor in the evolutionary chain. There may well be such a chain; it is the best theory to explain the multifarious perceptions we have of our creaturely past on this earth. But to give credence to the biblical story we need not appeal to the latest anthropological theory that affirms all human beings as derivative from a common gene pool sourced in a woman 200,000 years ago, nor to the claim to have found a common male ancestor who lived 188,000 years ago. These theories may or may not be accepted scientifically, but revelation does not depend on the vagaries of scientific theory which are as volatile as the Wall Street stock market. The faith claim of revelation is for the certainty of creation and the universality of sin, as the doggerel says: "In Adam's fall we sinned all." Adam is the generic name for all of us because we are all members of the family that was expelled from the garden when this world we now live in was fashioned. If each of us is one's own Adam, it is not a matter of particular sins that cause separation from God but a matter of being in sin that produces particular sins.

The so-called "Eve" of mitochondrial fame cannot be compared with the biblical Eve. The biblical story and the scientific story are not at all the same. The scientific "Eve" has neither sin nor expulsion from the garden in her story. She belongs to the story of nature and history, but the Eve of revelation belongs to the story of reality that transcends both nature and history. History records our experiences and memories. Science is a method

The Sinking Sadness of Death

of rationally organizing our perceptions. Both are limited to human percepts and concepts. God alone knows what really is and what really happens. Revelation, however, gives us glimpses of what God knows about what really is and what really happens, not by imparting facts or information, but by establishing a relationship with the person of Jesus Christ through the power of the Holy Spirit. As Jesus said, "I am the way and the truth and the life." One pole of this relationship is empirical since Jesus was fully historical and we meet him in succeeding generations in the Church through the Bible. The other pole is given to us as faith, a transforming experience which cannot be compared with any other human experience but which cannot be denied once it has been given. As the blind man at the Pool of Siloam said, "Before I was blind, but now I see."

It is equally nonsensical and wrongheaded to try to get a nod of approval from science for our faith from the big bang theory of the origin of the universe. Some people like to say that the big bang is consistent with creation out of nothing; the Bible and science are saying the same thing. Not so! The scientific theory says the bang exploded not from nothing but from a soft ball-sized concentration of light, space, time, matter, and the forces that hold matter together. It might be better to say that the expulsion from the Garden of Eden was like the big bang. This may or may not be a fruitful speculation, but the other analogy, the analogy of the bang with creation, is definitely false. The bang produced a universe different from Eden, one which has the ambiguity of life-giving rain and life-destroying floods. Eden was a peaceful paradise and a garden of delight. The two stories are radically different.

The story of the serpent and Adam and Eve is strange in a scientific age with its success in bringing wealth and comfort and power. This is all good and we can believe God smiles when he sees our progress, but science cannot bring us peace and justice and community. And with each new scientific advance there is also the danger of abuse. Peace and justice and community, however, involve personal relationships and the exercise of freedom, which are the stuff of story. The story of the fall of Adam and Eve under the temptation of the devil tells how peace was lost and judgment was made.

What was the sin that had such cosmic, cataclysmic repercussions? Adam and Eve were beguiled by the devil. Beguiling includes both deception and free choice. Adam and Eve freely chose to be trapped; they willingly and responsibly believed the devil's lie. Our sin is both victimization and rebellious defiance. Satan is the angel who is the prince of this world, the ruler of darkness. He has been cast out of heaven and his defeat is sure, but his power remains as long as his nefarious lies are believed. We cannot shift blame, for this is only the expression of our original grasp for independence, as both Eve and Adam tried to do when God confronted them with their sin.

Our first parents' sin, which we all share, is the defiant attempt to know what God knows, and therefore to be able to live without him. It has to do with knowledge of right, wrong, good and evil, which is wisdom, not the knowledge of science and technology. There was no proscription against such search and use. The biblical revelation is quite different from the myth of Prometheus who stole fire from heaven and incurred the wrath of Zeus because people could now forge tools and weapons and were no longer dependent on the providence of the gods. But the biblical God is not jealous of our creativity. He simply cannot abide the loss of his uniqueness, and when we try to be God rather than to be under him we challenge that uniqueness and lose our own.

The irony of our defiant grasp for the knowledge of good and evil is that now we know that there is a difference but we are forever quarreling about what that difference is. Human justice is ambiguous and seldom brings peace. We are living in a world under a spell, in which there is both good and evil, but the natural world does not of itself distinguish between right and wrong. Big fish eat little fish; this is good for the big and evil for the little, but neither right nor wrong for either. Nature's rhythm has only pluses and minuses and no moral judgment; but God has an adversary and so there is judgment in his wrath and redemption in his mercy. Nature has the cycle of birth and death. Natural religions see death as necessary to keep the cycle going with the renewal of life through death. Mysticism ambiguously and more mistakenly sees death and life as one and the same thing, so escape from the cycle is sought by denying it. Christian revelation, in contradistinction to both natural religion and mysticism, reaches beyond good and evil and proclaims the distinction between right and wrong. The cycle of good and evil, birth and death, is not endless. This time-frame concludes with an Eschaton that propels us into a new kingdom even more dramatically than when we entered this world through expulsion from the Garden of Eden.

As we wander and stumble through our exile we wonder with dismay why we suffer so much evil. What kind of God is reigning in heaven when earth is cursed with so much pain? Is it possible that God is infinitely good but only partially powerful? No! Such a God would be subservient to what is more powerful. Then is God responsible for both good and evil? Isaiah said God is the author of weal and woe; Job said the Lord gives and the

Lord takes away; Jesus said God makes the sun shine on good and evil alike. Insurance companies call natural disasters acts of God. Does God in his holy wrath send us evil to destroy what he has made? Again No! God does not create evil as if evil were a thing that could be called bad in the same way that the original creation was called good. Evil is not a thing; it is a relationship. We are in the good world that God made but we are out of joint with it because we separated ourselves from God, and so we are trashed by its force and reduced to its dust. This is evil to us but not wrong. God indeed shakes the earth with seismic disruptions and we are swallowed by this impersonal force. But in the midst of all the evil of fallen nature the gracious presence of the redeeming God brings us hope through the promise of Christ.

When the full story is told our wonderment turns from dismay to awe. We see ourselves as we are seen by God: rebellious sinners who deserve the pain we receive because we have chosen our death. All attempts to justify God with rational systems are arrogant because they fail to consider the great weight of sin. The sin that produces crime and war and oppression we know we must confess as our own, but what is the sin that brings disease and tornadoes and earthquakes? What sin did the child commit who was incinerated by the lava from Vesuvius? She committed no sin but she was born into a world cursed by sin. She was part and parcel of a world apart from God, a world in which we know, except for the coming of Christ, only the alien presence of God. It is our being in sin, not just doing sins, that has cursed us to suffer alienation from God, which is the separation of death that comes to us whether peacefully in bed or horrifically through natural disaster. Death is always an awesome terror, but it is also always deserved. Death is the wage of sin (Romans 6:23).

Although God ordains this world with its disjointed disasters in the midst of bountiful goodness, he is not a petulant angry Zeus who sends thunderbolts from heaven to punish specific deeds. Vengeance is mine, says the Lord, but his wrath is manifest when he delivers us up to our own unbridled wickedness (Romans 1:24). God does not send evil to us; he lets us walk in the wickedness we choose. We do not choose tornadoes, of course, but we have chosen to defy God and so we must accept a fallen, natural world which has only God's alien presence. This is a world doomed to decay, designed that way for our own good; and ironically when we cling to it in a desperate attempt to avoid the disaster of death we only sink deeper into its sadness.

In the biblical revelation, therefore, death is seen not as a natural necessity, nor as a sinking into nothingness, but as an enemy which enters through sin. Death is separation from God, from one another, and from ourselves. God did not make us to be separated. In defying God we sought to be alone. By breaking our community we found ourselves to be naked; we are no longer clothed with the glory of God through his loving companionship. We are now, by our choice, alone; and the pain of loneliness is unbearable. So we cover ourselves with fig leaves and the latest Paris fashion, and we strive to protect ourselves with a DEW line and a Strategic Defense Initiative, even pre-emptive war. We put on tinseled diadems and fustian robes and we walk with the pretense of holiness. But we are cursed to be alone because that is what we choose, and that is the meaning of death. Return to dust is just another step in the process of dying which begins with conception, but again ironically it is the necessary step that leads to Paradise. There is that mysterious and wonderful intimation in the revelation that an offspring of the woman will crush the head of the serpent.

In our discussion of the Fall, which is the biblical story of the human condition in our exile from Eden, we have discovered that we should make a distinction between nature and history. In nature there are cycles, seasons, and repetition. In history there are surprises, novelty, and freedom. In nature we can speak only of good and evil. In history we can speak of right and wrong. I have said it is good for big fish to eat little fish but not right or wrong for either. Human beings are creatures of both nature and history. We have the goodness and the evil of nature and we participate in the rights and wrongs of history.

Death keeps nature in balance. But humans are more than the natural dust of the earth. We also have the unique life the Spirit breathed into us, and hence we have freedom, and so history. And therefore we also have right and wrong. It is not natural for us to die. It is wrong. It is a wrong that must be righted. We chose our death. God chooses our life. God chooses to right the wrong that we chose by giving us righteousness and a new birth.

Because we are a part of nature we must share its goodness and its evil. The balance of nature, the ecological economy, must include us lest we render ourselves extinct along with passenger pigeons. But because we are also apart from nature as historical beings who exercise responsible freedom, we must endeavor to right the wrongs we perpetrate. Ultimately, of course, only God can redeem the wrong of sin and death. This is not keeping balance. It is a radical shifting of balance from death and destruction to life and construction.

We need more than ecological balance. The cycle of nature and the religions devoted to its preservation keep people going, but more than a circle is needed for our human destiny. A line must be drawn with a historical vector that has a cross in it. Natural religions celebrate the circle. The circle embraces and includes, and, like a womb, gives us warmth and protection. But the circle also excludes and does not go anywhere. The Christian revelation breaks free like birth from the confining limits of the circle. The Christian revelation projects us forward into a life of novelty and surprise.

The power that overcomes death and builds new life is *agape*, love, God's grace of renewal. The fool says there is no God and hence there can be no victory over death. No one has ever seen God and so, he says, there is no evidence for God's grace. But there is love. Ingmar Bergman produced a movie about love which he called *Through a Glass Darkly*. It is a story about a young woman who was terminally ill with a mental disease. At the end of the movie she is taken away to a hospital, and her younger brother cries in utter despondency, "I will not be able to care for her anymore." Her father replies, "But there is someone who will." The boy angrily shouts, "Do you mean God? There is no God. Where is the proof?" Gently the father says, "Love is the proof. You love her, her husband loves her, and I love her. She is surrounded by love. And God is love."

Death

One of the supreme paradoxes of Christian faith is the celebration of death, death which we declare is an enemy. Death is not natural, not in the sense of being in the created order of things, as if it were God's way of preventing over-population. God did not make us to die. If death is separation from God nothing could be more absurd than the notion that God separates us from himself in death. Rather the biblical story tells us that death is an intrusion, an interruption, a dividing wall that comes between us and God. Yet we Christians preach Christ and him crucified. We proclaim the death of Jesus as the atoning power that heals the breach, that breaks down the wall. The good news we preach is that God has nullified the things that are so that no one may boast before him. He has crossed out our arrogant human wisdom and substituted it with the divine offense and foolishness of the cross (1 Corinthians 1:18-31).

If anyone asks from the point of view of right reason how God could deal with the continuing multiplication of living creatures, we can answer only with speculations that are fanciful, idle, and humorous. We can never say more than we know. Wherever we have no empirical, rational or revelatory knowledge we must remain silent. We do not know the structure of the world before the Fall. We do not know what its structure will be after the Eschaton. We do know the balance that nature requires in this world and era of exile. In it we have death, and that contributes to the balance. Surely God is able in his wisdom to structure a newly redeemed world that will not suffer from excessive population.

How can we celebrate death? Death is dark and cruel. Death is furious and final. But this is precisely what St. Paul is talking about to the Corinthians: an offense to religious people and nonsense to the smart. So Christians celebrate death—Christ's death and our own—because we abandon the religion and wisdom of this world and embrace the wisdom of the Holy Spirit.

People react to death in various ways, all the way from laughter to tears. Humans are the only creatures who really laugh and weep. The lower animals can rejoice and sorrow, but they do not seem to have the power of reflection that produces laughter and tears. This is because we know the difference between what is and what ought to be. Humans are also the only creatures who can anticipate their death and so prepare for it. We buy insurance and we prettify our corpses. Sometimes we joke and laugh about death, but when we meet it face to face we react mostly with fear and anger. Shakespeare's Macbeth shouts in a fit of rage: "Life's but a walking shadow, a poor player that struts and frets his hour upon the stage and then is heard no more: it is a tale told by an idiot, full of sound and fury, signifying nothing" (*Macbeth*, Act IV, scene 5, lines 16–19). Thomas Hobbes complains: "The life of man is solitary and poor, nasty, brutish, and short." St. Paul speaks of the whole creation groaning together with the Spirit with sighs too deep for words. All nature throbs with pain, and even the Holy Spirit shares this death. The wail of the loon and the shudder of an earthquake join in a symphony of sorrow with the whimpering of a child. The poet Tennyson sings: "The woods decay, the woods decay and fall; the vapors weep their burden to the ground. Man comes and tills the soil and lies beneath, and after many summers dies the swan."

Now what meaning is there in the tearful bondage to decay? When the young widow was stoned to death by the villagers Zorba the Greek asks his friend, "Why do the young die? Why does anybody die?" The friend says, "I don't know." Zorba shouts, "What good then are all your damn books? If they don't tell you that, what the hell do they tell you?" Quietly the friend says, "They tell me about the agony of people who can't answer questions like yours."

We have a book that tells about the agony of death. It tells of the murder of Abel. It tells about the sacrifice of Jephthah's daughter, about Samson pulling the pillars of the temple down upon himself and the Philistines, about Moses going up a mountain to sleep with his fathers, about the weeping of David over the death of his son Absalom, about Jezebel's being devoured by dogs, about Samuel's dismembering the king of the Amalekites, about John the baptizer's head being served to the king on a platter, about the slaughter of the children by Herod, about Simeon sweetly welcoming his death because he has seen his salvation, about Judas hanging himself and bursting his guts because he betrayed Jesus, and finally and most important about Jesus nailed to a cross and accused of treason and blasphemy.

And this last agony, the story of Jesus, gives us a revelation that provides meaning for both death and life. It does not tell us how to escape from life. It does not tell us how to avoid death. It tells us how to meet death and turn it into life. The story of Jesus tells us that God himself suffers death. The Jews have asked where God was in the Holocaust. The cross tells us that God was in the gas chambers dying with the victims. God has revealed this by taking upon himself our sinful, mortal human flesh; and by walking with us wherever we go, all the way to death itself. This means that it is not God who takes away our lives; he certainly does not kill little children. When a child dies, or anybody dies, God weeps for the loss just as we do. Jesus showed this when he wept over Jerusalem. We are all his beloved children, more dear to him than any child is to human parents or grandparents. God receives us in death with his compassionate arms, but he does not take us. God does not bring death to anyone. Jesus said an enemy sows the evil tares, and St. Paul said the wages of sin is death. Death is deserved but it is not punishment, certainly not for particular sins, even though they may be its occasion.

Paradoxically, because in sin we are both rebels and victims, we are both responsible for our death and dupes of the devil's lies. Death is both something we do and something that happens to us. Death is the earning we get for our disobedience and faithlessness; and it is the fiery dart of the devil, the jealous rage of the evil one who attacks God and his creatures. When one person is attacked all are wounded, including God himself. As John Donne said: "Any man's death diminishes me for I am involved in mankind."

Then if death is the devil's doing does he win or does God win? And if death is deserved is this the final end? Not so! In faith we celebrate the victory of Christ Jesus over death and the devil. Death is not to be feared because with death's judgment there is also forgiveness and new life. We can face death's defeat and not be crushed by it. Indeed we will enter into the crisis with courage and relish it because we will be both chastened by its consuming judgment and challenged by its creative promise. We will be elevated by an experience in which we are struck down precisely as our liturgy of confession and absolution repeatedly declares. The Christian is exalted in dignity when death comes, and so we can pray with Johann Sebastian Bach: "Come, sweet death!" And we can sing with St. Francis:

> And you, most kind and gentle death,
> Waiting to hush our final breath,
> Oh, praise him! Allelujah!
> You lead to heav'n the child of God,
> Where Christ our Lord the way has trod.

When our vision of death is based on such a revelation of life we can sing in our sorrow and laugh through our tears. This is human wisdom crossed out. It is a wild dream, a fantastic vision, but it is indeed our Christian faith. Thanks be to God!

3

Power and Pain

Psalm 51

Have mercy on me, O God,
according to your loving-kindness;
in your great compassion
blot out my transgressions.

Wash away thoroughly all my wickedness,
and cleanse me from my sin.

For I acknowledge my transgressions,
and my sin is always before me.

Against you, you only, have I sinned
and done what is evil in your sight.

And so you are justified
when you speak
and upright in your judgment.

Indeed, I have been wicked
from my birth,
a sinner from my mother's womb.

Behold, you desire truth
deep within me;
you teach wisdom in the inmost place.

Cleanse me with hyssop
and I will be clean;
wash me and I will be whiter than snow.

Let me hear joy and gladness
that the body you have broken
may rejoice.

Hide your face from my sins
and blot out all my iniquity.

Create in me a clean heart, O God,
and renew a right spirit within me.

Cast me not away from your presence
and take not your Holy Spirit from me.

Give me the joy of your saving help again,
and uphold me with your bountiful Spirit.

I will teach your ways to the wicked,
and sinners will return to you.

Deliver me from bloodguilt, O God,
and my tongue will sing of your righteousness,
O God of my salvation.

Open my lips, O lord,
and my mouth
will proclaim your praise.

Had you desired it,
I would have offered sacrifice,
but you take no delight in burnt offerings.

The sacrifices of God
are a troubled spirit;
a broken and contrite heart, O God,
you will not despise.

Do good and be gracious to Zion,
and rebuild the walls of Jerusalem.

Then you will be pleased
with sacrifices of righteousness,
with burnt offerings and whole burnt offerings.
And they will offer young bullocks
on your altar

Romans 7:15-25

I do not understand what I do.
What I want
I do not do,
but what I hate
I do.

*And if I do
what I do not want
I agree that the law is good.
But now it is no longer I myself
who do it;
it is sin dwelling in me.
I know that nothing good lives in me,
that is, in my sinful nature.
The desire to do good
is present with me,
but the performance I find not.
For the good that I want
I do not,
and the evil which I hate,
that I do.
Now if I do what I do not want,
it is not I who do it,
but sin living in me that does it.
So I find this law at work in me:
when I want to do good,
evil is right there with me.
For in my inner being
I delight in the law of God;
but I see another law
at work in the members of my body,
waging war against the law of my mind
and making me captive to the law of sin
that gnaws within me.
O wretched man that I am!
Who will deliver me
from this body of death?
Thanks be to God
through Jesus Christ our Lord!*

Romans 5:1-20

Therefore, since we have been justified through faith,
we have peace with God through our Lord Jesus Christ,
through whom we have gained access
by faith into this grace
in which we now stand.
And we rejoice
in the hope of the glory of God.
Not only so,
but we also rejoice in our sufferings,
because we know
that suffering produces perseverance,
perseverance, character;
and character, hope.
And hope does not disappoint us,
because God has poured out his love
into our hearts by the Holy Spirit,
whom he has given us.

You see, at just the right time,
when we were still powerless,
Christ died for the ungodly.
Very rarely will anyone die
for a righteous man,
though for a good man
someone may possibly dare to die.
But God demonstrates his own love for us in this:
While we were still sinners,
Christ died for us.

Since we have now been justified by his blood,
how much more shall we be saved
from wrath through him!
For if, when we were God's enemies,
we were reconciled to him
through the death of his Son,
how much more,
having been reconciled,
shall we be saved through his life!
Not only is this so,

but we rejoice in God
through our Lord Jesus Christ,
through whom we have now received
reconciliation.
Therefore, just as sin entered the world
through one man,
and death through sin,
and in this way death came to all people,
because all sinned—
for before the law was given,
sin was in the world.
But sin is not taken into account
when there is no law.
Nevertheless, death reigned
from the time of Adam to the time of Moses,
even over those who did not sin
by breaking a command,
as did Adam,
who was a pattern of the one to come.

But the gift is not like the trespass.
For if the many died
by the trespass of the one man,
how much more did God's grace
and the gift that came
by the grace of the one man, Jesus Christ,
overflow to the many!
Again, the gift of God
is not like the result of the one man's sin:
The judgment followed one sin
and brought condemnation,
but the gift followed many trespasses
and brought justification.
For if by the trespass of the one man,
death reigned through that one man,
how much more will those
who receive God's abundant provision
of grace and of the gift of righteousness
reign in life through the one man, Jesus Christ.

*Consequently, just as the result of one trespass
was condemnation for all people,
so also the result of one act of righteousness
was justification
that brings life for all people.
For just as through the disobedience
of the one man
the many were made sinners,
so also through the obedience
of the one man
the many will be made righteous.*

*The law was added
so that the trespass might increase.
But where sin increased,
grace increased all the more,
so that, just as sin reigned in death,
so also grace might reign through righteousness
to bring eternal life through Jesus Christ our Lord.*

Sacraments

The story of our life with God and with one another is of the earth earthy, but occasionally our earthiness is lifted heavenward and given a transcending meaning. We shuffle through life episodically with significant rites indicating stages along life's way. Throughout its history the Church has developed seven such rites. They are called sacraments. Christians dispute among themselves over the number of sacraments and their exact definition. If you proceed to determine truth by definition you can make truth into anything you want, but if you look at reality through the window of experience you will discover that in fact the Church performs a ministry for a variety of fundamental needs, and the sacraments, all seven, serve those needs.

If you define a sacrament as an outward sign of an inward grace which has been instituted by Jesus, the number of sacraments must be limited to two. Baptism and holy communion alone satisfy those criteria. If you define a sacrament as a token or sign of some greater, hidden reality then confession and absolution, confirmation, marriage, ordination, and extreme unction may also be included.

The truth is that, whether we are Protestants or Roman Catholics or Eastern Orthodox, clergy of all denominations serve their parishioners in all seven ways and some kind of rite marks this performance. Besides the sacraments the Church also has other ministries which serve human needs such as teaching, preaching, prayer, and welfare. These functions also lift us above our earthiness, but we may distinguish them from sacraments in that they are not tokens of a divine gift. Unlike the sacraments, these ministries all begin with human devotion and decision. Sacraments are pledges of divine grace. God gives us forgiveness when we confess our sin. God raises us to newness of life in the Spirit when we die with Christ and join his Church in baptism. God confirms us with the gifts of the Spirit in confirmation. God blesses the bonds of faithfulness and love in holy matrimony. God guarantees the authority and service of ministry in ordination—and this sacrament should rightly be expanded to include all the vocations of Christians as they witness and work in the world. God commends us with his compassionate grace as we leave this life on earth—and we should extend this sacrament of extreme unction to the healing grace that we receive throughout our lives. And finally God is really present with us when he gives us forgiveness, atoning sacrifice, a memorial celebration, and a foretaste of the Messianic banquet in the sacrament of holy communion or eucharist.

Revelation has shown us that as we grow in faith God takes the initiative graciously providing us with the power to live and live abundantly through all the stages of our earthly voyage.

Revelation is the disclosure of what is unseen, the opening of what has been hidden. God is unseen and hidden, but he has made himself known by a general unveiling of his nature through his creation and a special disclosure through his coming to us in the person of Jesus. St. Paul said this to the Romans: "For since the creation of the world God's invisible qualities—his eternal power and divine nature—have been clearly seen, being understood from what has been made, so that humans are without excuse" (Romans 1:20). The great religions of the world have confirmed the disclosure from creation, and their cultures have been sustained by it. But the special revelation of Jesus helps us to see the difference between the creation and the Creator.

Human religion confuses God and nature. In our sinful separation from God we see nature in all its splendor from a benign source of life to the awesome destroyer of life. Our response is varied. We give thanks and we bargain for bounty, control, and escape. Elaborate religious structures are erected, always under the influence of Satan's temptation to twist our approach to God into a phony imitation of worship rather than the real thing. Satan is the father of lies; he cannot create, so he tries to imitate, and his copies are always fake. They cloud and cover the reality and do not disclose. They take from us and never give.

God, on the other hand, gives himself to us. His giving is grace, which produces faith. Grace and faith are two sides of the same coin. As a coin has a head and a tail, so grace is the head and faith is the tail; and the tail does not wag the head. Grace is always prior because it plants in us faith, not the other way around. Faith does not bring to us grace; it is grace that brings us faith. Because of the reality of time there is always an interval between the giving of grace and the receiving of faith. The interval may be infinitesimal, almost instantaneous; or it may be inexplicably, even painfully, long. Because God has made us free in his image the gift of grace is not forced. We may respond with gratitude or indifference or rejection. We may accept at once or delay for a time or forever.

The grace of God is initial and active. Our faith is receptive but not passive. When we receive grace we enter into an activity of response; we are responsible for what we receive and accountable for what we do with it. Thus as Augustine and the Reformers said, there is no sacrament without faith. They meant that the grace given in the sacraments must produce the response of faith which becomes evident in a vocation in life of love to God, to one's neighbor, and to oneself.

Christians have ritualized the giving of God's grace in the sacraments. It has been a mistake to quarrel over whether God instituted two or three or seven sacraments. The truth is that the word sacrament does not occur in the Bible, but the mystery of God's grace coming through material means is indisputable. And the presence of this grace is evident in the occasions of importance in the stages along life's way. From birth through the various passages and transitions we encounter until death God has provided his mercy and strength so that we may have a safe voyage. Every Christian pastor knows that his or her ministry is a blessing at the birth of a child, at the confirmation of a youth, at the confession of a sinner, at the communion of a congregation, at the marriage of a couple, at the ordination of a vocation, at the healing of the sick, and at the burial of the dead. Grace is given at these moments and faith endures from the giving.

But grace is not a magical substance that can be manipulated. The Aristotelian substance metaphysics which prevailed in the Middle Ages was accompanied by a superstitious religious practice that encouraged people to believe they could win their salvation by the appropriation of the sacraments. But grace is not a thing to possess; grace is the giving of the person of God to his creatures, thereby establishing a living, growing, powerful relationship. Grace cannot be handled; it can only be enjoyed.

The relationship between grace and faith is not causal. The determinism of a causal connection does not describe what happens when God comes to us in the presence of Jesus. The category of causality is useful in scientific investigation and explanation of natural sequences, but the sequences that follow in the divine-human encounter have a mystery that can only be celebrated, not explained. The category is not causality but relationship.

Sacramental grace is the presence of God giving us his power to live, to forgive, to heal, to love, to sanctify. We do not initiate this presence and power; we cannot merit it by behavior or knowledge; but after God gives us himself we can in faith transform both our behavior and our knowledge. The states along life's way then become what the Eastern Orthodox call theosis and the Western Protestants call sanctification: the restoration of the lost image of God to sinners who now become saints. Rather than having to grow into a position of worthiness through what we learn or do in order to effectually receive the sacraments, we receive from the sacraments the worthiness that transforms our life into holy service in the world.

The fantastic transforming power of grace is described dramatically by Dale Wasserman in his Broadway play *Man of La Mancha*, a retelling of Cervantes' *Don Quixote*. Wasserman, however, tells a different story, not the tale of a Medieval man who lost his faith in the chivalric code and died a cynical modern man, but the story of a true Christian who showered grace upon a miserable bar wench who deserved contempt but was changed by his love. Aldonza was an ugly peasant girl with a plain face, smelling of garlic and without morals. Quixote saw her as a princess with sweet beauty, and so he called her Dulcinea. At the end of his life when he is about to despair of his dream about Dulcinea she comes to him and he finds that she has really become Dulcinea. Not magic, not effort, but the power of Quixote's presence has transformed her into the person he considered her to be. The hairy warts on her face literally became beauty marks. Her crude lack of morality became a clean fullness of holiness. Such was the sanctifying grace of love from the knight of the woeful countenance. So God changes us from sinners to saints, from mortals to immortals, not with magic of fiat, but with the free gift of grace in the transforming presence of the risen Christ.

We have been considering the revelation from God through the grace of his sacraments. We are saying that God discloses through our earthly experiences something of what is hidden. Why is God hidden? Luther speaks often about the difference between the *Deus Absconditus* and the *Deus Revelatus*, the hidden God and the revealed God. We cannot see God face to face. Why not? Because, as the medieval theologians said, "*nondum considerasti quantum ponderis peccatum est*"—you have not yet considered the great weight of sin. Our sin is so serious that God and we cannot stand in each other's presence.

When we chose to separate ourselves from God in sin God ironically for our own good masked himself so that we are not blinded by his glory. Moses could see only God's hinder parts, only what God had done after he had passed by. So no one has seen God at any time, but we see what God has done, and the sacraments are these very masks which give us God's grace. They paradoxically both hide God from us to preserve his sublime integrity and reveal to us his transforming power to make us holy. These sacramental masks of God freely infuse in us good works that change us from confused sinners to serving saints.

Confession and Absolution

The ancients personified their desires and thereby gave birth to gods who became their lords. We call them idols: Mammon, Moluch, Astarte, Sophia—wealth, power, love, wisdom. Paul says these idols are demons which are really nothing (1 Corinthians 10:19-20), but they have power because of the perversity of our sin. We make them, these monstrous nothings, into our rulers. If in our modern sophistication we do not personify our desires and offer sacrifices to them we just as fervently bind ourselves to their demonic rule, and we worship at their altar by dedicating our lives to their service.

In our loneliness, because of our sinful rebellion against God, we have ironically engaged in an anxious quest for God. We who have tried to be independent of God think that if only we can have God we will have all our desires. This is the story of human religion throughout the world. This quest has produced, humanly speaking, the highest truth, goodness, and beauty. It has also produced the lowest deception, evil, and dread. The magnificent pyramids of Cheops and Cholula still groan with the slaves that built them. The exquisite temples at Nikko and Delphi have seduced with oracles of deception. *Gita* and *Koran* inspire. Cultures thrive and people live by their lies. In all this human religion there is the black curse of idolatry. The gods eat their devotees and the devotees eat their gods. When God is nature, or the epitome of natural desire, worship becomes cannibalism. Life is for death and death is for life, an inexorable cycle of devotee devouring deity and deity devouring devotee. Without the special revelation of Jesus the human quest for God has produced cultures of colossal courage, terrible tenderness, and cruel perversity. Witness the legacies of the priest-kings, Akhenaten among the Egyptians and Ce Acatl Topiltzin Quetzalcoatl of the Toltecs. The story of Quetzalcoatl began with a prince whose legend combined the revenge of Hamlet and the mercy of Christ. But history dissolved into myth and the priest-king became a god who, when worshipped by the Mayans, demanded human sacrifice at Chichen Itza, the same sacrifice Quetzalcoatl had abolished among the Toltecs. Some quests, however, have been tempered with practical wisdom. The jolly jokester Zhuang-zi nurtured China for centuries with his worshipful accommodation to the benignity and inevitability of the forces of nature. For Zhuang, *Dao* is the wisdom that says you cannot have the cooling shade of clouds without the drenching cold of the rain.

The search for God in Hinduism and Buddhism has an ironic twist. It is always our pain that prompts us in our human religiosity to look for surcease from a power beyond ourselves, but Hinduism and Buddhism face pain in the world by not facing it, by denial of all reality. Hindus lose pain and themselves by absorption into the deity (*atman* is *Brahman*). Buddhists deny the reality of both the individual self and the deity. But this is only for the scholars and seers, who are very few. The masses of people in their piety frenetically seek release from suffering not by denial but by the merit of *puja* (ritual) and prayers and yoga meditation. Whether the temples are Hindu, Buddhist, Daoist, or Shinto, the people there have come to buy candles, incense, and prayers to get favor from the gods and release from their *karma*. Again ironically the release they seek is foiled by the relentless return in reincarnated existences. The *moksha* (release) that is desired must not be desired because desire is the cause of suffering, and the denial of self and all reality cannot be denied because the wheel of *karma* grinds out an inevitable return. This bargaining with gods for favor, whether for health, wealth, power or longevity in this life or the next, is different among the various religions throughout the world only in external forms; and this includes selling masses and exploitation of relics and manipulation of prayers from medieval Catholicism to modern Protestant television religion.

In our Western culture today, our quest for a gracious God has developed a peculiar dichotomy between fact and value. We know the gods do not exist and we offer them no sacrifice. But we still want to do good, and we find ourselves gamboling in our guilt, so we turn again to religion. Originally this dichotomy was drawn by Immanuel Kant to protect faith in God. Miracles, the virgin birth, and the resurrection of Jesus could not be established by empirical fact, and so to preserve belief in them they were described as values worth believing. But this reduced faith to the private domain of subjective fancy. A more recent attempt to rescue objectivity of values has been the rendering of values as meanings. The semantic word game of Ludwig Wittgenstein, however, only makes the values meaningful to the group that accepts them. This politicizes religion. Groups or even masses are then described as moving to act together by the hysteria of the moment or season.

But reality includes and transcends empirical facts of nature and history. Therefore if we would speak with comprehension we must use the poetical language of story. Facts are not limited to sense experience. The word "fact" comes from the Latin *facere*, to do. It refers to something that is done, that actually and really happens. *Poesis* is making something happen, and the poetry of revelation is the performative speech of God who makes by his Word both creation and redemption. The story is about God making poetical, factual realities. But we must distinguish these realities from fantasies that arise from human imagination. These fantasies may be healthy or sick but always they are radically different from the reality of God's Word, as different as Santa Claus is different from Christ. Revealed facts transcend the senses and are peculiar in that they are wonderfully, poetically nonsense, with the added surprise that they could not be humanly conceived. Facts of our behavior also transcend the senses and are known to be either sinful or holy because, when seen in the light of Christ, their perversity is exposed or their goodness revealed. We could not have known this behavior to be either sin or holiness without the revelation that came through Jesus Christ (John 12:32; 14:6-7).

We therefore confess that we are in a condition of bondage to sin in which we can in no way set ourselves free. It is this confession that led to the great debate between Luther and Erasmus over predestination. This debate was about sin and grace, however, not about freedom and determinism. The philosophical antinomy between free will and determinism is not the issue. Islam, Hinduism, and Buddhism teach the fateful laws of *kismet* and *karma*, but biblical revelation declares our freedom and responsibility as creatures in the image of a God who is free and responsible. The biblical doctrine of predestination, therefore, has nothing to do with determinism of any kind. Predestination means that God has chosen in advance a course for his people both as communities and as individuals. He has prepared beforehand the good things we can do (Ephesians 2:10). For communities this means God has chosen the Jews to be a light to the Gentiles, and then in due time God has chosen the Christians to be a light to the world (Romans 9–11). For individuals, this means God has chosen each by name to be his witness in our unique and various ways (Ephesians 1:5; Romans 1:1).

During the Reformation, predestination was discussed also in connection with our bondage to sin as over against our freedom before God to save ourselves. The Reformers insisted that before God we have no freedom or ability to justify ourselves, and therefore if we are to be saved at all, salvation must come by the predestined grace of God. We have freedom of choice and action in matters within the created order, but with regard to redemption and our eternal destiny we have no choice or ability. Indeed to try to exercise such false freedom is the most grievous sin. It is the refusal to let God be God by rejecting the grace of Christ. Honest realism must face up to the overwhelming facts of our sin and death. We can freely vote for a demagogue to rule over us, and then we must live with the consequences of our perversity. We cannot freely choose to vote for or against God. He chooses us. He is forever beyond our power. Moreover, we are always free to fall from grace (Galatians 5:4). Just as grace is freely given it may be freely rejected.

The religious person will always ask, what must I do to be saved, and expect to find himself or herself by doing good things; but both the question and the answer are wrong. Christian revelation shows us that we must stop seeking for our salvation and trust God's grace. It is not a better self that we need but another, and the other is never our own but Christ's. As Luther said in *The Freedom of a Christian*, a Christian lives not in oneself but in Christ and one's neighbor; in Christ through faith, in one's neighbor through love.

We cannot offer to God our past and expect to get credit for it. We can only keep our past as that for which we have been forgiven. Does this mean no human production is pleasing to God? Nonsense! The Taj Mahal, Taliesin West, the cathedral at Chartres, Bach's *Passion According to St. Matthew*, Mozart's *Requiem*, the jazz rhythm of Duke Ellington, the fragile understatement of *ikebana*, the lacquer miniatures of Palekh, *The Brothers Karamazov*, *Anna Karenina*, *Hong Lou Meng* (*A Dream of Red Mansions*), Michelangelo's *David*, Van Gogh's self portraits, the *Oresteia* of Aeschylus, Shakespeare's *Hamlet*, the Magna Charta, the Declaration of Independence, a mother's sacrifice for her child, a father's care for his family, a city's planning of parks—these creative, loving works of human endeavor, are they not pleasing to God? Indeed, we dedicate them to his glory. But they would not be possible without his providence and they do not save us for eternity. Even the most magnificent of our human creations are only magnificent temporalities. They crumble as the earth itself crumbles. But we believe God is pleased.

Moods change in different ages, different cultures. In the Middle Ages people sought a gracious God because they felt their sin, confessed it, and worked at religion to merit God's favor. In the Orient people sought release (*moksha*) from a world of illusion because their desires deluded them and they felt they could escape by denial. Some people work at religion and others rebel against it. In the present age many people seek satisfaction apart from God because they feel his absence and they think it makes no difference whether they acknowledge God or not. Modern existentialism affirms the death of God. Submission is the problem for modern sophistication. The original sin of Adam—and Judas—also involved the refusal to submit. We rebel against submitting to the Creator; we would be our own creator, the determiner of our own destiny (Camus: *L'Homme Revolté*). We would be our own savior; to receive grace and forgiveness puts us in God's debt and we resent that (Sartre: *Les Mouches*). Therefore we must, as Nietzsche said, kill God and be free to become superman, to transcend our submissiveness.

The moods of a culture are moved by warring spirits. The Holy Spirit moves people with legitimate concerns for justice but an evil spirit warps those movements. The spirit's justice sought by Feminism and Liberation Theology is twisted when these movements join the existentialist rebellion in the denial of our dependence on God. To be free from oppression we must not only kill the king and the male, they say, but also the God who ordains their rule. Christ's death, according to this modern sophisticated rebellion, which is as old as Adam, does not set us free. It only makes us all obliged to worship in abject repentance. We still have religion. We still live in a city cursed with flies. We still have the wrath of God. So speaks modern cynicism.

To this the Christian revelation has a resounding answer. It is true we must rebel against oppression and be free. It is true that religion curses us to live under the wrath of an angry god. But it is not true that the cross of Christ obliges us to live under this curse. In fact the cross alone liberates us from religion and such dependence. The veil of the temple has been rent. Instead of religious ritual we now have liturgy. A liturgical act in ancient Greek secular usage was a beneficence given by a wealthy person on behalf of the people. The word did not refer, as some have mistakenly used it today, to a work of the people. Liturgy is not what we do in worship to please God. Our Christian liturgy is what God does in his sacramental and Wordly presence. It is God's wealth benefiting his people.

We become free in our worship, but paradoxically we realize this freedom only when we let God be God. He is the creator and redeemer, and we must not rob him of his self, his uniqueness. Then we too can be ourselves, free to fulfill our destiny, not as gods but as humans, with responsibility and creativity. As I have said before, we must see the distinction between religion and revelation. It is the difference between Christendom and Christianity. Christendom is what Christians in their sin have made of Christianity. Christendom is another religion which ambiguously lifts us and warps us. Religions are human quests to get to God. Revelation is God's quest to come to us. Our quest brings us beauty and communion, but invariably also destruction and division. God's quest alone absolves us and sets us free.

The coming of Jesus has made the difference. It has not yet brought us the fulfilled kingdom of God, but it has brought its vision, its hope, its seed, its dream. We do not yet have justice and peace but we have the struggle for it. We have not complete freedom from oppression and slavery but we have the weapon of the Word that liberates. We have no complete knowledge that transcends the sinful spell of our benighted ignorance, but we have the liberating power of scientific prowess which acknowledges mistakes and discloses truth as the pragmatic fruit of "sinning on bravely." Scientific method is simply the practical application of the Christian grace of confession and absolution. Confession is the admission of error. Absolution gives us the chance to start over again, to embrace the future in spite of the past. Scientific experimentation using absolution makes it possible for us to throw the rock of Sisyphus over the mountain.

The distinction between religion and revelation is all important. As a religious institution Christendom has overtly perpetrated enormous crimes in history such as the Crusades, the Inquisition, the obstruction of scientific advances by people like Galileo and Darwin, the burning of witches, the exclusiveness of Puritans and Pietists, the subjugation of slaves and women, and many other covert crimes of omission. Yet in spite of this monstrous behavior the revelation of grace has brought to our sinful world a wonderful emancipation and correction of many of these evils. We still have far to go to rid the world of its many wrongs, but it would be ungrateful of us to fail to acknowledge the blessings we have received in historical advances due to the revelation of God's grace. Political freedoms, scientific discoveries, artistic creations, and advances in social relationships have rightly been inspired by the creative impetus of the Holy Spirit.

Being careful not to gloat over the historical success of Western culture, and being ever mindful of our many egregious faults, we cannot deny the fact of stagnation in Chinese, Indian, African, and Muslim cultures. What is the reason for this stagnation? China at the time of Marco Polo was the envy of Europe, India flourished under Shah Jahan, the Muslims produced the Ottoman empire and the Moors thrived in Spain, but all these cultures went only so far and then disintegrated. Undoubtedly the reasons for decay are multifarious, but I submit the most important is religious. For example, the fundamental driving force of Islam is the concept of submission. Islam literally means submission, which when institutionalized becomes subjugation, first to the mullahs and then to the males. This is quite different from the freedom that is proclaimed in the Christian Gospel in which a graciously free God grants freedom to his children to create their own destiny with all its risks, and he also provides a stage on which rich opportunities abound for advance.

When Christ speaks to us through his Spirit we see that all we do, from our simplest mistakes to our greatest perversity, is a symptom of the broken relationship that came when sin took possession of our lives. Now absolution, not religious effort, is needed. When we see ourselves as shattered sinners we know we cannot go back to innocence; we can only go forward to repentance. God grants this repentance and we are absolved because Christ is the judge who justifies. This grace he gives when he draws us to himself on the cross (John 12:32). The absolution is possible because of the victory Christ won over sin and death in his resurrection. All these other religions attempt to gain God's favor and merit our success, and so they wallow in penultimate efforts to retain the conditions of this world. Hence their culture stagnates. Jesus' resurrection, however, is the beginning of a new heaven and a new earth, and hence we spring forward proleptically already in history. We can become part of his coming kingdom through baptism and the eucharist in which we share Christ's death and rising again by the energy of the Holy Spirit

4

Time For, Place Where

Isaiah 9:2-7

The people walking in darkness
  have seen a great light;
on those living in the land of the shadow of death
  a light has dawned.
You have enlarged the nation
  and increased their joy;
they rejoice before you
  as people rejoice at the harvest,
as men rejoice
  when dividing the plunder.
For as in the day of Midian's defeat,
  you have shattered
the yoke that burdens them,
  the bar across their shoulders,
  the rod of their oppressor.
Every warrior's boot used in battle
  and every garment rolled in blood
will be destined for burning,
  will be fuel for the fire.
For to us a child is born,
  to us a son is given,
and the government will be on his shoulders.
  He will be called
Wonderful Counselor, Mighty God,
  Everlasting Father, Prince of Peace.
Of the increase of his government and peace
  there will be no end.
He will reign on David's throne
  and over his kingdom,
establishing and upholding it
  with justice and righteousness
  from that time on and forever.
The zeal of the Lord Almighty
  will accomplish this.

Isaiah 53:1-12

Who has believed our message
  and to whom has the arm of the Lord been revealed?
He grew up before him like a tender shoot,
  and like a root out of dry ground.
He had no beauty or majesty to attract us to him,
  nothing in his appearance that we should desire him.
He was despised and rejected by all,
  a man of sorrows, and familiar with suffering.
Like one from whom people hide their faces
  he was despised, and we esteemed him not.

Surely he took up our infirmities
  and carried our sorrows,
yet we considered him stricken by God,
  smitten by him, and afflicted.
But he was pierced for our transgressions,
  he was crushed for our iniquities;
the punishment that brought us peace was upon him,
  and by his wounds we are healed.
We all, like sheep, have gone astray,
  each of us has turned to our own way;
and the Lord has laid on him
  the iniquity of us all.

He was oppressed and afflicted,
  yet he did not open his mouth;
he was led like a lamb to the slaughter,
  and as a sheep before her shearers is silent,
so he did not open his mouth.
By oppression and judgment he was taken away.
  And who can speak of his descendants?
For he was cut off from the land of the living;
  for the transgression of my people he was stricken.
He was assigned a grave with the wicked,
  and with the rich in his death,
though he had done no violence,
  nor was any deceit in his mouth.

Yet it was the Lord's will that he be crushed
   and made to suffer,
   and though the Lord makes his life a guilt offering,
he will see his offspring and prolong his days,
   and the will of the Lord will prosper in his hand.
After the suffering of his spirit,
   he will see the light of life and be satisfied;
By his knowledge my righteous servant will justify many,
   and he will bear their iniquities.
Therefore I will give him a portion among the great,
   and he will divide the spoils with the strong,
because he poured out his life unto death,
   and was numbered with the transgressors.
For he bore the sin of many,
   and made intercession for the transgressors.

Luke 2:1-20

And it came to pass in those days,
that there went out a decree
from Caesar Augustus,
that all the world should be taxed.
This taxing was first made
when Cyrenious was governor of Syria.
And all went to be taxed,
all to their own city.
And Joseph also went up from Galilee,
out of the city of Nazareth,
into Judea, unto the city of David,
which is called Bethlehem,
because he was of the house and lineage of David,
to be taxed
with Mary, his espoused wife,
who was great with child.
And so it was,
that, while they were there,
the days were accomplished
that she should be delivered.

Divine Disclosure

*And she brought forth her firstborn son,
and wrapped him in swaddling clothes,
and laid him in a manger,
because there was no room for them,
in the inn.*

*And there were in the same country
shepherds abiding in the field,
keeping watch over their flock by night.
And, lo,
the angel of the Lord came upon them,
and the glory of the Lord
shone round about them,
and they were sore afraid.
And the angel said unto them,
"Fear not,
for, behold,
I bring you good tidings of great joy,
which will be to all people.
For unto you is born this day
in the city of David
a Savior, who is Christ the Lord.
And this will be a sign unto you:
you will find a baby
wrapped in swaddling clothes,
lying in a manger."*

*And suddenly there was with the angel
a multitude of the heavenly host
praising God,
and saying,
"Glory to God in the highest,
peace and good will
to all people on earth."*

*And when the angels were gone away from them
into heaven,
the shepherds said one to another,
"Let us go now even unto Bethlehem,
and see this thing which has come to pass,
which the Lord has made known to us."*

*And they came with haste,
and found Mary and Joseph,
and the baby lying in a manger.
And when they had seen it,
they made known abroad
the saying which was told them
concerning this child.
And all they that heard it
wondered at those things
which were told them by the shepherds.
But Mary kept all these things,
and pondered them in her heart.
And the shepherds returned,
glorifying and praising God
for all the things that they had heard and seen,
as it was told unto them.*

Prophecy

PROPHECY IN revelation is warning and hope. Prophecy is not prediction. God's Word to us in prophecy is always contingent upon our response because it is delivered in the arena of freedom, and it is intended to evoke a change in us when it comes as a warning. Or it may call for a response of joy, thanksgiving and sanctified service when it comes to inspire hope.

Prophecy does indeed speak to the future. God tells us his will for our destiny through the historical context in which we live and into which he enters in various ways through chosen servants, historical and natural events, and meaningful relationships. This future about which prophecy speaks is not fixed. Indeed the past tense of the verb "not fixed" is a clamant indication that the future is open, open to a multitude of possible courses of action. If the future were fixed it would not be future but past, or, more accurately, there would be no such thing as the passage of time.

It is an error to think of God in a timeless realm, or worse to think of God having neither time nor place. It is tempting to psychologize God and reduce him to a concept of the human mind. Such a deity really has no being and is ultimately merely a creature of our imagination. The God who speaks to us in prophetic revelation, however, has a past, present, and future and not only exists in a place, which may be everywhere but certainly is not nowhere. But he also has a spatial substance, however mysterious and ineffable this may be. This is not to say that the universe is God's body. That notion is popular today, but cannot be supported by the story of revelation that tells of a creation that receives an incarnation.

Place can be described as a creation of God. It is not so clear that time is a creation. Stories begin "once upon a time." The story of creation in the Bible says: "In the beginning God created heaven and earth." Was there a time before the beginning? Then it would not have been the beginning. But if a beginning was once upon a time, then the beginning was that event which is identified as the beginning of a sequence in the story that is being told. Perhaps time is what we share in the on-going life of God. Each of us has a portion in that life insofar as we are his creatures.

An alternate view might entertain the notion that God is outside time as well as outside space. Time and space then would both be conceived as creatures. This would render God ultimately mysterious and utterly beyond human comprehension. The notion of an incarnation would be impossible to envision.

If, however, we understand the nature of reality to be narrative and if revelation is the story God tells us through his creation, it would seem necessary to receive God as the author who speaks his mind as the chapters of nature and history unfold. The mind of the Master will always remain a mystery, but his speech will also have intelligibility. He speaks to us where we are and in the familiarity of our experience. We can understand, without minimizing or detracting from God's mystery, that God shares our time and place because they are also his time and place.

In the story God is telling there are times and places when events congeal so that a fullness of time arrives. This is a *kairos* moment as distinguished from a *chronos* sequence. There are times when decisive action takes place which changes the course of history. In nature such turning points may arrive too, as when an asteroid strikes the earth and slaughters the dinosaurs, if this did indeed happen. Or when supernovas explode. But such events occur within a causal sequence, and they must be distinguished from kairotic events that freely arise due to either divine or human decision. Prophets are lifted up to warn a community of impending disaster if the people do not change their ways, or to promise them a future blessing if they will receive it in faith. Nothing is determined in such a story. All is contingent upon our response. The Servant of Yahweh is promised in the context of the yearning of the people for release from their captivity. This has a special and precise pertinence to a specific time and place in the history of a single tribe of people, but it also has a general application to the experience of all of God's children who enter into his story at the time appointed for them.

The general application of revelation to particular peoples apart from the biblical account of the history of Israel deserves recognition. We might well ask what was God doing among his people in North America when they were forming themselves into tribes with social cohesion, with legally ordered structure, and with a life-giving tradition? The classic European and American interpretation of *Heilsgeschichte* (salvation history) too narrowly assumed that Israel's and the Church's history is the only history of salvation; but how could the God who is the creator and redeemer of all his creatures favor one tribe over the rest to the neglect of their salvation until missionaries could come to them? If prophetic revelation made it possible for Israelites to live in hope of redemption through the promise of the coming of the Suffering Servant, the Son of Man, and the Messiah, surely

God with his merciful compassion must have been active in guiding the peoples of Asia, Africa, Europe, and the Americas in preparation for their salvation.

An example of such revelatory preparation is cited by Bishop Steven Charleston in an article in the Lent 1991 issue of *Areopagus* titled "American Indian Tradition—Rediscovering an Old Testament." Long ago the Choctaw tribe of American Indians lived far to the west of the present state of Mississippi. They had not yet formed themselves into a stable society but were wanderers. Two great leaders rose up among the people, two brothers named Chahtah and Chikasah. "They led the people on a long migration, carrying before them a sacred staff. Each evening this staff would be planted into the ground at the center of the camp. Each morning it would be found leaning toward the east as a signal that the exodus was to continue. Finally, when the people reached the holy hill called Nanih Waya, the promised land, the staff stood upright as a sign of God's purpose that our people should live in the land and become a nation" (*Areopagus*, Lent 1991, page 6).

Among the tribes and peoples around the world similar stories abound which are taken to be revelation, the special guidance of God freely determining their destiny. The contradictory expression "freely determining" is deliberate. The destiny could not have occurred had it not been made possible by the intervention of God, and yet that intervention was freely given and freely received. The result of God's action could have been otherwise. It was not a deterministic, natural, causal sequence. It was a freely-chosen historical event.

The choice must be made. Either we are the sole determiners of our destiny and we stand alone in the world as the product of natural selection, or we are cared for by a divine Lord who has made us freely in his image. If the latter is true then our destiny rests upon the free decisions of both God and ourselves. This is not to say that our salvation is Pelagian cooperation. Rather the story of revelation tells us that we are saved solely by God's grace which is given to us freely and may be freely rejected. The prophecy is a warning, not a prediction; and it is a promise, not something predetermined. On this stage of freedom God is glorified by the fact that he is not omnipotent Fate but rather personal Father. And we, his creatures, can rejoice that we are personally responsible for what we do with God's free gift. We are not puppets; we are not animals who act on instinct; we are human earthlings who are accountable for our decisions because we are capable of communicating with the Holy Spirit.

Two themes derive from God's story of revelation: his destiny for us in this world and his promise for us in a new heaven and a new earth. Our destiny in this world involves our relationship to both nature and history. Inasmuch as all things in nature are interconnected our ecological responsibility is paramount for our health and welfare on this earth. Inasmuch as the politics and economics of our global village have universal repercussions our free decisions for our behavior with one another must be made in the light of God's will for us.

In both cases this will mean obedience to laws, but as the Bible clearly reveals the law is given for sin, is not eternal ("You have heard it said of old, but I say unto you . . ."), is relative to circumstances, and does not save. Every culture must have laws, but, as our contemporary democracy shows, those laws are constantly reviewed, revised, and honed for the welfare of society.

We need government protection and control of our environment. The balance of nature is a global economy. A pessimistic view looks upon nature as a war of all against all in which every species of plant and animal is competing for survival. The strongest and brightest, the human species, is the greatest threat to everything else on the planet. But our planet is only a small, spinning ball in a universe that is replete with violence as galaxies collide and black holes ingest all matter within their gravitational pull. We cannot control astronomical events but we must be responsible for all that is within our grasp. We have a royal responsibility to care for everything on the earth. Such is our stewardship. We are not the owners. We are servants employed with the task of keeping the earth beautiful, fruitful, and holy.

We also need government to protect our families and economies. Just as we need a balance in nature so we need stability in history. Our societal structure requires law and government to constrain our sinful nature from destroying one another. But the law and government can become the most destructive forces when they try to rob us of our personal freedom and responsibility. Continually and repeatedly society must carefully draw the line between license and liberty, between tyranny and toleration. An example of this dilemma is the tension that arises when a government tries to control art, thereby turning it into propaganda for the sake of a narrow ideology. The law is needed for the sake of sin, but also because of sin the law (all forms of government) can become tyrannical.

Prophetic revelation is most exciting when it leads us to see our destiny beyond this life on earth. We are appalled when we view the rotting bones in the valley of death. We ask with the prophet: Can these bones live? God's revelation is most edifying and joy-fulfilling when the story turns to his victory over death. It involves victory because death is an enemy, both to God and to us. The warfare is universal in that it involves not only earthlings but everything else on earth and indeed earth and the universe itself. Nothing short of a new heaven and a new earth are required, such is the enmity, such is the separation between God and his creatures.

The story of revelation is a high drama involving warfare in heaven between God and his angels. We look upon our sin and its enormity and we shudder, but when we consider the cosmic scope of the rebellion against God we must be stopped utterly short. Just as our planet is but a small element in the vast universe, so we earthlings are small creatures among the multitude of heavenly hosts. We only dimly see ourselves in the magnificent fullness of God's universe. And when we realize that his fullness will be replaced by a new world more magnificent and without this destruction of death, we will lift our hearts in praise and thanksgiving.

The awesome joy we experience from the promises of prophecy, both for our earthly future and for our heavenly destiny, is in marked contrast to the kind of response we get from the predictions of science. Scientific prognostication is based upon responsible observation of patterns of natural behavior projecting trends with the assumption of continued uniformity in the process of events. Whether we are talking about nature or nurture in scientific investigation we look for patterns that we think we can alter so as to change the future. We have discovered the molecular makeup of animal species and we know that the DNA of a human being commands the function of that individual. By manipulating the genes future diseases can be avoided. But it is mistakenly assumed that genes or a stretch of the DNA can control behavior. Genes do not produce behavior. They have no causal connection with emotions or thinking. They produce proteins. What we do with the proteins is still done by free choice, and therefore the future of an individual's behavior cannot be predicted or controlled.

Scientific investigation can successfully predict some patterns of events in the future, but cannot predict anything that results from free choice. There is another kind of prediction that should not have the respect that we give to science. This is the superstition of soothsaying which rests upon no controlled experiment for verification but only upon an arbitrary tradition of untestable relationships. Prophecy does not claim the kind of detailed precision in predicting future events that science seeks, but it also has nothing to do with soothsaying. The prophets were not astrologers reading the future in the celestial patterns of the stars. The prophetic word is not a horoscope. It was this kind of confusion which sent Simon Magus into a tailspin when he tried to buy the gift of the Holy Spirit so that he could use it for profit.

Nevertheless prophecy does deal with the future. The writers of the New Testament found a whole host of statements in the Old Testament pregnant with prophetic meaning in the events which they witnessed concerning Jesus of Nazareth. Matthew recalls the passage in Isaiah where the prophet tells of a virgin conceiving a child who will be called Immanuel. Also Matthew cites Hosea when he tells of the escape of the holy family to Egypt: "Out of Egypt I called my son." Mark asks, "Why then is it written that the Son of Man must suffer much and be rejected" (Mark 9:12)? And Luke tells us from his special source, "And beginning with Moses and all the Prophets, he explained to them what was said in all the Scriptures concerning himself" (Luke 24:27). The passion narrative itself is colored by the twenty second psalm. The nails, the bitter wine and hyssop, the seamless garment, the casting of lots, the division of clothes, the mocking mob shooting out their lips, the cry of dereliction—the whole drama is described not as an eyewitness account but in the familiar language of the prophetic psalm. This language was deliberate. The evangelist wanted to communicate the faithful conviction that what happened here happened under the prophetic guidance of God. Notice also how the author of 1 Peter describes the crucifixion in terms of Isaiah 53 and John 5:39 says: "These are the Scriptures that testify about me."

What distinguishes prophecy from any other language about the future is the factor of faith. Prophecy operates in the realm of faith not sight, and therefore it involves the hiddenness of God. The early Christian witnesses were convinced that what they saw happening in Jesus was promised beforehand and was now fulfilled under the will of the Father. Neither scientific prediction nor illusory soothsaying involve faith. And faith must be understood here to be an elemental gift from God, not to be confused with mere human trust, belief, confidence, feeling, or decision. Before one has received this gift one cannot describe it; after it has come one cannot deny it. Now faith says that these events are the actions of God in history fulfilling what was promised aforetime.

Without faith the death of Jesus is simply a strange occurrence in the course of history. It may be explained as the miscarriage of justice or an accident of fate. The fact that it changed the course of history would always be a cause of wonder, but even this could be fitted into some philosophy of history as the necessary catalytic agent in the fusion of cultures. Seen in this light Jesus would have meaning as the bridge between Semitic and Greek cultures, but he would have no meaning to the Orient or Africa or modern post-Christian secularism. But the biblical contention is that Jesus is the cosmic Christ who was sent by the Father to save the whole world. His work is the fulfillment of the promise given to Israel which we receive only through faith. And it is faith that sees miracles to be the free acts of God, parables to be the true teaching of God, prophecy to be the promise of God, and apocalypse to be the hope of God.

Apocalypse

Besides the prophetic word there is another word in Scripture that deals with the future. This is apocalyptic—from *apo* and *kaluptein*, which means to uncover, disclose, or reveal. Albert Schweitzer maintained that Jesus used apocalyptic language and thought patterns throughout his life and teaching. He concluded that Jesus was a thoroughgoing apocalyptic visionary who was finally disappointed that his visions of the final coming of the kingdom of God did not occur, and therefore he tried to force the hand of God by the desperate action of the cross in Jerusalem. Such far-fetched exegesis is clearly warped, but it is significant that Jesus used apocalyptic teaching along with rabbinic. In this respect Jesus was similar in his teaching to the Essenic people of Qumran. They expected an eschatological prophet, recalling Deuteronomy 18:15-18 ("The Lord your God will raise up for you a prophet like me from among your own brothers"), which Acts 3:22 identified with Jesus. They also expected the Anointed Priest, the Messiah of Aaron, which is reminiscent of the militant Lamb of the book of Revelation. And they expected the Davidic or royal Messiah which is dominant throughout the New Testament.

What is the nature of apocalyptic? It takes seriously the sovereignty of God. In this idiom God is the present Lord of the universe, quite contrary to the deist notion of God as an absentee landlord. The world and everything in it exist by the word of the Lord; nothing exists by itself. There is no self-sufficient continuity. Each moment proceeds from the mouth of the Lord and therefore each moment can be the last. We find apocalyptic thinking uncongenial today because we want the world to be in our hands to use as we choose. We think we have baptized deism by talking about God as the owner and ourselves as his stewards, but instead of a real stewardship we want to have independent managerial control. We think the world can be shaped by our wills just as, by vote, we settle political issues. But if God is really sovereign he is always imminently present and we live from moment to moment by his grace.

Another characteristic of apocalyptic, derivative from the sovereignty of God, is a recognition of the cosmic dimension of God's rule. All nature and all history bow to his Lordship. Moreover apocalyptic sees the rule of God over the cosmos to be challenged by a cosmic adversary. This in no way detracts from the sovereignty of God because in the drama apocalyptic sees God to be the victor. "I saw Satan fall like lightning from heaven" (Luke 10:18). "But if I drive out demons by the finger of God, then the kingdom of God has come to you" (Luke 11:20). And the gospel is told in the mythical language of apocalyptic in chapters 12 and 13 of the book of Revelation.

Apocalyptic literature uses language that is veiled in order to uncover the truth. It is a species of poetry which uses symbolic imagery to reveal what is hidden while at the same time keeping it hidden. Here in apocalyptic we find the same dialectic of revealment and concealment that occurs with miracles, parables, and prophecy. God wishes to make himself known to us but he cannot do so on our terms because we would invariably make him into an idol. He must remain himself in the revelation, and so he remains hidden except through faith. And in our faith we come to know him as the mystery of the Unknown.

Apocalyptic tells strange and wonderful stories. A woman is clothed in the sun with her feet on the moon, and a beast with seven heads and ten horns sweeps a third of the stars out of the sky. The Son of Man comes at the end on clouds of glory with a shout and a final trumpet blast. John in Revelation, and Jesus in the Synoptics, and Paul in 1 Thessalonians all used apocalyptic language to refer to eschatological events. This language is veiled, not to be taken literally, and to an ordinary observer apart from faith it is nonsense.

Apocalyptic in the New Testament is careful never to predict the time of the end. There is no calculation or even a hint of any kind, only repeated warning that it is not for us to know the times or the seasons. Men will come and say it is here or there, but no one knows the time of the coming of the Lord, not the angels, not even the Son, but only the Father. He comes as a thief in the night when no one expects him. Yet Matthew's special source says, "You will not finish going through the cities of Israel before the Son of Man comes" (Matthew 10:13). To his disciples Jesus said, "This generation will certainly not pass away until all these things have happened" (Mark 13:30). And Jesus said to the High Priest, "And you will see the Son of Man sitting at the right hand of the Mighty One and coming on the clouds of heaven" (Mark 14:62). These passages seem to contradict apocalyptic uncertainty. They declare specific prediction. Modern scholars indeed consider them to be authentic precisely because they were not fulfilled and so were unlikely to have been concocted by writers who came afterward in the early Church.

Actually Jesus' statements to his disciples refer to his first advent, not to his second. In Matthew he speaks in the context of the mission to Galilee, and he refers to the coming of the promised One to Israel. This promised One did come to Israel before the disciples went through all the towns as is indicated by the confession of Peter at Caesarea Philippi. The word of Jesus to his disciples in Mark is spoken in the context of his remarks about the ambiguity of the signs of the end. Terrible portents will occur but do not be deceived. They are not the signs of the end. Jesus said, "Let those who are in Judea flee to the mountains." He could hardly have advised that to warn people about the end of the world. What good would a mountain refuge do? In the same pericope Jesus says no one knows the hour or the day. And finally Jesus' reply to the High Priest does not specify when the Priest will see the Son of Man coming, and again Jesus' words may well have been understood by the early witnesses to refer to his first advent. In any case the precise timing of the coming of the Son of man, whether as Jesus or as the risen Lord, is not said.

The important thing to remember with regard to apocalyptic, as with prophecy and, as we shall see, with miracles and parables, is that biblical story is a kind of poetry that dialectically reveals and conceals. Always it comes in a context that is universally experienced but is reserved for those who see with the eyes of faith as given by Christ.

Another important divine disclosure that comes through apocalyptic is the penultimate nature of history. This revelation has been repeatedly misunderstood because people want to grasp their destiny according to their own time-line rather than God's. The early Christians in Thessalonica stopped working because they expected the imminent "ending of the world." At the other extreme people have sought by working to establish the kingdom of God here on earth within the span of history. Apocalyptic clearly distinguishes between the time of historical ambiguity and final resolution. Paul in his letters to the Thessalonians admonishes his readers "not to be shaken in mind" by anything that might lead them to believe that the day of the Lord has come. Everything before the coming of the Lord, i.e., everything in the time-line of history, is provisional. We can expect suffering, but in the midst of it we must work for the benefit of all. This is the time for work but our work is not the engine that establishes the kingdom. God alone does that. Our work has its value; it serves various needs in this life. It does not create the new heaven and the new earth. Augustine and Luther both recognized this distinction between the penultimacy of history and the ultimacy of God's kingdom with their doctrine of the two kingdoms.

Failure to see this distinction was the error of the Social Gospel in the nineteenth century. Rauschenbusch valiantly pled for a movement in history to establish peace, unity, and justice in society, but he failed to see the realism of historical ambiguity. Reinhold Niebuhr's Christian realism was a salutary antidote to the imbalance of the Social Gospel. But with typical swing of the pendulum Niebuhr's realism was felt to be too compromising with the evils of this world. Black Power, Liberation Theology, and Feminism called for action now. These movements were not so naïve as to think, as did the Social Gospel, that we could establish the kingdom of God in our time. They were simply angry protests against manifest injustice. As with all good movements of the Spirit, however, they became perverted by a demonic tendency to absolutize their demands, reducing them to little more than a power play.

The Christian Gospel is never a simplistic program. It always requires recognition of the fact that we are living in a story of struggle that leads to a conclusion of triumph. We would like to embrace that triumph prematurely. We must learn to accept from the Holy Spirit the hard gift of patience. But with patience we must also be prophetic in our protest and not grow weary in well doing. To keep these contrary forces in balance is the difficult task of Christian behavior. This is what Luther meant when he said we should sin on bravely.

It is naïve to think that the exercise of our love alone will usher in the kingdom of God. It is also naïve to think that power in itself is evil. Power is neutral. Realism requires power, and if an evil use of power reigns, then nothing but another power will overcome it. Thus God has revealed himself to be almighty. But it is cynical to think that just any use of power will suffice. The violent protests of "right to life" advocates against abortion clinics fall into the devil's trap of attempting to seize moral righteousness by force. The hateful holy war declared by Muslims against "the Great Satan" ironically places these religious zealots in the hands of Satan himself. Power does indeed corrupt and its use must therefore always be tempered with compassion. We can and must struggle to redress wrongs, but we must recognize that God alone can ultimately establish his righteous kingdom. Our efforts in this historical era will always be ambiguous, yet we are obligated to strive for justice and equity and unity and peace, knowing that our attempts will always fall short, nor can they justify our salvation.

Evil is rooted in both collective institutions and in our individual selves. It is not sufficient simply to change the structures of society. Sin is profoundly fixed in us personally. We can use power to protect what we consider to be our rights, but truthfully we do not have rights; we have only gifts. As St. Paul said, "What do you have that you did not receive?" (1 Corinthians 4:7). Sin will make us hang on to our rights as we perceive them, but gratitude is the proper posture that will grant us the freedom to use our gifts for the benefit of everyone.

The struggle for rights describes social conflict between classes, races, nations, generations, and sexes. Our American Constitution has a bill of rights. But the flaw in political idealism based on rights is that sin makes each one of us an island, and the struggle for rights becomes a battle for self-interest. Persons and groups isolate themselves. The balance of self-interests becomes intolerably precarious. What is needed to make a civil, stable society is the enforcement of obligations. If people acknowledge obligations to one another, they can allow for the other's interest. Then freedom will flourish for the sake of justice, for expression, for equitable distribution of wealth, for health care, for social welfare, for the preservation of the environment, for education. America needs to balance the statue of Liberty in New York harbor with a statue of Responsibility in San Francisco harbor.

But the Christian realism of apocalyptic tells us that nothing short of a new heaven and a new earth will heal the hurts of history. To assume the resolution of history's failure within the span of our historical era is optimism that fails to probe the depths of human sin. This naïveté, however, must not be countered by the cynicism that surrenders to antinomian license. We are obliged to be grateful, and our gratitude must show with lives dedicated to achieve the very kingdom goals that finally God alone can and will provide.

Birth and Baptism

The time was ripe. The time was right. It was the moment for deliverance. Mary gave birth to a son and the world was delivered of sin. Creation was by the Word spoken, redemption by the same Word born of Mary. His birth brings our rebirth. But unlike natural birth, which because of sin is in sorrow and pain, the birth of Jesus is by the Spirit in joy, a glorious miracle and mystery, a virgin birth with no human father, not generated by biological union, but indeed a new creation of the family of Christ to replace the old family of Adam. And therefore this birth was accompanied by the choir of angels who sang glory to God and peace to all people. The deliverance was complete and unlimited. No one was excluded because this is a new creation.

Yet at the same time along with this unfathomable mystery—what can we make of angels singing to shepherds?—the word given was that the sign verifying this gracious deliverance is a baby in diapers. What could be more common, mundane, ordinary, human? And when taxes are due!

The story of Jesus' birth sanctifies time and place. Our time and place are warped and shattered. God came to us to make a new creation out of the old. So Jesus came through Mary from the lineage of David. But this world, in spite of its spell, is God's good creation, and the incarnation of Jesus through Mary is the affirmation of its goodness. Sin does not make the creation bad; it makes our relationship to creation twisted. The birth of Jesus from the creature Mary restores our relationship to the goodness of creation when we become joined to Jesus in the communion of the Church. The conception of Jesus by the power of the Holy Spirit without Joseph reveals God's judgment on our sin. The new creation cannot be conceived by a sinner. Hence Jesus, the new creation, is without sin, although he came to us in the likeness of sinful human flesh and took upon himself our sin (Romans 8:3; 2 Corinthians 5:21). This does not mean that virginity is better than marriage or that masculinity is sinful. Our natural functions are good; it is only their abuse that is denied.

The particularity of Jesus is a scandal. He was not God incarnate in general humanity. He was not a Gentile, he was not a woman, he was not Chinese or American. He was a particular Jewish male of David's family born in Bethlehem about 2000 years ago, a time which the whole world uses now to date its happenings. All this refutes Gnostic and mystic rejection of time and place. God saw in the beginning that what he had made is good. Neither Satan nor sin could destroy his good creation. Although because of sin this world is out of joint, it has its original beauty, and its final destiny is affirmed in the birth of Jesus.

Jesus' birth brings our baptism. By coming into sinful human flesh Jesus assumed also our mortality. We do not escape death thereby. He shares our death. He puts himself in the particular place of a sinner who has separated himself from God. He knows the loneliness, the nakedness—"Why have you forsaken me?"—and so he goes to the realm of the dead by way of the cross. Mary's heart was heavy. As he goes with us to death, we go in baptism with him to resurrected life. In the water with the Word we die with him to sin. We are separated from sin. That is what death means—separation. We are delivered from our old selves and born anew to righteousness and everlasting life. Baptism is our virgin birth. It is not the bloody, painful birth which was conceived in sin, but a new birth conceived by the power of the Holy Spirit—glorious, clean, holy, joyous, faithful, loving, with all the fruits of the Spirit.

Philips Brooks sang to Bethlehem about the birth of Jesus, "The hopes and fears of all the years are met in thee tonight." The people of the Old Testament waited for the Lord to deliver them from their enemies. They expected Yahweh to send his Messiah, or his Servant, or the heavenly Son of Man. Their faithful hope took a variety of shapes, just as ours does. None of these figures, however, was conceived as the progeny of a deity, as with pagan gods and goddesses. All were considered as angelic beings to be sent by the most high God to rule with victory, to serve with suffering, and to judge with equity. The great contribution of Old Testament revelation is not only monotheism, but also the notion that God is a transcendent Father who, as Creator, is not metaphysically continuous with his creation, yet is immanently present with his creatures, caring and providing for their needs. And it is the peculiar contribution of New Testament revelation to declare that all these expectations, those of Gentiles as well as Jews, are not only fulfilled in Jesus of Nazareth but that God himself was in Jesus Christ reconciling the world unto himself. It was Yahweh, not just an angel, who came to us in his Messiah, Servant, Son of Man. God was not just sending another to do his work; he incarnated himself. He sent Christ, incarnate by the power of the Holy Spirit, to be our victorious King and suffering Servant and gracious Judge.

And this incarnation by the Holy Spirit raises us in our baptism to newness of life by the laying on of hands. We have died with Christ in the water of baptism and we rise with the Spirit through the laying on of hands. Then we are knit together and woven into the seamless garment of the Church. A member of the congregation of the faithful clothes us with a white garment and brings forth a lighted candle and our names are written in the parish register. With the sign of the cross on our foreheads we have an eternal destiny of life and love and blessedness.

The Real Presence in Baptism

We need to take a new look at the meaning of baptism. The history of the Church produced three views of baptism: the sacramental view, believers' baptism, and Spirit baptism.

The sacramental view of baptism says that baptism is God's act in which he gives us a new creation through water, the laying on of hands, and incorporation into the Church. Baptism is God's gift to his sinful creatures in the form of a token or pledge or promise which has outward signs of inward grace. Both Christ and the Spirit are present in this gift. Christ is present to share with us his suffering death and his victorious resurrection. The Holy Spirit is present to raise us to new life so that we can bear his fruits of love, joy, patience, and hope.

The danger in this sacramental view is that we can turn it into a magical ritual. If we think erroneously of the gift of grace as a supernatural substance, rather than a new relationship, then it can be manipulated by an elite priesthood. The sacrament can be perverted into a superstition that can be exploited. This was one of the issues of the Reformation, and we can say that most Christians have gladly learned from Martin Luther on this matter.

Those who teach and practice believers' baptism reject the notion that it is a sacrament. For them baptism is not God's act. Baptism is not a sign of God's gift of grace, but rather a sign of a human decision to respond to God's grace. Baptism is not God's promise to renew us in Christ, but rather a human promise to dedicate oneself to God. Baptism is the believer's vow to be faithful. Obviously for such human decision and dedication one must reach the age of discretion and infant baptism is precluded.

Interestingly, in such a view and practice, water, the laying on of hands, and incorporation into the Church are involved just as they are in sacramental baptism, except that a whole tank full of water is used. But apart from the form, believers' baptism in meaning and significance is related to the baptism of John in the River Jordan, not to the baptism of early Christians. It is a baptism of repentance in preparation for the coming kingdom. Believers' baptism is really not dying with Christ and rising into the Spirit for membership in the Church as new creatures. It is the faithful and conscious recognition that the life of Israel is coming to an end, so that now we must intensify our dedication to live a life worthy of the coming Messiah. Often associated with this decision is an emotional experience of great depth. One becomes alert to the feeling that one's whole life is beginning anew. Obviously we are not talking about a gift from God, a sacrament, but rather we are talking about a human experience consciously and responsibly engaged in.

The danger in this believers' view is that 1) we make it into works-righteousness, and 2) we mistake our own emotion for the gracious action of God. To think that we are saved because we have decided for Christ is an easy error. But Jesus said, "You did not choose me, but I chose you to go and bear fruit that will last" (John 15:16). Baptism is not our emotion-charged born-again decision to live a life of dedication in preparation for heaven. Baptism is the regenerating power of the Holy Spirit building us up in Christ, enriching us with his grace, so that we may walk in the good works God has prepared for us before hand. Baptism is like a trust fund established for us before we are aware of it, but when we become aware we are free to draw on it with responsibility or to neglect it with disuse or to waste it with profligacy.

Spirit baptism is seen to be a divine act in which the Spirit gives new life and special gifts, chiefly the gifts of prophecy, healing, and tongues. When the Spirit comes he may be tested by his gifts. Ordinarily this manifestation of gifts requires adult behavior, hence infant baptism again is precluded. Sometimes, but not always, water is used as an external sign of the presence of the Spirit.

Those who believe in Spirit baptism say little about dying with Christ or sharing his suffering or completing his affliction with a life of sacrifice for the neighbor. The emphasis, and the danger, is upon what one receives as power from God. Prophecy, in the testimony of these Pentecostal people, is usually a simple word of comfort for one's daily life. Among the electronic preachers and more confident leaders of this movement prophetic utterances make more portentous claims about the destiny of the world. Isolated passages from the Hebrew prophets are twisted to provide political comment on current events. Ezekiel's enemy from the north, for example, was once identified with the Soviet Union attacking America across the North Pole.

Healing becomes an even more dangerous abuse when linked to Spirit-led prayer, because when it fails one is left bereft of the Spirit. The most common gift claimed is speaking in tongues, and the danger here, apart from sheer hypocrisy, is the self-righteousness that comes from the deception that you actually have something that others do not have. Other than the self-imposed feeling of religious satisfaction, no communal edification or revelatory communication has ever been provided by speaking in tongues.

But let us speak of baptism in terms of what it really is. Baptism is a new creation. To get that in perspective we must look at the first creation in terms of the story that is told. Or perhaps we should say stories, because there are several stories involved. The important thing is that we shall use the language of story, and not the language of the sciences, nor the language of philosophy. We will use the language the Holy Spirit uses in Scripture.

In the beginning God created the heavens and the earth. And God said, "Let there be light;" and God saw the light, that it was good.

But the goodness fell. There was rebellion in heaven when an angel, Satan, desired to be God and tried to usurp God's authority. There was temptation on earth when Adam and Eve believed Satan's lie; and they too rebelled.

Now God was confronted with a problem.[1] He could not leave his creatures in the garden he had made for them. Adam and Eve and all under their dominion were expelled, and ever after the earth and all its creatures have been groaning in anguish, suffering separation from God, waiting to be delivered from this exile, waiting to be restored to God. God waits too, and he cannot abide the rebellion and separation from his creatures. How could God restore them?

What would you do if you were working on a problem and it did not come out right? You would start over from the beginning. You would go back to the beginning and carefully work over every step to see what went wrong. This is what God did with himself and his creature, and this is what he wants us to do with our lives. We must go back to the beginning, to the start of everything before all the mistakes were made, so that we can be born anew with a fresh start.

What will you find in the beginning? When you started your life you were a baby in the arms of your mother. Your father was close by with his love and strength. That is the way God starts with his revelation of himself to us, with a tiny baby wrapped in swaddling clothes and sleeping in the arms of his mother, Mary. But if you go back beyond your parents and beyond your parents' parents and back beyond and beyond there will come a time when this world will lose form and all will become empty. There will be darkness brooding on the face of the deep before the sunrise brightened the morning, before the moonlight softened the night, before there ever was a sky above and an earth below. You will ultimately go back to the loneliness of God in the limitless seas of eternity.

When you come to the loneliness of God you will see that it was no accident that he decided to correct all the mistakes in humanity by going back to the beginning with the sighs of the Spirit and fashioning himself as a baby. There in Christ is the starting point. It was Christ in the first beginning whose Word created the world, and the Spirit gave it life. It is Christ again in the incarnate Word conceived by the Spirit in the womb of Mary that brings the new beginning, the new heaven and the new earth. Christ begins as a baby. This is an important reason why we baptize babies, because we must all become as babies to start over again. "Except you become as a little child you cannot enter the kingdom of heaven," Jesus said. Christ and our baptism are the hope of our renewal. In baptism we leave the fam-

---

[1] Cf. also: Roth, Robert Paul, *The Theater of God*, (Eugene, Ore.: Wipf and Stock, 2005), 117–19.

ily of Adam and Eve and enter the family of Christ. We leave our earthly parents to become the bride of Christ. To leave an old family means to be separated from it, to be dead to it, never to return. So baptism means dying to Adam's family and rising to the family of Christ.

But in the history of salvation God did not start with baptism. Indeed he tried a couple of things before he decided to go all the way back to the beginning.

First he tried to clean up the world by means of the flood. His intention was to save a few, eight people, so that all would not be lost. In the biblical version of the flood story God repented of his method of salvation, and so he tried a new method by electing Abraham to be the means of saving humankind. A covenant was made and Abraham and his seed were called to be a blessing to many nations, a light to the Gentiles. Henceforth God preserves Israel against his enemies. God wanted Israel to endure so that Israel could save the Gentiles. Now some are saved so that all can endure. This method failed too; the chosen people took their election to be a privilege instead of a commission.

In the New Testament the story shifts to a tale of redemption not in spite of suffering but through suffering. In the New Testament the elect one does not endure; he dies. The old covenant, in which God promises to preserve Israel, is replaced by a new covenant, in which God neither saves some and drowns the rest, nor elects some for the sake of the rest, but he slays his elect one and indeed all the rest in order to make a new creation. Or rather we should say he delivers up his elect one and all the rest to sin, and so they suffer death. His wrath is to let us have the consequences of the sin we chose.

The Christian story alone among all redemption stories faces up to the scandal of death as the wage of sin for everyone. Hence our story says we must give up all power and wealth and wisdom and become a little child in order to enter the new kingdom. We must die to ourselves and rise to new life in the Spirit, and in that way we become alive in the family of Christ. We become incorporated into the body of Christ, the Church.

These are the three dimensions of baptism. The first is dying with Christ with its visible sign of water. The font is a watery grave, and it has cosmic scope because it is the sign of our personal death to the old creation along with the entire world. There are stories within the great story to illustrate this. The story of Jonah is a watery tale that tells about the pagan notion that one evil person endangers all the rest. When Jonah was on board ship, running away from God, he was blamed for the storm that threatened the ship and all on board. So they threw him overboard to save the rest. This is just like the flood story. Only the numbers are changed.

But the Christian revelation is just the reverse. If one good person can be found, all the rest who are wicked can be saved. This was the story of Sodom and Gomorrah. This was the story of Paul and his shipwreck off the coast of Malta. God has something good for this one man to do and so all who were with him shared in this goodness. And, of course, this is the story of Jesus, the Lamb of God who takes away the sin of the world. For the sake of this one good man the whole world is raised again.

The second dimension of baptism is rising in the Spirit to newness of life with its visible sign of the laying on of hands. Out of death we come to life, and the new life in the Spirit brings us into a new heaven and a new earth, a whole new creation which God is fashioning according to his glorious imagination and according to his table of times. And this new creation itself has a visible sign in the Church. Hence the Church is the sacrament of the new kingdom, the visible token, pledge, promise of the final victory.

In the baptismal rite we have a sign of this third dimension in the lighted candle that is presented by a representative of the congregation. The Church, as the sacrament of the new kingdom, is not a voluntary fellowship nor a cultural development, although it provides fellowship and produces a culture. The Church is the called assembly of the Lord, the members of which constitute, as in the great mystery of marriage, a living organism which is one flesh, holy, catholic, and apostolic. The Church is a ministry of sacrifice. As Christ was elected to be the suffering servant, so the Church has been called out of the world to be sent into it to serve.

Baptism is the ordination of the people of God for this living sacrifice. Baptism then makes a difference in all that we do, not that as born-again Christians we can claim a special holiness for ourselves, or to possess special gifts from the Spirit, but as born anew in the family of Christ we can suffer and serve joyfully in our various vocations. In our baptism we acknowledge the ambiguity of our situation as sinners and saints in a world that is both good and evil, but a world in which we can always serve with love and joy and patience and faith and hope, for these are the fruits of the Spirit.

5

And Gladly Wolde He Lerne, and Gladly Teche

Geoffrey Chaucer: The Canterbury Tales

Matthew 5:3-10

Blessed are the poor in spirit,
  for theirs is the kingdom of heaven.
Blessed are those who mourn,
  for they will be comforted.
Blessed are the meek,
  for they will inherit the earth.
Blessed are those who hunger and thirst for righteousness,
  for they will be filled.
Blessed are the merciful,
  for they will be shown mercy.
Blessed are the pure in heart,
  for they will see God.
Blessed are the peacemakers,
  for they will be called children of God.
Blessed are those persecuted because of righteousness,
  for theirs is the kingdom of heaven.

Luke 7:36-50

Now one of the Pharisees invited Jesus
to have dinner with him,
so he went to the Pharisee's house
and reclined at the table.
When a woman who had lived a sinful life in that town
learned that Jesus was eating at the Pharisee's house,
she brought an alabaster jar of perfume,
and as she stood behind him at his feet weeping,
she began to wet his feet with her tears.
Then she wiped them with her hair,
kissed them and poured perfume on them.

When the Pharisee who had invited him saw this,
he said to himself, "If this man were a prophet,
he would know who is touching him
and what kind of woman she is, a sinner."
Jesus answered him,
"Simon, I have something to tell you."
"Tell me, teacher," he said.
"Two men owed money to a certain moneylender.
One owed him five hundred denarii,
and the other fifty.
Neither of them had the money to pay him back,
so he canceled the debts of both.
Now which of them will love him more?"
Simon replied,
"I suppose the one who had the bigger debt canceled."
"You have judged correctly," Jesus said.

Then he turned toward the woman and said to Simon,
"Do you see this woman?
I came into your house.
You did not give me any water for my feet,
but she wet my feet with her tears
and wiped them with her hair.
You did not give me a kiss,
but this woman, from the time I entered,
has not stopped kissing my feet.
You did not put oil on my head,
but she has poured perfume on my feet.
Therefore, I tell you, her many sins have been forgiven—
for she loved much.
But he who has been forgiven little loves little."
Then Jesus said to her, "Your sins are forgiven."
The other guests began to say among themselves,
"Who is this who even forgives sins?"
Jesus said to the woman, "Your faith has saved you;
go in peace."

And Gladly Wolde He Lerne, and Gladly Teche

Luke 10:25-37

On one occasion an expert in the law stood up to test Jesus.
"Teacher," he asked,
"what must I do to inherit eternal life?"
"What is written in the law?" Jesus replied.
"How do you read it?"
He answered, "'Love the Lord your God
with all your heart
and with all your spirit
and with all your strength
and with all your mind'
and, 'Love your neighbor as yourself.'"
"You have answered correctly," Jesus replied.
"Do this and you will live."
But he wanted to justify himself, so he asked Jesus,
"And who is my neighbor?"
In reply Jesus said,
"A man was going down from Jerusalem to Jericho,
when he fell into the hands of robbers.
They stripped him of his clothes,
beat him and went away,
leaving him half dead.
A priest happened to be going down the same road,
and when he saw the man,
he passed by on the other side.
So too, a Levite, when he came to the place and saw him,
passed by on the other side.
But a Samaritan, as he traveled,
came where the man was,
and when he saw him, he took pity on him.
He went to him and bandaged his wounds,
pouring on oil and wine.
Then he put the man on his own donkey,
took him to an inn and took care of him.
The next day he took out two silver coins
and gave them to the innkeeper.
'Look after him,' he said,
'and when I return I will reimburse you
for any extra expense you may have.'

Which of these three do you think
was a neighbor to the man who fell among thieves?" The expert in
the law replied, "The one who had mercy."
Jesus told him, "Go and do likewise."

Luke 11:1-4

One day Jesus was praying in a certain place.
When he finished, one of his disciples said to him,
"Lord, teach us to pray,
just as John taught his disciples."
he said to them, "When you pray, say:
'Our Father in heaven,
hallowed be your name.
Your kingdom come.
May your will be done on earth as it is in heaven.
Give us each day our daily bread.
Forgive us our sins
as we forgive everyone who sins against us.
And lead us not into temptation
but deliver us from the evil one.'"

John 9:1-39

As he went along, he saw a man blind from birth.
his disciples asked him,
"Rabbi, who sinned, this man or his parents,
that he was born blind?"
"Neither this man nor his parents sinned," said Jesus,
"But this happened so that the work of God
might be displayed in his life.
As long as it is day,
we must do the work of him who sent me.
Night is coming, when no one can work.
While I am in the world, I am the light of the world."

Having said this, he spit on the ground,
made some mud with the saliva,
and put it on the man's eyes.
"Go," he told him, "wash in the Pool of Siloam"
(this word means Sent).
So the man went and washed,
and came home seeing.
His neighbors
and those who had formerly seen him begging asked,
"Isn't this the same man who used to sit and beg?"
Some claimed that he was.
Others said, "No, he only looks like him."
But he himself insisted, "I am the man."
"How then were your eyes opened?" they demanded.
"The man they call Jesus made some mud
and put it on my eyes.
He told me to go to Siloam and wash.
So I went and washed,
and then I could see."
"Where is this man?" they asked him.
"I don't know," he said.

They brought to the Pharisees the man who had been blind.
Now the day on which Jesus had made the mud
and opened the man's eyes
was a Sabbath.
Therefore the Pharisees also asked him
how he had received his sight.
"He put mud on my eyes," the man replied,
"and I washed, and now I see."
Some of the Pharisees said, "This man is not from God,
for he does not keep the Sabbath."
But others asked,
"How can a sinner do such miraculous signs?"
So they were divided.
Finally they turned again to the blind man,
"What have you to say about him?
It was your eyes he opened."
The man replied, "He is a prophet."

*The Jews still did not believe that he had been blind
and had received his sight
until they sent for his parents.
"Is this your son?" they asked.
"Is this the one you say was born blind?
How is it that now he can see?"
"We know he is our son," the parents answered,
"and we know he was born blind.
But how he can see now, or who opened his eyes,
we don't know. Ask him.
He is of age; he will speak for himself."
His parents said this because they were afraid of the Jews,
for already the Jews had decided
that anyone who acknowledged that Jesus was the Christ
would be put out of the synagogue.
That was why his parents said, "He is of age; ask him."
A second time they summoned the man who had been blind.
"Give glory to God," they said.
"We know this man is a sinner."
He replied, "Whether he is a sinner or not,
I don't know. One thing I do know.
I was blind but now I see!"
Then they asked him, "What did he do to you?
How did he open your eyes?"
He answered, "I have told you already
and you did not listen.
Why do you want to hear it again?
Do you want to become his disciples too?"
Then they hurled insults at him and said,
"You are this fellow's disciple!
We are disciples of Moses!
We know that God spoke to Moses,
but as for this fellow,
we don't even know where he comes from."
The man answered, "Now that is remarkable!
You don't know where he comes from, yet he opened my eyes.
We know that God does not listen to sinners.
He listens to the godly person who does his will.
Nobody has ever heard of opening the eyes
of a man born blind.*

*If this man were not from God,
he could do nothing."*
To this they replied, "You were steeped in sin at birth,
how dare you lecture us?"
And they threw him out.

Jesus heard that they had thrown him out,
and when he found him, he said,
"Do you believe in the Son of Man?"
"Who is he, sir?" the man asked.
"Tell me so that I may believe in him."
Jesus said, "You have now seen him;
in fact, he is the one speaking with you."
Then the man said, "Lord, I believe,"
and he worshipped him.
Jesus said, "For judgment I have come into this world,
so that the blind will see
and those who see will become blind."

Teaching—the *Didache*

OF THE scholar, Chaucer said, "And gladly wolde he lerne, and gladly teche." Because Jesus was a teacher the Church has throughout its history been a school to its members. One of the earliest Christian writings was a collection of the teachings of Jesus called *Q*, the source; and the *Didache* was a teaching manual already in use throughout the Church early in the second century. As the healing ministry of Jesus produced hospitals in the service of the Church, so the teaching ministry produced schools. Learning and teaching have been to the glory of God, although it must be said that in practice the Church has not always magnified the Lord with its stewardship of learning and teaching. The preservation of classical texts by the transcription of manuscripts by medieval monks was marred by the persecution of Galileo and the prejudice against Darwin. Nevertheless the Church has always given something special from the revelation of God in Christ to the enterprise of education.

Education is a science, a craft, and an art, but the revelation of Christ makes it something more. In fact Christian education requires the unlearning of what we learn from the world. The world today is ambiguously both intensely secular and religious. Society has become secularized in the twentieth century in a way unknown to Christian history since Constantine. The patterns of chivalry no longer govern the conduct of nations at war. The ethics of personal respect no longer governs the conduct of couples in marriage. Manipulation of the masses is a psychological tool (or weapon) employed with equal finesse by advertisers, union leaders, business management, and politicians. This calls for unlearning. Far from emulating the world, the Church must teach with a prophetic word of warning and hope. Ironically alongside the new secularism a new religiosity has arisen which is just as inimical to the movement of the Spirit for peace and justice. Fundamentalist exclusiveness and legalism flourish alongside New Age mysticism and a revival of old age Gnosticism. We must guard carefully against an easy compromise with religiosity.

Egregious mistakes are made when wrong models and metaphors are applied to pedagogy. Just as the Church cannot be modeled after business, government, or entertainment, so likewise the teaching and learning process cannot be modeled after a business transaction, or governmental structure, or entertainment. Truth is not for sale. Students are not consumers. Teachers are not entrepreneurs. To turn the university into a marketplace where students pick and choose their education turns teaching into a popularity contest. Eventually money will be the bottom line in building a curriculum just as it has become with athletics. The university will become an asylum run by the inmates. Moreover the political model turns teaching into propaganda, and, of course, entertainment reduces the university to a playschool.

In the past fifty years colleges and universities in America have dramatically increased funding for research that brings a substantial monetary return. Curricula have become shaped to satisfy students' demand for training in occupations or professions that promise high earnings. Faculty salaries in the sciences, engineering, and business far exceed those in the humanities. Grants from government or private foundations abound for research in applied sciences, computer sciences, business, and engineering, but go begging for philosophy, religion, literature, languages, the arts, and interestingly also for theoretical physics. The growing imbalance between financially rewarding fields and the humanities is a striking indicator of the spiritual demise of our culture.

We will surely slip into a dark age if we do not produce leaders in our schools who have a profound command of language, the precise meaning of words, rhetoric, aesthetics, and especially logic. We cannot survive as a stable, democratic society without the ability of our citizenry to distinguish between a cogent and a false argument. We can never stop dealing with ethics and the choosing of values in human relationships. We need knowledge of the legacy of the past with sound logic to avoid making the mistakes of the past. If we cannot expose the fallacies of a specious argument and convince our fellows with a sound argument we will flout good reason, one of God's most fruitful gifts. Medical practitioners, however skilled, who sell their care in an open market to get the highest fee for service, without learning in school the values needed for a healthy society, fail to provide the care they sell. Lawyers who compete in an adversarial system for the judgment of a jury without considering the truth, only the victory, in a court case fail to provide the justice they sell. Scientists who discover and develop products which can be sold to enhance the well being of our society must also ask whether their products may in fact by detrimental. Business courses in a capitalist system that ignore the need to curtail human greed will not be good for business. Education without the humanities is no education at all. What is needed is education in the liberal arts which seeks to liberate people in all fields from their sinful ignorance and for a freedom to produce the society God intended for us.

It was the Church with its monasteries that kept alive classical culture through the Dark Ages. The clergy were the learned class. But with the secularization of modern society the Church has lost its monopoly on learning. Now a tension has arisen over the need for the Church to be involved in education. It is correctly argued that truth is not sectarian. Should religious institutions, therefore, leave education to the public sector, either private or government? It is said that there is no such thing as Christian mathematics. Numbers and equations are true or false in themselves regardless of the faith of the one computing them. There is no such thing as a Christian basketball team or a Christian swimming pool, only Christians playing basketball or swimming in a pool. Being a Christian does not make one a better mathematician or athlete or teacher. If this is the case, and it is, one may well ask why the Church should be involved in education.

But there is more involved in education than imparting the truth. It makes a difference what we do with the truth. We are ethical and political beings. Politics, as Aristotle said, is the extension of ethics to the public sector. Schools must wrestle with ethical and political decisions in every arena of life.

Fifty years ago people in the Church worried about the secularization of education, the growing monopoly of public schools, and the ability of the Church to compete. Today the public schools are failing in their task, unable to keep discipline, and many people are turning to private and religious schools. I doubt that our society will abandon the public school system entirely, nor should we, because a parochial, sectarian education is a poor substitute.

The crisis in our schools at every level calls for a critique of education that goes beyond what both secular and religious movements are offering. The nature of the Church requires us to present to the world a pedagogy that is something more than what is taught in the schools. Søren Kierkegaard began his *Philosophical Fragments* with the question: "How far does the truth admit of being learned?" Socrates posed the dilemma that if we have the truth we cannot seek it since we have no need to, and if we do not have the truth we cannot seek it because we do not know what we are seeking. In the face of this dilemma Socrates remained humble, not claiming to have found the truth so as to be able to teach it to someone else. He was the wisest of the Greeks because he knew that he knew nothing. All other wise men thought they had the truth which they could impart to others. Moreover they even charged money for their teaching. Hence they exercised power over others, and therefore they were a friend to nobody. Socrates alone was wise and humble and a friend.

But what then becomes of the teacher? Socrates resolved his dilemma by means of the doctrine of recollection of ideas (*anamnesis*). Each person has truth in himself or herself. We therefore need no teacher to tell us what we know. We need only a midwife to help us bring to birth what is already within us, to awaken to consciousness the slumbering ideas which we have forgotten when our souls passed from eternity into this confused world of time and space. If truth is within us then self-understanding is the key to God-understanding.

Kierkegaard rejected this humble Socratic wisdom because it does not allow for the unique significance of the single Moment in history, the Moment of Jesus of Nazareth, in which truth breaks in upon us from without, not from within. If each individual has one's own truth within, it may well be that one will not violate another with dogmatic imposition, but then others are only occasions to us. They do not count. If we have the truth within us personal piety can easily be substituted for learning.

Instead of Socratic subjectivity suppose things are otherwise. Suppose the occasion in time has decisive significance so that I will never be able to forget it, neither in the present time nor in eternity. If the moment is decisive, then when it occurs the learner must become dependent on the teacher. One does not have the truth within; rather one gets the truth from the teacher in the decisive moment. One is in error and another brings the truth. Moreover the error is one's own fault; it is what the Bible calls sin. Thus the teacher not only brings us out of error into truth; the teacher also brings us out of sin into faith. Truth is now seen to be more than the possession of information and skills; truth is a relationship that brings creative empowerment.

But how then does the individual avoid enslavement to the teacher? This was the question that prompted Nietzsche to kill God. The Church has a different answer. Rejecting Socratic wisdom but retaining Socratic humility the Church insists that no individual be violated in teaching the truth. Because we are in error there is need for a teacher, not a midwife; but we must not allow the occasion, nor the other person in the occasion, to rob the individual of one's integrity and freedom. This is a problem of authority. How can we avoid the tyranny of the teacher? In practice, of course, this goes beyond the classroom to tyrannies of all hierarchical systems in Church and society.

Gotthold Ephraim Lessing, like Kierkegaard, also had chosen occasional truth over eternal truth, and so Lessing became one of the fathers of modernism; but he did not acknowledge the decisiveness of the moment. Jesus was for him just one occasion among many, even if the highest and best. In a fuzzy way Lessing settled for an approximation to truth by studying the accumulative effects of history. This produced the abortive liberal faith in progress. Kierkegaard reaffirmed the Christian revelation which takes the moment in time seriously because it has eternal, that is everlasting, significance. Not just every moment, nor the growing sum of all moments in some kind of process naturalism, but one Moment, the Moment of Jesus of Nazareth, has significance for all time and eternity. Also within the life of each individual the moment of one's baptism is temporally and eternally significant, just as the Moment of Jesus is to the cosmos.

Worship is what is needed, therefore, to realize truth in the learning experience, since truth is seen to be not just the imparting of ideas or skills but encounter with a Person, and subsequently with other persons. Not recollection in the myth of Socrates, but celebrative remembrance (*anamnesis* in the Christian sense) in the eucharist will provide living, integrated flesh and blood to the learning process. Worshipful learning is the way the Church unlearns the wisdom of this world. Truth comes occasionally when a teacher imparts it, but teaching is not tyrannical if it is always indirect so that a personal relationship is created. Truth is not simply an idea or a thing or an impression, or a process, or an experience, all of which are real and may be good or bad; but truth is the coming of a Person; and all these other things receive reality, meaning, and value from that Person. It is from the abiding presence of Jesus in holy communion and confession and baptism that we learn what it means to be human. And the teacher does not collect disciples who are bound to him or her, but rather apostles are created who are sent to serve.

Parables

Miracles, prophecy, and apocalypse were all teaching tools used by biblical writers, and the most characteristic pedagogical method employed by Jesus was the parable. Jesus was called rabbi, master or teacher. He gathered disciples, learners. He used words to communicate in a special way; sometimes he taught without words as when he put a child in the midst of his disciples, or when he took a coin to show the difference between obligation to Caesar and obligation to God. Whether Jesus used words or objects his method in teaching was indirection. He had to point to a reality by getting around the surface meanings to the hidden secret that needed disclosure. The language of the Bible is not abstract scientific prose; it must point to truth to effect an encounter. The purpose of the teacher was to produce a new relationship.

Jesus used metaphors. A metaphor carries us from one level of meaning and understanding to another. The literal meaning of a word must be abandoned in the step to a higher meaning. Jesus said God is our Father. He had to use familiar human images, yet he had also to disabuse us of our sinful understanding of those images. The Jewish family of his day had a legacy of patriarchal connotations in which the father presides over his family with authority but also serves with suffering sacrifice. No doubt this was an image preferable to the pagan picture of God as the Great Mother (*Magna Mater*), which was the prevailing deity worshipped in the Greco-Roman world at the time. But no patriarch would send his son to a cross. Jesus' Father is not the image of any human father, but we are called freely to make our fathers in the image of the heavenly Father.

Today the father is pictured on television as the all-American breadwinner, the pitiful, harried business man who has abdicated his domestic throne to his domineering wife and his tempestuous teen-aged children. The father is Big Daddy in Tennessee Williams' great play *Cat on a Hot Tin Roof*. Surely God is not Big Daddy; nor are the children of God Williams' little no-necked monsters who make a shambles of the home and range over the neighbors' yards screaming like banshees. Jesus proclaims the gift of the kingdom, but to us a king is an exiled playboy or at best a beloved but disempowered symbol of empire. Feminists want to avoid the term altogether because they read it only in a literal sense.

Literalism leads to idolatry and renders revelation impossible. The Bible uses words to point to reality. When we translate we must be sure the new words point to the same reality. We are not free to change the reality in order to make the message relevant. The word is like a snapshot, not a dead picture, however, but a living, moving snapshot like one finds in children's books. The word only gives glimpses. The constant temptation of the theologian is to think that we can get rid of the pictures and put the words into abstract language. We think that if only we can systematize the attributes of God we will have him in our possession. This is nothing but intellectual idolatry. God cannot be abstractly defined. God says through the psalmist, "You thought I was altogether like you" (Psalm 50:21). Thus the parable as a means of teaching the unknown simply points to the truth and comes closer thereby because the parable brings us to the unknown while keeping him known to us as unknown. Abstract systematic theology fails because it makes the unknown merely known.

As an example let us examine in depth the parable of the sower in Mark 4:3-20. I choose this because it contains within the pericope its own interpretation. Is this interpretation authentic from the lips of Jesus? Hermeneutical procedure requires us to examine the text for authenticity, source, form, historical meaning, and then the Christian meaning for us today. Many scholars (Otto, Julicher, Dodd) say this interpretation is not authentic, but is rather an interpolation which indicates how the early Church misunderstood Jesus. These scholars say that Jesus was a Semitic teacher but his long interpretation is a Hellenistic corruption from a later time. Let us examine the record.

Jesus tells the parable. A sower went out to sow. 1) Some seed fell on a path and birds devoured it. 2) Some seed fell on rocky ground where it withered after it grew. 3) Some seed fell among thorns and was choked. 4) Other seed fell on good ground and yielded thirty, sixty, and one hundred fold. He who has ears to hear let him hear.

When Jesus was alone with the twelve the disciples asked him to interpret and he said, "The secret of the kingdom has been given to you. But to those on the outside everything is said in parables so that they may be ever seeing but never perceiving, and ever hearing but never understanding; otherwise they might turn and be forgiven" (Mark 4:11).

And then Jesus says if you do not understand this parable how can you understand any of them? But if you understand this parable you will have the key to all of them. The sower sows the word. 1) Satan devours what is sown on the path. 2) Persecution destroys the seeds on the rocks. 3) Worldly cares kill the seeds sown among thorns. 4) But what has been sown on good ground bears more seeds thirty, sixty, and one hundred fold. This is what the record says.

It is not apparent from the Greek text that this is an interpolation. To say there is interpolation requires historical and exegetical analysis. What then of the source? The source is Mark textually, and there are parallels in both Matthew and Luke with little change. The pericope does not seem to have any affinity with the Q source found elsewhere in Mark, nor does it appear to have come from the tradition of Peter as found in the story of the calming of the storm in this same fourth chapter. The source therefore seems to be the oral tradition of the Roman Church with probably Galilean background rather than Jerusalem. But according to an analysis of the form of the text a later Hellenistic interpretation has been added. Is this acceptable analysis?

First let us consider how the text says Jesus begins to interpret. He says to you is given the secret of the kingdom. The Greek text is *mysterion dedotai tes basileias tou theou*. In the Septuagint in Daniel the word *mysterion* refers to the secret purpose of a king. If we give it that meaning here Jesus is speaking of the secret purpose of God's kingly rule. The disciples have related themselves to Jesus in a decisively new way, hence Jesus is saying that in this relationship to him they have been given the secret purpose of God. To be related to Jesus is to be related to God. He who has this relationship then has the key to the parables. The requirements for discipleship can be demonstrated to be identical with requirements for entrance into the kingdom.

Next everything hinges on the Greek word *hina*—so that they may be ever seeing but never perceiving. *Hina* in the koine may be either purposive or resultant. It may mean what is said in parables is for the purpose that people will not perceive, or with the result that people do not perceive. A purposeful failure of perception makes no sense except in a fateful determinism, but a descriptive result makes good sense. The faithful elect are given truth upon truth so that their blessings are compounded but the unfaithful are given confusion upon confusion and wrath upon wrath, which is of their own choosing. Thus to those who have faith the parable reveals, but to those who do not the parable is meaningless. Hence there is both revelation and concealment in the telling of the parable.

The contention of modern form critics is that the form of Semitic teaching presents a single thrust of meaning, whereas later Hellenistic form sought for a variety of allegorical meanings. In the Middle Ages allegory became very popular. Thus in the parable of the good Samaritan the two coins supposedly represented the law and the gospel, the inn represented the Church with its comfortable hostelry, the thieves were the ministers of Satan, etc. This Hellenistic approach is considered not congenial with the style of the Old and New testaments. We must rather, say these modern form critics, expound the parable from the plain teaching which is clearly known. Discounting the details in the parable, therefore, the single thrust is that there are various soils and one should be sure to be the good soil so that one may increase.

But such an interpretation flies in the face of the main thrust of the gospel itself. It lends itself to unevangelical works-righteousness: work hard to be a good soil! This exegesis applies a theory of history concerning Semitism and Hellenism which is arbitrary. The parable must fit into this theory before we can understand it. But a better, because more open and unprejudiced, method is to let the parable speak to us. At the beginning we have the sower; at the end we have the harvest. We begin with seeds of the sower and we end with seeds of the harvest. There is a main single thrust here, but it is not the thrust of soils. This is a parable of seeds, for the main thrust is the strange miracle that the sower sows seeds and at the end of the season he reaps seeds. This is both familiar and strange. In farming this happens all the time. And so the preacher sows the word and at the end he or she reaps the word. The preacher puts Christ into the world, and from this good seed in good soil comes the surprising and strange result of a harvest of more Christs! The evangelistic process is the multiplication of the word. The preacher reproduces himself or herself. But along the way the word is vulnerable to various kinds of waste and attack. Hence the details of the parable are not arbitrary or inconsequential but structured. They belong to the whole not in an allegorical way but in an organic way. Look for the single thrust in the parable in the light of Christ, examine the beginning and the end and show how the end results from the beginning, and then show how the details in between help to support the whole structure. This is not a parable of soils but a parable of seeds—the word. The missionary meaning of the parable is the thrust of the gospel in all its fullness.

And when the thrust of the parable is seen it must be grasped not with the senses, nor with the mind, nor with the heart, but as a revelation by the power of the Holy Spirit. Throughout these essays, whether we are talking about parables, teaching, preaching, prophecy, apocalypse, miracles, sacraments or any form of communication it is presupposed that no human ability given to us in creation is adequate to perceive the hidden word of God. It is not by reason or by empirical evidence or by feelings of the heart or by decisions of the will that we come to God, but rather it is by faith given through revelation that God comes to us. And then our faith informs and shapes our intellect and our emotions and our decisions. This is why the Lord said to Isaiah that he should tell the people to be hearing but not understanding, seeing but not perceiving, and he should make their hearts calloused. The people should not be deceived into thinking that they have the power in themselves to grasp and comprehend God. We live only by grace!

Miracles

The biblical word for miracle is *semeion*, not a supernatural event deviating from the known laws of nature, but a wonderful sign. In biblical times the fixed system of natural laws was not established. Generally, but vaguely, it was assumed that there is a difference between the hidden, unseen world of God and angels, principalities and powers on the one hand and the visible world of human experience on this planet. Interaction between the two worlds was affirmed as an occasional wonder. Angelic beings visited humans, even identified with names as Gabriel or Satan. Strange and unusual events, especially connected with healings or demonic seizures, were considered the result of such intervention. The notion of nature and supernature, however, was not yet developed, neither as a philosophical world view nor as a scientific system. We would do well to consider the stories in Scripture about miracles simply as wonderful signs that tell us something about our relationship to God.

Today we have two different notions about natural events, both of which make problematic the stories about wonderful signs in the Bible. One notion comes to us from the middle Ages, especially the philosophy of Thomas Aquinas. It affirms a system of natural laws which have been ordained by God in the created order of things. These laws are the pattern we observe in nature, and they are conceived to be unvarying for all times and places. Any interruption of the sequence they describe can only be ascribed to the supernatural work of God. Raising Lazarus from the dead is an example of such supernatural intervention.

The other notion is our modern scientific assumption that every natural effect has a natural cause. This is the principle of sufficient reason which we have inherited from the Enlightenment. According to this notion there can be no miracles since there is no transcendent reality beyond what is empirically verifiable. Miracles, as described in the Bible, and in the piety of the devout, are superstitions and hence fraudulent. They have no foundation in fact.

It is true that accounts of miraculous events are sporadic. Reports of strange and wonderful happenings occasionally occur in the histories of people all over the world and at various times. It is significant that they are not continuous. Miracles were reported at the time of Moses and Elijah but not at the time of the great prophets of Israel. Again we have the many stories of miraculous healings at the time of Jesus. Is this because God chooses to intervene only at certain times when the kairotic moment is right? Or are these times peculiarly susceptible to the reception of miracles because of the psychic conditioning of the times? In modern times our scientific world view rejects the possibility of miracles because they are not verifiable. A natural explanation is assumed. The Roman Catholic Church still affirms miracles, howbeit reluctantly, with the canonization of saints. Also the visions of Bernadette and other young women are given credence. But in America where, unlike Europe, the vast majority of people devoutly believe in God, the general sophistication affirms a faith without the need for miracles to support it.

What can we say about the stories of Scripture in view of our contemporary world view? If we are honest and precise we must rest with a humble agnosticism about miracles. We do not have a general experience of healings that can be ascribed to the special intervention of God. Mysterious remissions of a disease do occur, but they occur among people with or without prayer. There is no way we can demonstrate they are the direct intervention of God. Instances of such miraculous healings have invariably been exposed to be fraudulent. Are the stories of the Bible simply the product of wishful imagination? We need not charge pious people with fraud, although they may be duped by charlatans.

It is my view that the method of science, which requires empirical verification, must be respected for all human experience, but it does not require a world view of complete determinism. This means that there is always and everywhere the possibility of a free decision on the part of both God and his people which can begin a new sequence in the order of things. Faith can affirm the substance of things unseen, but we must be especially wary of credulity. We must test every event in terms of its edification or its destruction, and all the wastefulness in between. There seems to have been times when miracles occurred giving us revelation of wonderful signs concerning our relationship with God and our destiny. And there are also times when such revelation is absent.

We do not know what is in the mind of God to decide when such wonders are appropriate for our spiritual welfare, but we may say that in a world created by God who is a free Spirit such miraculous wonders are possible. It should be recognized that Jesus was not quick to perform miracles; indeed he seemed at times extremely reluctant. It should be recognized also that the human desire for miracles can be downright demonic. "Why does this generation seek for a sign?" We have signs in the regular course of events; we do not need special supernatural portents. The story of Jesus should be sufficient for us. The appearance of the risen Lord was a miracle, a wonderful sign not in the natural course of events, but Jesus told Thomas, "Because you have seen me, you have believed; blessed are those who have not seen and yet have believed" (John 20:29).

The most astonishing miracle, the wonderful sign of God's grace, is the story of Jesus in which we are taught that God is the friend of sinners, and from which we have the proclamation of good news to all the world that God was in Christ reconciling the world unto himself.

We are talking then about signs in the Bible which tell us about our relationship to God, but there are two different kinds of sign: one is an ordinary event and the other is wonderful and special, and both bring revelation from God. In the Greek texts of the Septuagint and the New Testament sometimes the word *semeion* (sign) refers to something within the natural order of events, howbeit unusual and significant, as the swaddling clothes of a baby in a manger, or the preaching of a man like Jonah. At other times the word is used to refer to a wonder of divine origin as performed by Christ or by men of God, such as the feeding of five thousand and Peter's healing of the crippled beggar; or the wonder may be of a demonic nature performed by Satan or his agents (Revelation 13:13). The beast brings fire down from heaven in the sight of people and the coming of the lawless one is accompanied with pretended signs and wonders.

Both uses of the concept of sign in Scripture differ from later interpretations which have received broad acceptance in Christendom. I have referred to the notion that a miracle is the interruption of God's system of natural laws, and I have said this is false because there is no verifiable evidence of such a system. God never enters a scientific equation. The laws of science are convenient constructs of human imagination which we find useful in understanding our experiences. These laws change from generation to generation according to what we think is useful. They are operational statements, shorthand formulae, sometimes mathematically constructed in areas where we are able to describe our experience with great precision. They do not describe God's laws or his government, only human perceptions.

Another interpretation, which tries to accommodate this scientific critique, follows Schleiermacher's idea of religion as human dependence upon God. According to this notion every event is a miracle because God is in every event. Our feeling of dependence on God supposedly gives us a sense of the miraculous in all human experience. This notion is false because it fails to distinguish between the created order of things and the special revelation which God brings to us in the story of Jesus. Christianity cannot be described as the feeling of dependence upon God. Such a feeling signifies something about us and describes human religion, not divine revelation.

It must be granted that we are left with much ambiguity with regard to biblical accounts of miracles. People call for miracles in order to establish faith, but Jesus says no such sign will be given (Mark 8:11-12). The people of Jesus' day thought of supernatural powers as being either angelic or demonic, and both angels and demons could perform miracles. Jesus was accused of casting out demons by Beelzebub (Luke 11:15).

If we must rest with this ambiguity and mystery we can rejoice in the faithful certainty that there are signs which reveal to us the will and the work of God among his creatures. The mark of genuineness is the story of

Jesus. We need not quarrel over whether any report is historical or not; we need only to ask whether any report edifies the body of Christ. It is true that much in the biblical account is not helpful because it is manifestly human in origin. Some accounts in Scripture are even contradicted by later revelation. "Now that faith has come, we are no longer under the supervision of the law" (Galatians 3:25). This is certainly true with regard to dietary laws, circumcision, the relationship between Jews and their neighbors. It is foolish, misleading, and wasteful scholarship to investigate the historicity of various biblical records. Jesus said, "This is a wicked generation. It asks for a miraculous sign, but none will be given it except the sign of Jonah. For as Jonah was a sign to the Ninevites, so also will the Son of Man be to this generation" (Luke 11:20-30).

It really makes no difference whether the perception sought is of a divine intervention or a historical verity; in both cases the criterion of judgment is a human perception. In both cases, ancient superstition and modern sophistication, faith and the Holy Spirit are absent. Genuine miracle is the revelation that gives us the faith in the Christian community to see and hear the Holy Spirit shaping us as new creatures in the body of Christ. Whereas before we were blind to see the beauty and holiness of this community, now we see in faith by the power of the Spirit the sacrificial service of the living Christ in whose life we share. Miracles must be understood then as teaching tools in the story of revelation.

6

Paradox and Contradiction

Mark 15:33-38

*At the sixth hour
darkness came over the whole land
until the ninth hour.
And at the ninth hour
Jesus cried out in a loud voice,
"Eloi, Eloi, lama sabachthani?"—
which means, "My God, my God, why have you forsaken me?"*

*When some of them that stood by
heard this,
they said,
"Listen, he is calling Elijah."
One man ran,
filled a sponge with wine and vinegar,
put it on a stick,
and offered it to Jesus to drink.
"Now leave him alone," he said.
"Let us see if Elijah will come to take him down."*

*With a loud cry,
Jesus breathed his last.*

*The curtain of the temple was torn in two
from top to bottom.
And when the centurion,
who stood in front of Jesus,
heard his cry
and saw how he died,
he said,
"Surely this man was the Son of God!"*

Mark 16:1-8

*And when the Sabbath was past,
Mary Magdalene,
and Mary the mother of James,
and Salome,
brought spices
to anoint Jesus' body.
Very early
on the first day of the week,
at the rising of the sun,
they came to the sepulcher.
And they asked each other,
"Who will roll away the stone
from the entrance of the tomb?"
But when they looked up,
they saw that the stone,
which was very large,
had been rolled away.*

*As they entered the tomb,
they saw a young man
dressed in a white robe
sitting on the right side,
and they were alarmed.*

*"Do not be afraid," he said.
"You are looking for Jesus
the Nazarene,
who was crucified.
He is risen!
He is not here.
See the place where
they laid him.
But go,
tell his disciples and Peter,
that he is going ahead of you
into Galilee.
There you will see him,
just as he told you."*

Trembling and bewildered,
the women went out
and fled from the tomb.
They said nothing to anyone,
because they were afraid.

1 Corinthians 15:35-58

But someone may ask, "How are the dead raised?
With what kind of body will they come?"
How foolish!
What you sow does not come to life
unless it dies.
When you sow, you do not plant the body that will be,
but just a seed,
perhaps of wheat or of something else.
But God gives it a body as he has determined,
and to each kind of seed he gives its own body.
All flesh is not the same:
People have one kind of flesh,
animals have another,
birds another and fish another.
There are also heavenly bodies
and there are earthly bodies;
but the splendor of the heavenly bodies is one kind,
and the splendor of the earthly bodies is another.
The sun has one kind of splendor,
the moon another and the stars another;
and star differs from star in splendor.

So it will be with the resurrection of the dead.
The body that is sown is perishable,
it is raised imperishable;
it is sown in dishonor,
it is raised in glory;
it is sown in weakness,
it is raised in power;
it is sown a natural body,
it is raised a spiritual body.

*If there is a natural body,
there is also a spiritual body.
So it is written: "The first man Adam became a living being,"
the last Adam a life-giving spirit.
The spiritual did not come first, but the natural;
and after that the spiritual.
The first man was of the dust of the earth,
the second man from heaven.
As was the earthly man,
so are those who are of the earth;
and as is the man from heaven
so also are those who are of heaven.
And just as we have borne the likeness of the earthly man,
So shall we bear the likeness of the man from heaven.*

*I declare to you, brothers and sisters,
that flesh and blood cannot inherit the kingdom of God,
nor does the perishable inherit the imperishable.
Listen, I tell you a mystery:
We will not all sleep, but we will all be changed—
in a flash, in the twinkling of an eye, at the last trumpet.
For the trumpet will sound,
the dead will be raised imperishable,
and we will be changed.
For the perishable must clothe itself with the imperishable,
and the mortal with immortality.
When the perishable has been clothed with the imperishable,
and the mortal with immortality,
then the saying that is written will come true:
"Death has been swallowed up in victory."
"Where, O death, is your victory?
Where, O death, is your sting?"
The sting of death is sin,
and the power of sin is the law.
But thanks be to God!
He gives us the victory through our Lord Jesus Christ.*

*Therefore, my dear brothers and sisters, stand firm.
Let nothing move you.
Always give yourselves fully
to the work of the Lord,
because you know
that your labor in the Lord is not in vain.*

Crucifixion

"Jews demand miraculous signs and Greeks look for wisdom, but we preach Christ crucified." (1 Corinthians 1:22-23)

THE CHRISTIAN revelation alone proclaims the sacrifice of God for his creatures. Religions all present offerings to the gods, sometimes in the form of sacrifices, even human sacrifices, sometimes in the form of prayers, whether of confession, petition, lamentation, praise, or thanksgiving, sometimes in the form of behavior as in the piety of moral rectitude or in charitable service. Invariably the action is from us to the gods. Christianity alone brings God to us in a mind-bending, heart-rending, world-shaking paradox and contradiction.

The paradox is the cross, the contradiction is the Incarnation. A paradox is something that seems to be other than what it really is. The Cross seems to be an ugly execution; it really is a loving redemption. It seems to be the defeat of a good man; it really is the defeat of sin, death and the devil, a victory that through sacrifice redeems sinners. What seems to be an execution of justice, whether a miscarriage or not, is really the triumphant justification of a fallen world.

A contradiction is something said against itself. The Incarnation is a contradiction in which God says he became human in Jesus. The Incarnation is not a paradox. Jesus does not just seem to be human; he is really and fully human. Logic requires consistency. A is A and not Not-A. God is God and not Not-God. Humans are Not-God. But revelation says that Jesus is both God and Not-God. This contradiction cannot be resolved. The rational tool of logic, as valuable as it is in many other ways, simply does not work here. The surprising marvel of revelation, however, declares that this inconsistency can not only be accepted but it can be celebrated. As Luther said in his Catechism: "I believe that Jesus Christ, true God, begotten from eternity, and also true man, born of the Virgin Mary, is my Lord." And we confess in the Nicene Creed: "We believe in one Lord, Jesus Christ . . . true God from true God, begotten not made, of one Being with the Father. . . . For us and for our salvation . . . he became incarnate from the Virgin Mary and was made man." Moreover we can believe this contradiction not by our own power but only by the revelation of the Spirit, as Luther says further in his Catechism: "I believe that I cannot by my own reason or strength believe in Jesus Christ my Lord, or come to him, but the Holy Ghost has called me . . ."

Paul says there are two kinds of people in all the world. His metonyms are Jew and Greek. By Jew he means the religious person who wants to get to God but always on human terms through signs and wonders. The religious person is deceptively humble and pious, but really demanding. The religious person never believes on the faith given by God. This person believes on the evidence that satisfies one's preconceived notion of reality. The Greek is the sophisticated person who thinks he knows all he needs to know, and therefore God is unnecessary because human wisdom is sufficient for all our needs. The sophisticated person is the primordial Prometheus who stole fire from heaven and thus rendered the gods superfluous because with fire humans can provide their own weapons to defend themselves and their own food to satisfy their hunger. The wise person is coolly arrogant even when such a person is tolerant and magnanimous.

Whether we are fearfully anxious in our religion or pridefully oblivious in our sophistication, St. Paul says we are contradicted by God. Hence God's revelation on the Cross is an offense to the Jew and nonsense to the Greek. The religious person stumbles over the Cross and finds it a monstrous scandal to one's piety. How could God, who is holy and infinite and eternal, be subjected to such humiliation? The sophisticated person sees the Cross as a simple mistake, folly, foolishness, perhaps regrettable for the victim but of no consequence for the world. Why should we be concerned overmuch with such a pathetic story?

Yet this story turned the world upside down. The great promise of the resurrection cannot be told without the crucifixion. The crucifixion has captivated the hearts and minds of both religious and sophisticated people ever since that first Good Friday, troubling them, fascinating them, and ultimately creating in them new persons. The great artists through the centuries have represented Christ on the Cross in sculpture, painting, hymnody, and passions. What is the awesome and poignant power of the hideous scene on Golgotha that so overwhelms our creative imagination? Why is the depiction of the death of this particular individual celebrated as the most uplifting beauty?

Perhaps Matthias Grunewald's triptych, the Isenheim altar piece, now in Colmar, most dramatically portrays the horror and the beauty of the crucifixion. Christ is dead on the Cross. His body exudes bloody sweat. Life has left his face. John the baptizer anachronistically stands beside the cross with his enlarged index finger pointing to the dead Jesus, and a caption reads in Latin: "He must increase; I must decrease." On the other side Mary shows her shocked grief. Her face is as white as the shawl that covers her head. Why do we celebrate this monstrous horror? What loveliness draws us to this grief and pain? The crucifixion is the supreme example of the mysterious wonder of God's revelation turning inside out and infinitely exploding all human expectation.

Religion seeks to appease an angry god or to satisfy a hungry god. In our sinful ambiguity we think God is either angry or hungry, but in truth we really try to assuage our own anger and satisfy our own spiritual hunger with our religious quest. The cross reveals that God is neither angry nor hungry. He was pleased to give himself in love and sacrifice so that we might rise and be his friends.

Ostensibly the crucifixion was a legal execution. Jesus was accused of blasphemy and treason. Before the high priest and the Sanhedrin Jesus declared, when asked if he is the Christ, "Yes, it is as you say, but I say to all of you: In the future you will see the Son of Man sitting at the right hand of the Mighty One and coming on the clouds of heaven." Notice the subtlety of Jesus' answer. Is he the Christ? Yes, and for a mere man to claim this is blasphemy; but Jesus reveals in his answer that Christ will come in the future. The man perceived by the high priest, who speaks blasphemy to human ears, is really not what the high priest sees and hears. He is really the Christ hidden to the mind and senses but open to faith. And therefore Jesus was not guilty of blasphemy.

The same twist of revelation occurred when Jesus was brought before Pilate. When the governor asked him if he is the king of the Jews, a treasonous threat to Caesar, Jesus answered, "Yes, it is as you say." Again Jesus made a qualification: "My kingdom is not of this world." To claim to be king of the Jews is treason, but Jesus' kingdom is not a threat to Caesar because it is not of this world. Jesus was not guilty of treason. What the high priest and Pilate thought they saw in Jesus was contradicted by God who came to us not as a man pretending to be God and a man pretending to be a king, but Jesus was truly God incarnate as Christ the King of kings.

From the standpoint of sinful human perception Jesus was guilty of blasphemy and treason, and he was legally crucified under both Jewish and Roman law; but from the standpoint of revelation perceived by faith the crucifixion was a travesty. The highest and best in human justice is judged to be the greatest human sin, comparable universally with the sin of Adam. In both cases all humanity is implicated, for as the psalmist says:

> All have turned aside,
> they have together become corrupt;
> there is no one who does good,
> not even one.

What is blasphemy and treason to human perception is holiness and beauty to faith!

Only art and liturgy can express the height and depth of the passion of Jesus Christ. And in Johann Sebastian Bach's *Passion According to St. Matthew* art and liturgy become one. The *Passion* music is artfully suited to the text. Most emphatically Bach expressed the dramatic change in Pilate's judgment of Jesus. Pilate washed his hands and declared himself innocent of the blood of this just person. The true innocence of Jesus and the ironic hypocrisy of Pilate resound with crashing contrast. The cruelty of the cross and the comfort of its song in the heart of the believer are equaled only by the setting Bach gave to the *Crucifixus etiam pro nobis* in the *B Minor Mass*, which Bach adapted from the cantata *Weinen, Klugen, Sorgen, Zagen*. The sorrow and the joy one feels in the face of such passion reveals how God heals through suffering. Only, however, when suffering is guiltless, as in the passion of Jesus, can this healing and redeeming love be effective for us. We receive this grace when we enter into communion with Christ in the sacrament. The pulsating poignancy of Jesus' passion lifts us from the depths of our despair.

The final chorus in the *St. Matthew Passion* sings this solace. It is a lullaby to Jesus as he hangs dying on the cross. The faithful sing: "My Jesus, good night!" Softly and calmly Jesus is comforted, and just as softly and calmly we rest in his passion:

> "We sit down in tears and call
> to Thee in the tomb:
> Rest softly, softly rest
> Rest, ye exhausted limbs,
> Rest softly, rest well.
> Your grave and tombstone
> Shall for the unquiet conscience
> be a comfortable pillow
> and the soul's resting place.
> In utmost bliss the eyes slumber there."

And just as edifying as the sounds of music are the stones of buildings. The vaulted arches and flying buttresses of Notre Dame of Paris, the rose window and stained glass of Chartres proclaim the glory of the Lord as he himself declared when he marched to Jerusalem to undergo his passion. At his triumphal entry into Jerusalem Jesus' disciples joyfully began to praise God in loud voices: "Blessed is the king who comes in the name of the Lord!" Some of the Pharisees in the crowd told Jesus to rebuke his disciples for their unseemly exuberance. Jesus replied, "If they keep quiet the stones will cry out." And here we have in the magnificent cathedrals and churches throughout Christendom the shouting of stones beautifully extolling their frozen music in the name of the Lord.

The arts in worship lift our spirits and make the crucifixion, this most horrible of tortures, into a comfort that strengthens us for any and every trial. Thus we can sing: "Komm, seusses Kreuz!" Come sweet cross, my Jesus, give it always to me. Should my pain become too heavy, then help me to carry it. Think of the almighty Creator God coming close to each of us and lifting our crosses as he bears his own!

Resurrection

The gospel story is unique among all religious tales. It tells us that a man, who was also God, really died as all people do, and then really rose from his grave, as no one ever does. Moreover, it is a great irony that talk about the resurrection stirs up a hornet's nest. The women who came to Jesus' grave were so frightened they could not speak about it to anyone. Every time Peter and Paul and Stephen proclaimed the good news that Jesus was raised from the dead they encountered resentment and disbelief. One might think people would be delighted with such news, but instead they became angry, and the early Christians were martyred for it.

The reason for this strange reaction is that people want resuscitation, not resurrection. What the early apostles preached required people to be changed radically from what they are; but people want to continue as they are and not be made new. The prevailing view of human destiny at the time of Jesus and Paul was the Platonic teaching of the immortality of the soul. People thought of themselves as individuals having a body and a soul, the body being earthly and temporal, the soul being heavenly and eternal. Death could even be welcomed as the release of the soul from the prison of the body. The soul could live on without dying as a reward for righteous behavior.

The revelation of Jesus' resurrection, however, rejected the notion of an immortal soul as distinct from the body. The soul is not an entity alongside the flesh. The soul is the name for the life of the person. When death comes this life is snuffed out. The whole person dies—body, soul, spirit, brain, mind, heart, guts, blood, bones, cells. And the whole person rises in a new body, a changed body that will not die. This is not simple resuscitation of the old earthly flesh. That flesh returns to the dust of the earth from whence it came, as we all know from empirical experience. But the resurrection of Jesus reveals to us that our future destiny with him involves a new creation.

When Peter and the disciples were confronted with the resurrection of Jesus their thoughts were not centered in themselves as individuals, as if to say, "Hallelujah, Jesus lives, so now I will survive too," None of the biblical reports and sermons say that. Rather their thoughts centered on the vindication of God's purpose in the establishment of his kingdom. God's goodness won the victory over evil, life over death. Jesus' resurrection was the first fruits of this harvest. It was an operation headstart on the coming kingdom. It was resurrection to something radically new, not resuscitation of something old.

The Christian view sees humans as God's good creatures who have fallen by their own choice into the temptation of the devil, so that we are both personally guilty and victims of sin. But God is not defeated by this sin. He has conquered it by suffering it, absorbing it without himself becoming sinful, without becoming like the enemy he defeated. We, as sinners, invariably become like the enemy we fight. This is every nation's foreign policy and every individual's personal defensiveness. But God wins with the power of weakness and so he remains God. We lose because we try to win by force; we try to become powerful like God and thereby we do not remain ourselves. We try to become God in the process and so we lose our humanity. Christ remains himself, as true God and true man, and so he does not become a demon. And we through baptism and the Eucharist become members of Christ's body the Church, and thereby we share his victory. Thus we keep our humanity in the humanity of Jesus. Thus the Church is the sacrament of the coming kingdom.

So then, when we think of resurrection we must turn from selfish concerns and ego trips and see our personal resurrection as entrance into a new community, a kingdom not made with hands but a kingdom which is now being planted and is growing in secret and manifest in weakness. The salvation of ourselves in the future is in God's hands. We can do nothing about it. We cannot win it, or earn it, or deserve it. We can only believe God's promise, and celebrate it with thanksgiving, hope, joy, and faith. This is our reasonable worship.

But if the future is in God's hands, the present is in ours. We can do something about the here and now. It is this difference in the lives of the early apostles that caused the trouble. It will produce trouble in our generation too if we harness its power. But the resurrection assures us that God has won our salvation, and so we can joyfully leave it to him. The present, however, is ours. We can do something about the present, and the injustice and disunity here need serious attention. Justice and peace are humanity's doing. We have power to change the present. Indeed the problem is we have too much power. We split and fuse atoms, we create nuclear waste that we cannot dispose, we fly to the moon, we rearrange the organs of our bodies, we splice genes, we tamper with the chemicals of nutrition and upset the balances of nature. We should look to that balance and get into closer vibration with it. The fault is not in the power but in our misuse of it. We seem to be hellbent to trash our environment with our greed. A symbol of this greed is the plethora of billboards that clutter up our highways, the graffiti of corporate business.

Resurrection, however, gives us a new perspective on creation and ourselves. Why do some people react against it? They fear that their cherished notions of personal identity might be threatened. But the biblical denial of immortality of the soul does not reject personal resurrection. Greek dualism of body and soul fails negatively to consider the great weight of sin as a contamination of the whole person, and positively this dualism fails to recognize the future identity of the person in a deathless body. Our personal destiny is affirmed through baptism. To cling to the self, however, makes it impossible for God to make us new. Jesus clearly taught that if we are to inherit the kingdom we must first go down into the ground like a seed and die. We must lose ourselves if we want to gain eternal life. To die does not mean to pass into nothingness or to be annihilated. To die means to be separated so that we can be changed. We must be separated from this world of flesh and devil so that we can rise as new creatures.

We are naturally curious about what this new creature will be like. It is tempting to describe the streets of heaven. The passages of Paul and John are sketchy and poetic, not intended to be literal descriptions. We can only know that heaven is a place and a time where there is no death, no separation, no tears, no fears, no loss. Is heaven a garden or a city? It is not a return to Eden, and it certainly is a community. It is neither a dictatorship nor a democracy, but a kingdom with a single monarch whose benevolent rule is our greatest joy. But the more we try to say about heaven and resurrection life the more we realize our speculation is futile. The reason is that we ask the wrong questions. We are not called by resurrection faith to look for a different world, but to see this world differently. We do not need to know what heaven is like, but knowing that Christ rose from the dead we need to look for peace and justice in this world. We need to consider the lilies of the field and the birds of the air. We need to look at the children and learn from them and then set aside our greed and our fear so that we can work fruitfully for the kingdom of God.

The story of Jesus' resurrection necessarily includes his ascension. It is the ascension that sent the apostles out into the world with zeal to bring peace and justice and unity. This is what happens when we teach all nations and baptize in the name of the Father and the Son and the Holy Spirit. The marvelous irony of the ascension is that God takes away in order to give. Here we have another instance of a pattern in divine behavior that mysteriously is always a surprise to us even though it happens repeatedly in salvation history.

God took away the nation of Israel and sent the people into exile in Babylon in order to give them a new nation and a new temple as preparation for the coming of his Messiah. God gave us his Messiah in Jesus but then took him away in the crucifixion in order to give him in greater glory in the resurrection. God then took the risen Lord away in the ascension in order to give him to all the world through the sacraments of the catholic Church. The historical flesh of Jesus went into the grave and the resurrected Lord came forth only to be removed so that Jesus Christ could be received in every place and every time, not just in Israel at the time of the disciples. The absence of Jesus through the ascension made possible the real presence of Jesus in the Eucharist. And so we too must participate in this irony of taking and giving. We must lose ourselves for Christ's sake so that we can be given a new self of everlasting glory. God took away the temple of Israel and circumcision in order to give us the Church and baptism. God took away the priesthood of the Levites in order to give us apostolic ministry. God takes in order to give. Be prepared to be surprised when the Eschaton comes. But in the meantime the ascension sends us into the world with a mission to bring the good news that God does not take away.

Resurrection and ascension reveal to us what we need to do for our lives in this world. They tell us the ethical principles for our communal behavior. We learn from death what life is and we learn from life what death is. The disruption of life by death tells us that life is togetherness, community. Our community as creatures enlivened by the breath of the Spirit is in the image of the community in the Trinitarian God. In God there is communication because of this community. Father speaks to Son and Son speaks to Holy Spirit and the responses reverberate throughout eternity with celestial music. Life therefore is constituted by community and communication. Our life in God's image then reflects the divine intelligence, communicability, and freedom. God made us like himself so that we might have meaningful relationships with him and with each other. The resurrection teaches us that to live is to be together with responsible personal integrity in which the whole is enhanced by the diverse, unique contributions of the individuals, just as the distinct persons of the Trinity magnify the glory of God. So we communicate and contribute in our human relationships as the Father communicates within himself with the Son in the freedom and creativity of the Holy Spirit. Living means changing and growing in time as we participate in the changing and growing life of God through this community and communication.

If life is growing together then death is the enemy of life, opposite in every way. Death is the breakdown of community and communication. Death is separation. Death is not simply the absence of life, not simply a negation. Death is not the passing, nor even the threat of passing, from existence to nothingness. Death is a positive, active process that separates us from God, from our neighbor, and from ourselves. Death is a series of stages in our existence in which we grow apart and change in time through a process of decay. Both living and dying are changing in time; living is growing together and dying is growing apart.

Obviously it would seem from these observations of the revelation that comes through the resurrection that we should seek life and avoid death. That would be our ethical principle if it were not for the irony and paradox of the gospel. The revelation of Jesus Christ, however, teaches us that if we seek life we will lose it and if we lose life we will gain a new life. The point is that we see in faith that resurrection comes only through death, and it brings not resuscitation but a changed life eternal. This means that life as we know it in our exiled world is not absolute. Jesus delivered himself into the hands of Satan to die. Life is given by God. It is good and should be preserved, but it is not absolutely inviolate. Indeed if we seek it for ourselves we will lose it for ourselves as well as for others and for God. Life is not for itself. It is for God. God alone is absolute. To make anything other than God absolute is idolatry. Life is inviolate, therefore, only when it serves God's glory, when the neighbor is loved, and when we can be a joy to ourselves. It goes without saying that when the neighbor is loved and we are a joy to ourselves God's glory is served. The interesting paradox of our faith is that we can be a joy to ourselves only when we love our neighbor and thus glorify God. In ethical questions on the preservation of life, such as abortion and euthanasia, the answer for Christians in the hope of resurrection is that death can be welcomed when God is no longer glorified, when the neighbor cannot be loved, and when we cannot be a joy to ourselves, i.e., when community and communication break down.

We do not know how the streets of heaven will be paved. We do not know what our life with Christ will be in paradise between our personal death and the final resurrection. It may be a sleep; it may be a waiting at the altar where the Lamb is enthroned; it may be that we will be somehow clothed with Christ—all these intimations given by Paul and John are poetic and symbolic, not literal. We do not need to know anything more than what Paul tells us in First Corinthians 15: "The body that is sown is perishable, it is raised imperishable; it is sown in dishonor, it is raised in glory; it is sown in weakness, it is raised in power; it is sown a natural body, it is raised a spiritual body. . . . Therefore my dear brothers and sisters, stand firm. Let nothing move you. Always give yourselves fully to the work of the Lord, because you know that your labor in the Lord is not in vain." In this spirit of ethical obligation in view of the resurrection Luther said if he knew the world were coming to an end tomorrow he would go out and plant a tree!

7

A Water Droplet Yearning

Isaiah 40:1-8

"Comfort, O comfort my people,"
says your God.
"Speak to the heart of Jerusalem,
and call to her,
that her time of slavery has ended,
that her guilt is paid in full,
that she has received from the Lord's hand
double for all her sins."

A voice calls:
"In the wilderness clear the way for the Lord.
Make straight in the desert a highway
for your God.
Let every valley be raised up,
and every mountain and hill brought low.
Make rough ground into a plain,
and rugged heights into a valley.
Then shall the glory of the Lord
be revealed,
and all humankind will see it together;
for the mouth of the Lord has spoken."

A voice calls:
"Cry out!"
And I said, "What shall I cry?"
"All people are grass,
and all their beauty
is like the flower of the field.
The grass withers, the flower fades,
when the breath of the Lord
blows upon it.
Surely the people are grass!
The grass withers, the flower fades,
but the word of the Lord will stand forever."

Psalm 46

God is our refuge and strength,
a sure and certain help in trouble.
Therefore we will not fear,
though the earth be shaken
and the mountains collapse
into the heart of the sea;
though its waters roar and foam;
though the mountains quake
at its uproar.

There is a river
whose streams make glad
the city of God,
the holiest habitation of the Most High.
God is in the midst of her;
she will not crumble.
God will help her
at the break of the day.
The nations roar, the kingdoms collapse,
the earth melts.
The Lord Almighty is with us;
the God of Jacob is our fortress.

Come, see the deeds of the Lord.
He makes wars to cease everywhere;
he breaks the bow and shatters the lances;
he burns the chariots.
"Be still and know that I am God!
I will be exalted among the nations;
I will be exalted in the earth."
The Lord Almighty is with us;
the God of Jacob is our fortress.

Psalm 130

Out of the depths.
I cry unto you, O Lord!
O Lord, hear my voice!
May your ears be attentive
to my cry for mercy.

If you, O Lord, should record iniquities,
O Lord, who could stand?
But with you there is forgiveness;
therefore you are revered.

I wait for the Lord,
my whole being waits,
and my hope is in his word.
I wait for the Lord
more than watchmen wait for the dawn,
more than watchmen wait for the dawn.

Hope, O Israel, in the Lord,
for with the Lord is unfailing love;
and with him is plentiful redemption.
He will redeem Israel
from all their sins.

Matthew 11:28-30

Come to me,
All you who are weary
and over-burdened.
I will give you rest.
Take my yoke upon you
and learn from me,
for I am gentle
and humble in heart,
and you will find rest
for your spirits.
My yoke is easy
and my burden is light.

Luke 12:22-34

Then Jesus said to his disciples,
"Therefore I tell you
do not worry about your life,
what you will eat
or about your body,
what you will wear.
Life is more than food,
and the body more than clothes.
Consider the ravens:
they do not sow or reap,
they have no storehouse or barn;
yet God feeds them.
And how much more valuable are you
than birds!
Who of you by worrying
can add a single hour to your life?
Since you cannot do this least thing,
why do you worry about the rest?

Consider how the lilies grow.
They do not toil or spin.
Yet I tell you,
not even Solomon in all his splendor
was dressed like one of these.
If that is how God clothes the grass of the field,
which is here today
and tomorrow is burned in the fire,
how much more will he clothe you,
O you of little faith!
Do not set your heart
on what you will eat or drink;
do not even think about it.
The pagan world runs after all such things,
and your Father knows that you need them.
But seek his kingdom
and these things will be given you as well."

John 3:1-8

Now there was a man of the Pharisees named Nicodemus,
a member of the Jewish ruling council.
He came to Jesus at night and said,
"Rabbi, we know you are a teacher
who has come from God.
No one could perform the miraculous signs
you are doing if God were not with him,"
In reply Jesus declared,
"I tell you the truth,
no one can see the kingdom of God
unless he is born again."
"How can a man be born when he is old?"
Nicodemus asked.
"Surely he cannot enter a second time
into his mother's womb to be born!"
Jesus answered, "I tell you the truth,
No one can enter the kingdom of God
unless he is born of water and the Spirit.
Flesh gives birth to flesh,
but the Spirit gives birth to spirit.
You should not be surprised at my saying,
'You must be born again.'
The wind blows wherever it pleases.
You hear its sound,
but you cannot tell where it comes from
or where it is going.
So it is with everyone born of the Spirit.

Acts 2:1-36

When the day of Pentecost had come
they were all with one accord in one place.
And suddenly
a sound came from heaven
like the rushing of a mighty wind.

Divine Disclosure

*It filled the whole house
where they were sitting.
They saw what seemed to be tongues of fire
that separated
and came to rest on each of them.
They were all filled with the Holy Spirit,
and they began to speak
in other languages
as the Spirit gave them utterance.*

*Now there were staying in Jerusalem
God-fearing Jews
from every nation under heaven.
When they heard this sound,
a crowd of men came together
in bewilderment
because each one heard them speaking
in his own tongue.
Utterly amazed, they asked:
"Are not all these who speak Galileans?
How is it that each of us hears them
in his own native dialect?
Parthians, Medes, and Elamites;
residents of Mesopotamia, Judea, and Cappadocia;
Pontus, Asia, Phrygia, and Pamphylia;
Egypt and the parts of Libya near Cyrene;
visitors from Rome
(both Jews and converts);
Cretans and Arabs—
we hear them
declaring the wonders of God
in our own tongues!"
Amazed and perplexed,
they asked one another,
"What does this mean?"
Some, however, made fun of them and said,
"They have had too much wine."*

*Then Peter stood up with the Eleven,
raised his voice,
and addressed the crowd:*

"Fellow Jews
and all of you who are in Jerusalem,
let me explain this;
listen carefully to what I say.
These men are not drunk,
as you suppose.
It is only nine in the morning!
No, this is what was spoken
by the prophet Joel:
'And it will come to pass
in the last days,
says God,
I will pour out my Spirit
on all people.
Your sons and daughters will prophesy,
your young men will see visions,
your old men will dream dreams.
Even on my servants, both men and women,
I will pour out my Spirit in those days,
and they will prophesy.
I will show wonders in the heaven above
and signs in the earth below,
blood and fire and billows of smoke.
The sun will be turned to darkness
and the moon to blood
before the coming of the Lord
in that great and glorious day.
And everyone who calls
on the name of the Lord
will be saved.'

"Men of Israel,
listen to this:
Jesus of Nazareth was approved of God
by miracles, wonders, and signs,
which God did among you through him,
as you yourselves know.
This man was handed over to you
by God's set purpose
and foreknowledge;
and you, with the help of wicked men,

*put him to death
by nailing him to the cross.
But God raised him
from the dead,
freeing him from the agony of death,
because it was impossible for death
to keep its hold on him.
David said about him:
'I saw the Lord always before me.
Because he is at my right hand,
I will not be shaken.
Therefore my heart is glad
and my tongue rejoices
and my body will live in hope,
because you will not abandon me
to the grave,
nor will you let your Holy One see decay.
You have made known to me
the paths of life;
you will fill me with joy in your presence.'*

"Men and brothers,
I can tell you confidently
that the patriarch David died
and was buried,
and his sepulcher is here to this day.
But he was a prophet
and he knew that God had promised him on oath
that he would place one of his descendants
on his throne.
Seeing what was ahead,
he spoke of the resurrection of Christ,
that he was not abandoned to the grave,
nor did his body see decay.
God has raised this Jesus to life,
and we are all witnesses.
Exalted to the right hand of God,
he has received from the Father
the promised Holy Spirit
and has poured out
what you now see and hear.

*For David did not ascend to heaven,
and yet he said,
'The Lord said to my Lord:
"Sit at my right hand
until I make your enemies
a footstool for your feet."'
Therefore let all Israel be assured of this:
God has made this Jesus, whom you crucified,
both Lord and Christ."*

The Confirming Fruit of the Holy Spirit

CONFIRMATION IN the Churches has been a rite of passage in which the sacrament of baptism is established for the edification of children as they become adults. Religious rites have marked this passage in cultures throughout the world. African bush people and American Indians have had testing periods coupled with ceremony for males and females at the age of puberty. Islam has circumcision; Judaism has bar mitzvah and bat mitzvah. Christian confirmation likewise follows a period of instruction and preparation, sometimes with public examination before the congregation.

But the mark of distinction, the point of contrast, in Christian confirmation is the revelation of the gifts of the Holy Spirit: the spirit of wisdom and understanding, the spirit of counsel and might, the spirit of knowledge and the fear of the Lord. Christian confirmation is not the dedication of vows of faithfulness when the child reaches the age of discretion, although that does also take place. It is the recognition of the continuing establishment of the gift of grace begun in baptism which comes through the Holy Spirit. The confirming work of the Holy Spirit, however, is not limited to the rite of passage. The Holy Spirit is both an abiding presence and a sporadic, surprising pressure. The Holy Spirit is always with us and the Holy Spirit comes and goes. Progress in history, evolution in nature, revolution in culture, creativity in the arts, invention in the sciences, justice in government, cohesion in the family, enrichment in commerce and industry—all these movements and stirrings are the result of the Spirit's prodding.

The fruit of the Spirit is love, joy, patience, kindness, goodness, faithfulness, gentleness, and self-control (Galatians 5:22). These are not deeds but manifestations of character that builds within us when the Holy Spirit moves us with his life-giving breath. We can know the unseen God to be our Father only by the power of the Holy Spirit. It is the Spirit who calls and gathers us into the Church where we are edified with the fruits that enrich our service in the world.

When we were baptized we were born anew into the family of Christ by the creative power of the Holy Spirit. This is not a bloody birth from a womb. It is the fashioning of a new creature from the old. The old is dead and divided into disparate individuals that are yearning for union and constantly fighting each other. The new is a seamless garment, the glorious clothing of Christ, his righteousness and grace. We walk now in the beauty of holiness as members of a communion of saints whose destiny is with the risen Christ. Our baptism is confirmed by the fruit of the Spirit.

It is the Spirit who gives us the future. Never fixed, always open, rich with infinite possibilities, the future beckons and tantalizes and frightens and challenges. Two things we know will surely come in the midst of the future's puzzling uncertainties—our death and our resurrection. This leaves us yearning because we do not know the how or the when. We long for this new birth to reach its fulfillment, and then we are surprised by visions and dreams for the future which the Spirit gives us. Slavery is abolished by the winds of the Spirit. Knowledge is stretched, problems are solved, painting and poetry and plays are produced, music is sounded, sculpture shaped—all by the inspiration of the Spirit. He blows when and where he wills. Even though this world is dying all about us, because the Spirit leads us, we can face the future with confidence and expectant joy. The God who would not let his Holy One see decay will raise us up and deliver us from this body of death.

If the Spirit is like wind it sometimes comes with thunder. Our prayer must then be that God will not take his terror from us. Let him smite us so he can save us. When blood is on the moon rejoice, for the healing Spirit is soon to come. Winds also blow with light airs. The Spirit comforts with whispering hope. Whether almighty waves roll up or tiny cats paws spread softly the winds of the Spirit bring a future that has the victorious destiny of God in it.

The Spirit calls us to worship in the Church and then sends us to witness in the world. In our liturgy Church and world meet. Because of the gift of righteousness and new life that comes through the real presence of Christ we lift our hearts in thanksgiving and invoke the Holy Spirit to bear his fruits in our lives. We would present our bodies as living sacrifices for this is our spiritual worship (Romans 12:1). The climax of the Eucharistic prayer is matched by a second climax in the dismissal. Our worship leads to mission. This is what makes the Church, first its worship and then its mission. In worship we thank God for grace; in mission we manifest the Spirit's fruits. With such a shower of blessing both death and the devil are drowned and a new heaven and a new earth are created.

When the Spirit moves us the natural religious quest for God is abandoned because now our energy turns to service in the world. We live not by way of religion but by way of revelation. We need not seek because we have been found. Instead of searching for God we are now sent on a mission. Our prayers ask not to change God but to change us. We do not bring to

God a wish list; we simply report for duty. And the things we now do are fruits of the Spirit which may be seen in our daily stewardship as we use the talents given to us in our various vocations.

God has had to teach us stewardship in different stages. In the process of salvation during this period of our exile we live in a story that has three acts: the period of pagan nature worship, the time of historical legal development, and the final act of creative Christian community. In this fallen world we have learned from nature, history, and Christian revelation.

In the first act of the drama of salvation God is found extremely close, if not identical, to the processes of nature. The great pagan religions declared this with their devotion to fertility and the cycle of birth and death. All of life, labor, and leisure found meaning expressed through periodic communal festivals of thanksgiving for nature's gifts. Progress and change are abhorrent at this level or place in the story because there is no thought of an eschatological goal in the future. Everything is caught in the cycle of nature which constantly repeats itself. Stewardship and vocation become a simple matter of dividing a pie. Ethics in such a culture rests on the principle of communal sharing. Individual ownership is not countenanced. So long as everyone respects community concerns a stable society is assured. And to perpetuate this system a token offering is brought to the gods with an attitude of appeasement at the least and gratitude at the highest. This pious awareness of nature's gifts and the need for dividing an offering in recognition of the divine source has sustained people in various civilizations for centuries. Even modern philosophers sometimes try to remain in this first act when they define God as the Ground of Being or the Natural Process.

But the story has moved on, and in the second act we find that human prowess over nature has become so successful we no longer stand in awe before its life-giving mystery and its death-dealing judgment. Appeasement and gratitude are now abandoned. With a sense of history we organize society around legal covenants, and instead of appeasing God with gifts we offer him our moral rectitude. Cain learned the powerful lesson that he was his brother's keeper, that right division of his offering includes care for others. The stewardship of gratitude for nature's bounty is now replaced by the stewardship of obligation to one's neighbor. Here the second act in the drama of salvation is played with God's covenant with Israel providing the lines of the Torah for the role of stewardship. The legal covenant found expression also in the principle of *suum cuique* (to each one's own) in Roman law and in the social contract of modern government. It arises from a sense of obligation, and when we are obliged to come together we form a community with law. Rights are respected. As a result history is set on its course.

But God's revelation does not stop with nature and history. He has come to us in the uniform, cyclical behavior of natural process and taught us to be grateful. He has come to us in the unidirectional thrust of history and taught us to be responsible. And he has also come to us in a third act in the unique disclosure of his Son and taught us to be creative as we share his new life in the resurrection community. It is not enough that we recognize our responsible stewardship in the management of the resources God has given us. We must also accept the challenge of creative development of these resources. We are not only to cut up a pie equitably. We must also create and produce new things in a burgeoning economy under the surprising direction of the Holy Spirit.

Humans have been trying in their checkered career to tame the wilderness and harness nature. We have been trying to bring order out of the irrational forces of nature and establish a lawful society. Rapidly we are coming to a point where we no longer have nature as our environment, as the thing around us which we work. Indeed our stewardship has been so bad we are in danger of obliterating our resources, and we have instead a society with services but no goods. Whereas before we had things which could be used for our needs, now we have people who need to be managed for their services. By manipulating people in the organization of our work we make them into things. Instead of loving people and using things, we use people and love things. Herein lies one of the deepest tragedies in the drama of salvation.

In the resurrection community, however, we can live in the presence of the risen Christ by the guidance of the Holy Spirit. This is because we do not live as impersonal parts of a natural process nor as cases in a legalistically constituted community. Our destiny goes beyond nature and history as persons who freely participate in the creative thrust of the Spirit. We live and walk and work by the Spirit, and therefore we must strive to find a meaningful place for all persons in the new community. The pressing problem in the modern world is to keep the computer age from dehumanizing and depersonalizing people. It is only the coming of the Holy Spirit that guarantees our freedom to be persons, and beyond this we can develop a reverence of personal concern for everything in the cosmos, great and small. The unique and surprising development in the drama of salvation is the coming of the Spirit. It is by the Creator Spirit that we know Christ and move forward in our destiny. In a piercing thrust as participants with God himself we pass from glory to glory (1 Corinthians 3:17-18).

The work of the Holy Spirit in stewardship brings people above the natural process and out of the historical community of law into a creative, personal community of resurrection. Already before the Eschaton we have a prolepsis of the glory that is to come. Here the right division of offering means that we do not exploit nature and simply give God thanks; nor do we only organize people with justice and say we are obliged to give them their rights. Rather we wait upon the Holy Spirit and jump with joy at his spontaneous direction, for he will lead us into truth and peace and freedom.

Obviously these three acts are not simple successive periods in linear history. They are stages which overlap in the historical process, yet there is movement from past to future and never the reverse. The problem is always to realize that movement in fact. The pathos in the play is the frustrating stagnation in which we wallow as we try to pursue our vocation. Franz Kafka expresses the ironic absurdity of our contemporary predicament when he describes with serious joy and pathetic humor the ridiculous situation of a land surveyor, the anonymous K, in his novel *The Castle*. At least the character thinks he is a land surveyor, although he is never quite sure what he has been called to do. This is his problem: he wants to work, he knows he must do something, and he wants to do what is required of him; yet he can never establish contact with his employer, the lord of the castle. He tries every device to discover the will of his employer. Sometimes this is felicitous, sometimes tragic, but always it is ephemeral, futile, and pathetic. At one time he comes to a tavern where he learns the telephone number of the master. He is told he may try to get a connection, others have tried before, but no one has succeeded. With plodding courage he rings up the number, and, miracle of miracles, the operator gives him a clear signal. With his heart in this throat and pulses pounding he waits to hear the voice of the lord; but all he can hear is the sound of little children laughing.

Christians have the revelation that makes the connection K sought, and so we can overcome the mordant cynicism of Kafka. But we do not get it by calling to heaven. It is the other way around. God calls us by his Spirit through the Word become flesh in Jesus. And the human condition is worse than Kafka pictured it. We are not just confused victims of a grim cosmic joke; we are defiant rebels guilty of heinous sin and deserving the death we chose. This is more realistic than Joseph Conrad's depiction of death as a dark enigma or Ernst Hemingway's story of death as a cheat; and it is also more optimistic, because if death is deserved and Christ is risen, our death is also redeemable.

The real characters in the drama of salvation are not anonymous archetypes like K, but flesh and blood persons like Judas and Peter and Thomas. Like these eager and sincere disciples we paradoxically betray and deny and doubt the God who suffers to save us. Our rebellious sin brings us down in divorce, in discrimination, in strikes, in war, in all the devastating divisions that cruelly cut us apart from God and one another. Our confessing hymn must always be:

> Who was the guilty? Who brought this upon thee?
> Alas, my treason, Jesus, hath undone thee.
> 'Twas I, Lord Jesus, I it was denied thee;
> I crucified thee.

But when we survey "the wondrous cross on which the Prince of glory died," the Holy Spirit reveals to us what true gratitude is and what lawful obedience can be for the human community in nature's realm. Now there is no need to show gratitude by appeasing an angry god, nor do we live fearfully under the enforcement of cruel law, because the spiritual fruit of love, joy, patience, kindness, goodness, faithfulness, gentleness, and self-control freely lifts us to an eternal happiness.

Christianity is replete with paradoxes. Nature is the mother that nourishes us with her bounty and beauty, but earth eats earth in the cycle of life and death. The law is given by God to provide order and save us from destroying ourselves, yet it is the law that kills when we enforce it to the letter. The Spirit is the person who saves us from both nature and law, but the Spirit blows where and when he wills and no one knows from whence he comes. The Spirit moves in time, and just as the past cannot be recovered so the future cannot be predicted. The paradox of the Holy Spirit is his unpredictability and his absolute dependability. We can never know what God will do in his mysterious wisdom for our destiny, yet we can always be absolutely sure that what he does will be for our good.

So long as we live in this realm of our exile we are bound to the mothering of nature and the learning of the law, but when we become born anew in the Spirit we begin to become free of both nature and law, and we begin to live in the new kingdom of grace. Now we see the wonders of this kingdom with clouded vision, as through a glass darkly, but we see in faith, hope, and love. These gifts of grace are far more sure than sight or reason because they bring peace to our troubled hearts and a will to establish justice. In such a marvelous way the Spirit leads us into truth and sets us free. Can the Spirit free us from the current idolatry of Nationalism?

Spiritual Comfort in Healing and Counseling

Jesus was a counselor who brought comfort and solace with strength to all who listen with the ears of faith. As he taught with the Holy Spirit guiding us into truth, so he counseled with the Holy Spirit lifting us from our anxiety and healing us for holiness.

Because Jesus was a healer it was the Church that established hospitals. As with education, which is in itself secular, so the medical arts and sciences are neither Christian nor unchristian. Why then should the Church have hospitals? Because the Church brings a special relationship between our spirits and God that heals the whole person. Christians in medicine will treat not just the disease but also the loneliness, the feeling of failure, and the guilt that accompany the disease. The healing process is understood with Christian revelation to be a sacrament in the sense that God is inwardly at work graciously giving us health through the physical means of chemicals and physicians.

The distinctive dimension in the therapy Jesus brings is the power of the Holy Spirit. This power comes with Jesus because Jesus is the incarnation of the second person of the Trinity, and the three persons of God are never separate. Indeed the three are one, not three. This is a contradiction for human logic. It is most mind-boggling and heart-rending. We cannot resolve it. God is one; there is only one God, and the one God is both three persons and one person.

Perhaps we can gain some human understanding of this mystery if we think of God as living in the temporal process. The early Church Fathers said the one Lord Jesus Christ is "the only-begotten Son of God, begotten of his Father before all worlds, begotten, not made, one in being with the Father." Jesus Christ is true God, begotten from eternity; and true man, born of the Virgin Mary. To be both God and man is sheer contradiction. It cannot be grasped by perception or intellect, but it can be celebrated by the faith given by the Holy Spirit. It is this surprising, transforming faith that gives us comfort in counseling. We cannot receive it if we allow our reason or our heart to resist the Spirit. For Jesus Christ to be begotten, not made, involves the living process in the being of God. This process continues as the Holy Spirit proceeds from the Father and the Son. The life of God grows and magnifies. God is revealed to us in three dimensions: while the Son is all God, not just partially God, he is not all that God is, for there is also the Father who sends him in the incarnate Jesus, and there is also the Holy Spirit who speaks by the prophets, who is the Lord and giver of life, and who is the advocate and comforter of people narrowed by fear and oppressed by all kinds of evil.

Begotten has various meanings outside the context of God. When applied to God begotten does not mean born. Begotten when applied to God has a meaning that is unique and restricted to God. It cannot be defined in terms of anything else. Its meaning is intelligible only to faith experience just as meanings that derive from perception can be grasped only by experience of the perception. One cannot define the taste of Coca Cola. One must drink it to know it. So likewise one cannot define the begetting of God. One must experience faithfully the revelation of God as the Father who begets the Word by which he creates and redeems, and who processes the Spirit. And Jesus was a healer because he was one with the Spirit who gives life.

Counseling people in trouble is a human need and has a history of successes and failures. Medieval counseling was done through the practice of private confession. The priest listened to the laments of parishioners as they struggled with their shortcomings. They thought that the grace of forgiveness came with cost. The "Our Fathers" and "Hail, Marys" required for penitence were symbolic. To enhance the assurance of forgiveness, however, indulgences were sold. Counseling was commercialized. Like Simon Magus who wanted to buy and sell the power of the Holy Spirit, medieval clergy engaged in a profitable business at the expense of the credulity of the devout. This corruption of the confessional called for reform.

Martin Luther, among his many reforms, addressed this problem. He denounced the medieval practice of enumerating sins in the confessional and paying for them with prayers, fasting, and alms. Luther gave us an example of how counseling should be done when the Elector, Frederick the Wise, fell stricken with a serious illness. Luther wrote for him a treatise which he called the *Fourteen of Consolation*. He described fourteen tablets "not of silver but of a spiritual kind for the strengthening of a pious heart." He wrote as a pastor comforting his parishioner.

Luther arranged his counsels in two groups of seven, the first series treating the evils within us, before us, behind us, beneath us, on our left hand, on our right hand, and above us. The second series treats of the blessings of the same positions. Counseling clearly requires not only the recognition of sin and the evils that assail us but also the awareness in gratitude for the blessings that enrich us.

Luther's theme throughout is that we should rejoice and be comforted in the knowledge that the evil we suffer—regardless of where it may strike from our enemies or our friends—is always infinitesimal compared with the evil we deserve, or the evil with which we are threatened were it not for the protection of God. This counsel requires us to appreciate the full depth of sin and the evils it brings. We cannot feel this depth directly, for if we could we would be in hell, but we are given external evils to show us what it could be, and to comfort us in comparison. Only by faith can we comprehend radical evil, just as only by faith can we know true eternal blessings. These teachings Luther derived from Jesus' instructions about the Holy Spirit as the Counselor who convicts us of sin and comforts us with his righteousness (John 15 and 16).

Luther's treatise is a devotional writing which shows that the truly pious Christian puts oneself trustingly within the care of God and accepts health, wealth, power, or the lack of these things, with equanimity as Job did, without questioning the mercy of God. Even if we receive no blessings God is still merciful to us, if we consider what evils we could have had without God's care. Distrust of God and his care is the cardinal sin, and faith is its cure. Faith is not a virtue we can cultivate and offer to God as merit for forgiveness. Faith is a fruit of the Spirit which we must receive gratefully so that it can become a controlling force in our lives.

Here we have a beautiful consolation, comforting us in sorrow and promising blessing and balm. And always the counsel is given in the hope and promise of resurrection. It is counsel that is strange to modern ears. Luther says God humiliates whom he would raise up. The first shall be last and the last first. He who seeks his soul shall lose it, and he who loses it for Christ's sake will find it. All that is said by Luther presupposes the resurrection. Everything rests on the promise of God for heavenly inheritance. Instead of preaching rebellion for a just cause, as we hear today, Luther preached martyrdom and patient suffering for the sake of Christ, as Paul and Peter did in their epistles (Romans 5:3-5; 1 Peter 2:18-25). True piety is faithful confidence in God's promise of eternal blessing. As Kierkegaard said, "the joy of it that we must suffer but once and triumph eternally." This is a spirit quite different from the modern cry for justice by pressure. Historically, however, it cannot be denied that a one-sided application of Luther's piety encouraged a debilitating political quietism. But Luther did not intend for us to choose martyrdom. If it is thrust upon us with no alternative, then the counsel of the Holy Spirit comforts us with the hope of resurrection. This does not in any way preclude the need for us to establish justice and peace in our time and place.

Also we must stress the positive dimension of the Spirit in counseling. While there can be no forgiveness without a full confession of sin, a masochistic guilt trip is never countenanced. Much anxiety and spiritual pain are wrongly inflicted on us by ourselves and by others, even though this may be well meaning. Job's comforters bring no true spiritual counsel. Casting blame on others is a sorry way to get revenge. Accepting blame falsely is no way to achieve reconciliation. If we are guilty we must own up to it, but if not we must maintain our innocence in the face of false accusation. Always it is the truth that makes us free.

Discontinuing private confession left a vacuum in modern times that was filled by secular therapy. As is true of all things secular the substitute was a poor imitation. The devil rushes in where we cast the Spirit out, and since he cannot create he imitates what God gives. We want what the devil imitates because it is pleasant, but since it is a fraud, whatever derives from the devil's world ultimately never satisfies, even though it may give temporary relief or even some benefit.

This is the story of secular therapy from Freud to Jung, Adler, Rogers, Erickson, and their current colleagues. A brief comment of Freudian analysis will demonstrate the validity of this critique.

Historically secular therapy became an ingredient of modern culture when, in the eighteenth century, a liberating spirit shattered the unity of the medieval establishment. The authority of the Church was challenged because people no longer found meaning in its sheltering dome. People suddenly wanted freedom to develop their own national and personal destinies, to explore new worlds of both mind and space, and to seek for meaningful values in this life on earth. A secular transvaluation of values shifted attention from the world beyond to this world, from the soul to the body, from the community to the individual.

At first this liberal spirit looked to right reason for the new secular meaning, but not for long. The nineteenth century brought a violent reaction to reason, the violence of which was inevitable because cool reason was replaced by hot passion. Emotion was set up as authority, but the name of the new tyrant is legion. The visceral drive of hunger was rationalized in the economic theories of Karl Marx, who imitated divine revelation with his slogan: "From each according to one's ability; to each according to one's need." (cf. Acts 4:34-35). Then the will to power was rhapsodized in the philosophical poetry of Friedrich Nietzsche. The drive for survival was described in the principle of natural selection by Charles Darwin. And finally the libido was identified by Sigmund Freud as the driving force for social behavior.

Sigmund Freud took the biological concept of the sex impulse and used it to explain the nature of humanity, society, and all history. The practical significance of Freud for the Church is that acceptance of his theories and methods renders nugatory the rites of the sacraments and the authority of the pastor in counseling. The secular claim is that the function of spiritual healing is adequately accomplished through the therapy of analysis.

Self-examination, says Freud, will show that in the subliminal range of human consciousness the sex impulse, or libido, produces four stages in the metamorphosis of humans: the narcissistic period of auto-eroticism of infants, the amnesia period of childhood sexual innocence, the Oedipus complex of love for the parent of the opposite sex, and the final maturity in which the sex urge is given outlet in love for the opposite sex of the same age. Since this can never be wholly gratified, however, there is need, says Freud, for sublimation with some kind of creative work or art, lacking which regression will set in with the result of mental illness. Hence the therapy to use is the technique of free-association to liberate the repressed desire. This involves a temporary transfer of love to the analyst in the hope that the patient will mature through all the stages of growth and find healthy expression for one's libido.

Freud does not make the distinction between religion and revelation that these essays declare to be essential. He says religion is a regrettable aberration in the development of the human race. For him all religion is an illusion that we will forsake once we know that our religious symbols are only myths without attachment to reality. People, he says, now obey laws because of religious sanction, but if we educate the race away from this illusion we can both retain morality and liberate our energies for fruitful expression in science and the arts. Christianity in particular was attacked by Freud as a dangerous illusion that arose out of the Oedipus complex of father love. In childhood we are helpless and we receive protection from our fathers. In adulthood we are still helpless in nature, so we project our ambivalent feelings of fear and fascination from our earthly fathers to our Father in heaven. We imagine a God of wrath and mercy. This projection, says Freud, stifles our growth, and the legalism of religion causes repression rather than expression of natural impulses.

The fraudulence of Freud is evident on several fronts. Even if all behavior arises out of irrational feelings, which in itself is doubtful, there are more feelings than sexual feelings. Moreover, childhood disturbances can hardly be the sole source of adult neuroses. It has been demonstrated that many so-called repressed memories are really fraudulently induced by the counselor. Psychic aberrations of individuals cannot be an explanation for the religious behavior of the race. Far from being a cause of mental illness, religion, from a clinical standpoint, often helps rather than hinders therapy. Religion is a necessary, natural, but sinful, human search for God after we have defiantly rebelled against him. Freud rightly condemned religious legalism, but so too did Jesus and Christianity. It is precisely the Gospel of forgiveness through grace apart from the law that speaks to this evil. Freud mistakenly thinks the God of Christianity is modeled after the human image of the father, but we have repeatedly emphasized that no human image can define or describe God. Nor is God a hypothesis that we can discard. God is not a hypothesis at all. He is the one who speaks to us in his silence.

Freud's theory and method pretend to be scientific but are not. He appeals to myths and stories to substantiate his analysis. This is a prime example of substituting an imitation for the real thing. Cure by the spoken word instead of by chemical medicines is intended to replace both medicines and the sacrament of confession and absolution. Freud substitutes myths, such as the myth of Narcissus, and classical stories, such as the story of Oedipus, for biblical stories and the story of revelation. Christian revelation, however, which is also basically a story, does not discount the value of scientific medicine nor any endeavor in any other human enterprise which uses the talents given to humans in creation. Freud's error is false pretense. His stories do not say what he claims. It is true that the spoken word heals, but that word is divine, not human. I cannot talk myself out of sin or insanity, but grace can liberate me from any demonism.

C.S. Lewis in *The Screwtape Letters* (New York: Macmillan, 1943; 37) has grasped the irony of a Spirit-denying materialism that substitutes a "Life Force" for the true life which the Holy Spirit breathes into us. Humans are attacked by a diabolical temptation in which Satan lies to us and gets us to disbelieve in the world of the Spirit and to believe instead in a thoroughgoing materialism, but then Satan slyly introduces subliminal drives, such as Freud's libido, to take the place of the true spirituality that we have as creatures of the Holy Spirit. Thus Lewis has Screwtape, a fiend of hell, instruct his nephew, Wormwood, in the nefarious technique of capitalizing on intellectual fads which govern secular therapy. "The 'Life Force,'" writes Screwtape to Wormwood, "the worship of sex, and some aspects of psychotherapy, may prove useful. If once we can produce our perfect work—the Materialist Magician, the man, not using, but veritably worshipping what he vaguely calls 'Forces' while denying the existence of 'spirits'—then the end of the war will be in sight."

In recent years the success of drugs in the treatment of mental illness and psychosocial disorders has rendered psychotherapy as a talk healer out of fashion. Of course, it never did heal and only exploited the rich who could afford its unending treatment. But the demise of secular psychotherapy leaves another vacuum in our time that can only be properly filled by spiritual counseling grounded in the grace of God for his creatures who have bodies that have the life of the Spirit breathed into them.

Today, in light of the deceptive success of secular medical therapy, the need is to recover the revelation of the comfort of the Holy Spirit in counseling. Isaiah spoke a word of comfort to the people of Israel when they were being assailed by enemies from without. Comfort means "with strength," not sentimental indulgence. When people suffer from war, hot or cold, they need strength for courage, patience, hope, and endurance. The same applies to personal trials and tribulations. The Psalmist said God is our refuge and strength, a very present help in time of trouble (Psalm 46). Luther was inspired by this psalm to write his powerful hymn, "A Mighty Fortress Is Our God," which gives strength to all who sing it, Lutheran and Catholic alike. When our spirits are low the Holy Spirit lifts us out of the depths (Psalm 130). Before we can be comforted, however, we must confess our sin. If we come with arrogance, which is to say that we do not think we are in need, then we will be unable to receive divine help. This is the unforgivable sin against the Holy Spirit, the defiance that refuses grace. But if we come to God with open hearts, with our whole being welcoming God's grace, then we will rejoice in receiving plentiful redemption which comes through the culmination of sacramental authority.

Good counseling will always tell the truth, even when it is severe, but it will always lift us from our worries and despair. Jesus said we should not be anxious about the things we need for life. God supplies our needs, indeed he gives us his entire kingdom (luke 12:32). Robert Louis Stevenson echoes this joyful revelation: "The world is so full of a number of things, / I'm sure we should all be as happy as kings." When we are weary and the burden of life is overwhelming, come to Jesus. He will give us rest (Matthew 11:28-30). Jesus taught us with practical wisdom. Coming to Jesus does not mean lifting a prayer in a vacuum; it means coming to the Church, the body of Christ, and laying your burdens on Jesus as a member of this community. Here the imbalance of wealth and poverty can and must be corrected. No society can survive when the rich get richer and the poor get poorer. The strong are obliged, not to coddle the weak, but to help them become strong. No one can bear one's full burden. I cannot carry all that I am responsible for. You cannot carry all you are responsible for. But I can help you carry your burden and you can help me carry mine. God made the world this way so we can live together by helping each other. The devil's world is just the opposite. C.S. Lewis in *The Great Divorce* (New York: Macmillan, 1946) describes hell as a grey town, a suburban subdivision, in which the people, far from helping each other, constantly move away from each other because they despise their neighbors. In God's kingdom people love their neighbors even if they seem to be enemies.

Counseling speaks to every human situation: sorrowful, threatening, joyful, hopeful. Perhaps among the many situations most seriously calling for counseling are bereavement and divorce, both involving the death of a relationship.

Death produces a series of reactions which must be worked through before the wound it inflicts can be healed. It has been observed by many that humans first refuse to believe the fact of death when it comes to a loved one. Immediately we say no! It cannot be. The second reaction is often anger. The death is a blow we refuse to accept and we fight it with a passion that can include hatred and revenge. When we realize the death is real and we must somehow deal with it we resort to bargaining. Often people in their anger blame God or themselves or someone handy. All of these reactions are much more complicated than psychotherapists usually consider. In fact each situation has its own dimensions because no two people are alike, and each one responds to crises freely according to one's own choice. We would like to reverse the situation, and we try to bargain for this but it is utterly futile, and if we remain in any of these stages of reaction we just compound the pain.

Only when we grow to accept the death as a reality that we cannot change can we begin to receive a solution. When we realize that death is both the devil's doing and the wage of sin we will quit fighting its wound. Then it will be possible for us to move forward to welcome death as the necessary entrance into paradise. We will see that the particularity of our sin is part of the cosmic battle between God and his adversary in heavenly places. Death will be seen to be the separation of our sinful selves from this worldly existence and the beginning of a new life with Christ in paradise.

Divorce, which before the Second World War was comparatively rare, has become so common that as many as one half the marriages in the United States are being terminated. The reasons given for the tolerance of divorce are 1) if a relationship is dead we should not cling to the corpse, and 2) where verbal and physical abuse are violent beyond correction the injured party must be protected, and 3) children in a dysfunctional family suffer unnecessarily, and 4) the traditional reasons of infidelity and desertion still apply.

I do not deny the legitimacy of any of these reasons. Counseling to accept them may be necessary, but I think we have been too quick to use these reasons to excuse a situation that could be changed. Just as we have developed a comprehensive system of medicine to combat physical illness and forestall death, so we should develop a comprehensive system of counseling to combat failures in relationships and forestall the death of divorce. Especially when there are children, no matter what their age, divorce should rarely be considered as a solution to a problem in marriage. The damage done to children in divorce has not been sufficiently recognized. Children are hurt by the bickering of their parents but not so painfully as by their separation. The damage is compounded when the parents fight over custody of the children as if the children were objects to be possessed. Gargantuan efforts must be made to school quarreling parents in ways to achieve mutual respect when love is lost. Parents can learn to live together peaceably for the sake of the children, remembering that they will remain parents of their children as long as they live.

The most common causes of friction between spouses involve sex, money, and the exercise of power. Spiritual counseling will restore trustworthiness and trust in both partners. It is true that there is no innocent person in a broken relationship, but it is not true that guilt is equal. Often one member in a marriage is overwhelmingly at fault, whether the fault is sexual aberration or financial irresponsibility or bullying. We are not equal in emotional irresponsibility or bullying. We are not equal in emotional drives. One will be stronger than the other in a marriage, or one will be more aggressive than the other. Counseling will bring the Holy Spirit to guide the dominant partner to defer to the weaker as God always opts for the poor. The exercise of power by those who are strong is best realized when it is used to help the weak become stronger. And counseling will bring the Holy Spirit to guide the weak to cease being the enabler in the abuse.

We would do well to hear the counsel the parishioners heard every Sunday in Thomas Kirche in Leipzig when Johann Sebastian Bach delivered his cantatas as part of the morning worship. Music speaks its own language and is often more powerful and articulate than speech. Bach's musical message was soundly biblical, and so the words to his cantatas are also instructive. To modern ears they are strange. We do not like to think our pain is deserved, but only in penitential confession can we be cured. In Cantata number 114 Bach sings:

> Keep up your courage, Christian folk.
> Why are ye thus despairing?
> It was the Lord imposed this yoke,
> So bear it bravely.

> This punishment deserve we all,
> On each we reckon it must fall,
> Alike we all are faring.

Bach's piety celebrates the rhythm of redemption with the full gamut of God's grace. Every human emotion is expressed. In counseling the pastor must empathize with the penitent parishioner. Pastors can feel the pain and share the joy of the counselee because they are together in the sinful condition that is being redeemed. Unlike secular counselors, who think of themselves as being well and healthy helping people who are sick, the Christian pastor is in need of God's healing grace as much as the sinner being counseled.

The comfort of the Holy Spirit can be received only when we acknowledge the wondrous paradox that the wealth of this world is but a fleeting shadow. It is true that this world has beauty and value for which we should be everlastingly grateful. Yet to cling to it greedily brings nothing but defeat and sorrow. True strength, health, and holiness can be experienced when we give up our sinful hold on this life and all its wealth, and trust completely in the grace and mercy of Jesus Christ.

May our final supplication be the prayer of compline:

> O Lord, support us all the day long of this troubled life, until the shadows lengthen and the evening comes and the busy world is hushed, the fever of life is over, and our work is done. Then, O Lord, in your mercy grant us a safe lodging, and a holy rest, and peace at last, through Jesus Christ our Lord. Amen.

Art as the Revelation of the Holy Spirit

The Holy Spirit is a revolutionary force moving us from death to life, from stagnation in history to new, fresh, vibrant, and growing forms of social, political, economic, and aesthetic structures. Wherever and whenever change occurs that produces a blessing it is the life-giving work of the Spirit. The chosen heralds whose warning and promising words announce—and therefore produce—this change may come from God's covenant people, like Jeremiah and Amos and Luther and Martin Luther King, but in broader and more subtle ways the Spirit also speaks through the arts. Artists first conceive a culture and give it form and color and sound and taste and fragrance. In our Christian mission to the world we should look for points of contact not only in religion, where they are often also points of contrast, but also in secular society, where all people alike have orders of family, marketplace, schools, government, and especially the arts, where the love of beauty stirs our souls universally.

The Greeks did not know it but Christ was on Parnassus when from their insight the muses inspired the incomparable architecture and sculpture of the Acropolis. Aesthetic creativity was recognized by classical culture to be a gift.

The peril of the artist is the constant temptation to idolatrous worship of the beautiful creature rather than the beatific Creator. This results in service of the holiness of beauty instead of the beauty of holiness. Nevertheless art and religion are inextricably bound and the Christian faith finds expression in artistic forms just as truly as it does in intellectual works of theology or practical works of mercy.

I submit that art is that form of service to the ruling spirit of the age in which people try to express the will of that particular spirit by means of some kind of patterned arrangement of space. This means there are various spirits exerting their influence. While art is neither moral nor immoral, it is either spiritual or demonic depending on whether the spirit of the age is in the service of Christ or Satan. Art is never for art's sake, but often it is for the artist's sake or for Satan's. Only when it is for Christ's and the Spirit's sake is art true and beautiful and holy.

This view clearly cuts across Plato (art is a copy of a copy) and Aristotle (art is the representation of the universal in the particular for the purpose of catharsis) and Hegel (art is the manifest unfolding of the Spirit in history through conflict) and all the modern theories which try to reduce art to the will (such as Nietzsche and Freud) or the feelings (Santayana) or the mind (Maritain).

One example will show what I mean. When the Church in the late Middle Ages fell under the spell of an elemental spirit of this world, corruption attacked her from all sides, not only politically and socially, but also aesthetically. Her great culture lost its salutary grace and gradually became humanized. In the seventeenth century baroque art became a debased concern for nothing but the frilleries of nature. The Puritan reaction was healthy in its disciplined resistance against the intoxication of the pretty, but the priggishness of Puritanism was just as devastating to Christian art as was Plato's prudery to classic art. In each case art fell into the service of the spirit of the age and died with the demon of its choosing.

Art is a mystery which probes depths beyond and deeper than the human venture itself. For this reason Malraux called art a human protest against our fate, a brave, defiant attempt to say something that will live after we are gone. Certainly artistic creativity demonstrates one aspect of humanity's capacity to transcend itself, and therefore it exhibits at the same time the perils of a prideful hubris and the possibilities of a faithful service. There is a mysterious connection with Spirit that makes various definitions of art in terms of human enterprise inadequate, whether the definitions are formulated in psychological, sociological, or philosophical categories.

Art cannot be understood simply as the playful imitation of nature, nor the voluntaristic sublimation of basic biological urges, nor the aesthetic sensitization of intellectual pleasure. Although all of these factors and more may be present in the motivation of any artist, ultimately they must be seen as instruments in the hands of whatever Spirit happens to be ruling over the age in question. If Aristotle could say that art is the therapeutic catharsis of the emotions of pity and fear, it was only because healing, in the sense of reconciliation, is a proper concern of the Spirit. Any statement of the meaning of art will therefore require an examination of the *cultures* in which the various art forms are produced as well as the *styles* which vie for ascendancy in any given culture; and both culture and style will have to be studied in terms of the religious Spirit which motivates them. And then we shall have to discern what is divinely revelatory as over against what is merely human.

I. Art and Culture

Long recognized as a fruitful index to the meaning of culture, art is more basic than language itself to our understanding of ourselves, other peoples, and other ages. We have no extant literature nor any knowledge of the language used by the inhabitants of France and Spain twenty-five thousand years ago, but the drawings they left in their caves reveal more clearly than books the hopes and fears, the matters of ultimate concern, of those ancient people.

Christianity, however, is concerned with art not only because both religion and art are aspects and indices of culture. Christianity affects the whole person as well as the totality of society. Hence the problem of Christianity and art is more than cultural relationship. Christianity is both a culture and the critic of culture, both the product of a cultural legacy and the judge of all cultures, not the least its own. We shall see that this peculiar eschatological thrust of the Christian gospel is the key to our understanding of the relationship between Christianity and art.

Cultures may be analyzed in terms of their reaction to nature and the Spirit. Under the friendly Aegean skies the ancient Greeks sought a balance between the material substance of sensory experience and the spiritual stirrings within their souls. The word which best characterizes the height of Hellenic creativity is moderation (*sophrosune*), the proper equipoise between the Dionysian and the Apollonian phases of the Greek genius. Youthful ebullience is counterbalanced with the ideal of *mens sana in corpore sano*. The result is the search for perfect form. The idealization of natural forms arose concomitantly with the idolization of religious values. Indeed the idol of religious devotion was none other than the superman of aesthetic pursuit. Greek statues and paintings had expressionless faces because they were not simple imitations of nature nor even representations. They were idealized types. The same is true in both architecture and drama. The temples were not copies of anything in nature, but they exhibit the balance, symmetry, and proportion which the Greek mind abstracted from nature. The masks and artificial devices used to augment the voices of characters on stage rendered the actors utterly expressionless and made impossible the subtle nuances of voice inflection which are so important for modern drama. The Greek approached his art with a preconceived idea which he attempted to represent to the limit of perfection in his chosen medium. The idea of perfection stood at the apex of an architectonic hierarchy of rational values, making Greek aesthetic achievement predominantly intellectual. Art became the material formation of an idea.

The affinity of Chinese and Japanese culture with classical Greece is remarkable. Here, too, worship of nature with facile acceptance of the benignity of the Father of Heaven produced the same placid serenity in art forms as did the nature gods of Mount Olympus. The principle of *yang* and *yin* with its balance of opposites (male and female, sun and moon, heaven and earth) served for the Orient as did the golden mean in the West. The regal Guan Yin is simply the oriental version of Athene. The formalized figures of a Japanese print, cool and tranquil under the ideal of *shibusa*, are as typical as the painted ceramics found in the ruins of a Minoan temple. Even the symbolic gestures and grotesque masks of a *Noh* drama are reminiscent of the stereotyped strophes and the grimacing faces of the Athenian amphitheater.

When we turn to ancient Semitic culture, particularly that of the Hebrews, we find a marked contrast to the nature worship and naturalism in the art of Greeks and Orientals. The Hebrews viewed nature as the creature of God. Instead of exalting the forces of nature and divinizing them, the Hebrews extolled heaven and earth as the handiwork of the Creator Spirit. So fearful, however, were they of an idolatrous attachment to any created thing that they permitted themselves only symbolic, never representational, expression. When the Hebrews spoke aesthetically of "dragons and all deeps, fire and hail, snow and frost" (Psalm 148:7-8), they did so only to declare their faith that all creatures fulfill the command of the Lord.

The difference between the Hebrew and the Hellenic spirit is illustrated by their contrasting use of language. For the Greeks words defined and circumscribed idea. In the same way the artist's medium could contain and formulate an idealized concept. For the Hebrew words were windows which opened to reality and pierced the veil between one spirit and another. No surer grasp upon reality was available to the Hebrew than the glimpses afforded by fleeting words said or sung in a moment of faithful obedience. Any materialization through artistic media might falsely attempt to possess and control the hidden and unnamable God. This was not because matter was considered evil, but because as a created good it must not be identified with the Creator of all goods. The Hindu culture also exhibits an aesthetic indigence because of preoccupation with spirit as over against nature, but the Hindu subservience to spirit was accompanied by a world-negating denial of the flesh, while Hebrew release was sought in the apocalyptic longing for the courts of the Lord.

When Christianity entered upon the stage of history the glory that was Greece had already degenerated into the grandeur that was Rome. Gnostic fatigue with the frustrations of this world sought escape in mystic excursions to the ineffable world of the empyrean. Christianity at first did not foster artistic endeavor but rather "fasted from art." Christian reluctance, however, was not because of ascetic or spiritual odium for the things of this world. The central message of the Christians, after all, was that the Word had become flesh in Jesus! Yet for several centuries no serious attempt at artistic creation was made.

Was this because art is concerned with the beautiful while the Christian message proclaimed the ugly cross? Contrast the graceful beauty of the humanized god of Phidias with the formless, uncomely, rejected, bruised, defeated figure prophesied in Isaiah and fulfilled on Golgotha! Yet of the few Greek paintings known to us the most famous is Timanthes' depiction of the sacrifice of Iphigenia, a copy of which remains sketched on a wall of a house in Pompeii. Certainly Greek painting was not incapable of seeing the beauty in sorrow and tragedy, but here the tragic face of Agamemnon is covered with his robe, not due to inability of the artist or the medium to express tragic emotion, but because such horror would destroy the Greek sense of noble restraint. Perhaps a more profound interpretation of this restraint is that the Greek was ultimately unable to face the horror of human tragedy, a horror which is not avoided but accentuated in the figure on the cross. It is significant that the greatest Greek painting and the greatest among Christian paintings should both be concerned with the subject of sacrifice. Yet it is plain that Agamemnon's sacrifice is humanity's futile offering to God while the crucifixion is God's sorrow for humanity.

From the beginning, though their painting was halting, the Christians placarded before the world the ugly picture of the crucified Savior. From the scratches on the catacomb walls to the Isenheim altarpiece of Grunewald there has never been hesitation concerning the primary subject of Christian art. The reason for the Christian fast from art, however, must be found in the nature of the subject. The crucified Lord brings both judgment and mercy, death to the old world and life in the new. It was the eschatological judgment on the old that accounts for the slow development of a specifically Christian expression. The slaying of the old Adam in the classical world had to be done, the burial made, and the clearing of the debris completed before the new life could rise and produce the fruits of fresh culture. And since Christian culture still remains in the flesh while at the same time being born anew in the Spirit, the process of judging and slaying the past must continue and be repeated in each moment of the present.

II. Styles

Today it is not the subject that makes the difference in art but variation in styles. Beginning with the emphasis upon background in the Italian Renaissance painting but especially with the humane affirmation of Brueghel, the choice of subjects for painters in the modern world became infinitely various. Landscapes, portraiture, genre painting, still life—everything from guitars to guillotines became objects of the painter's interest. But the shift from ostensibly religious subjects to the infinite variety of the secular world was not so profound a religious shift as the innovation of different styles. Turning from Leonardo's *Last Supper* to Bonnard's *Breakfast Room* involves a religious difference in subject, but it is only a movement from consideration of the second article of the creed to the first. One is not less religious when one thanks God for daily bread than when one proclaims the Lord's death in the eucharist, and indeed both are as ineluctably related as the petals of a rose. But mere choice of subject will not reveal whether the artist's concern is reverence for the creature represented or for the Creator whose grace makes possible not only the creature but the artist and viewer as well. Here style becomes the revelatory factor.

The humanist return to classical forms, departing from medieval distortions, has often been described as an improvement in technique.

Certainly improvements were made, but why was the attempt made in the first place? The shift from the stilted, twisted figures of medieval painters and sculptors to the realistic, anatomically perfect form of the Renaissance was a change in ultimate religious concern from other-worldliness to this-worldliness.

Since this major transfer of religious concern with its consequent change in style, another shift has been made which is equally significant. Here the watershed is Cezanne, who stopped representing reality and started radically to reconstruct it. The result has become so complex that it almost defies analysis. Classical, romantic, impressionistic, expressionistic, futuristic, cubistic, surrealistic, particularistic, abstract, organic, idyllic, monumental, prophetic, propagandistic—these are some of the adjectives given to the many styles that have evolved.

Examination of styles and schools of painting may fruitfully reveal their relation to the existing philosophical theories of epistemology, assuming that art is basically communication. While painting is the medium under discussion the same observations may be made for all the art forms. According to such analysis the various styles may be classified as realism, impressionism, surrealism, and expressionism. It should not be assumed that the epistemological analysis will provide a complete understanding of the meaning of art. It offers only a key to the differing styles, and, as we shall see later, only a superficial one. For example, Picasso has used his medium for prophetic purposes or moral protest and propaganda with styles ranging from realism to surrealism, impressionism to expressionism.

Coupled with the classical revival realistic style recovered the simple Aristotelian correspondence theory of knowledge. Ideas are true to the degree that they correspond to their sensory images. Reality is thus a substance of this world and painting is true to the degree that it corresponds realistically to it. When the rules of the Academies became so fixed that painting became dull, the spirit of judgment and renewal reacted against realism and modified it into impressionism. Basically impressionism is not different from realism except that it seeks to capture a moment of reality rather than some timeless and formal truth. Monet, Pissaro, and Renoir thus freely experimented with light and color in a way which contrasted sharply with the tonal banalities of the Academies. The epistemology of the impressionists is empiricism. Each impact of the manifold world of the senses is a bit of reality which deserves to be recorded in both its pristine purity and in its provocative relation with its immediate neighbors.

Both realism and impressionism are this-worldly and life-affirming. Although the former is more concerned with universals and the latter with particulars, both are fundamentally humanistic. Surrealism and expressionism, however, are other-worldly and life denying. Mysticism is the way of knowing for the surrealists. Immediate insight into the subconscious is claimed as the source of all that is valuable in art. The limp watches of Dali are in the words of Alfred H. Barr, "irrational, impossible, fantastic, paradoxical, disquieting, baffling, alarming, hypnogogic, nonsensical, and mad—but to the surrealist these adjectives are the highest praise." Another characteristic of the mystical style is symbolism. From Ryder and Rousseau to Dali and Miro familiar objects are used only as suggestive symbols to lead the viewer into the world of fantasy, mystery, and magic. The expressionists, on the other hand, while just as gingerly with the things of this world, are far more comprehensible in their irrationalism. Existentialist theory of knowledge explains the style of the expressionists. No attempt is made to copy a preconceived form. Unlike the Greeks who sought to communicate a system of rational truth, the expressionists, whether they be cubists, futurists, fauvists, or the earlier experimenters like Van Gogh and Gauguin, have simply tried to convey on canvas in color and shape what is in their inmost souls.

The acids of modernity have eaten deeply into the souls of these disillusioned sophisticates, and weary with this world, they have set out to construct a new world of their own. Some, like Jackson Pollock and Willem de Kooning, have constructed an antinomian world of drips and blobs. Others, like Piet Mondrian and Mark Rothko, have shown their revulsion against the disorder of the given world by designing a world of pure and simple geometric forms. Both exhibit a recrudescence of ancient Gnosticism, antinomian and legalistic, a fevered and faithless attempt to escape fear and frustration in this world. Yet all these wild expressions proclaim more eloquently than realism ever could the basic Christian truth that the world is shattered and shorn of the image in which it was made. Not willing to claim an essential verity behind all existence, these painters "let the canvas speak to them." The result is the shocking positivism of the human spirit that wrestles not against flesh and blood but against principalities and powers.

III. Toward a Christian Critique of Art

How is it possible to choose between various styles? Can one be said to be better or truer than another? A work of art may be judged in terms of its integrity: has the artist honestly accomplished what he or she intended? Or in terms of skill in execution: has the artist successfully handled the medium in pursuit of his or her purpose? But these are questions which may be asked only within a given style. It appears no more possible to choose between styles than to choose between philosophers. Ultimately each rests upon a metaphysical root metaphor. Some prefer to look upon the world as an idea, and therefore everything in it is reduced to a formalized concept with art as its faithful representation. Clarity and adequacy then become the chief criteria of judgment. Others see reality in terms of the sense image. Purity and relationship become the critical concern. The mystics exult in their beatific vision because they find reality in the obscure. The expressionists thrash and wrestle with existence because they cannot accept what they see but are unable to create an adequate reality for themselves. But when we are asked to choose between metaphysical metaphors, all we can say is *chacun à son gout*. Indeed we may well wonder why it should be necessary to choose between Giotto and Van Gogh, Botticelli and Rouault, Gauguin and Klee. Each in his own way pierces the veil of truth and awakens in the viewer new life.

Regardless of philosophical orientation, a work of art may be said to be a vehicle of communication. Whether the artist sets out to say something or not, the product serves to speak to people in such a way as to move them. Christianly speaking we may ask if an art form communicates not just God, but the Father of our Lord Jesus Christ, and consequently does it move us by the Spirit to say, "Abba, Father!" We can ask this question as Christians because everything we have in this world is given by God and hence everything must serve to glorify him. Peter Blume's *The Eternal City*, which was at first received with critical disgust, conveys in stark realism the strident cadences of an Old Testament prophet as it blatantly shouts the judgment of God upon a city of sin. Who can say that the Spirit did not speak through this prophet? The tragic, bewildered face of Van Gogh with its mysterious bandage around his tortured ear earnestly but pungently asks the meaning of existence and leads us on our first step to repentance. And perhaps more clearly and profoundly Rouault says all these things—judgment, repentance, and the infinite plus of mercy—in his *Christ Mocked by Soldiers*.

The criterion is the relevance of the work of art to the Christian story in all its redemptive and eschatological force. The sentimental shepherds of Hoffmann, the calendar art of Coleman, and the many "beauty parlor Christs" that are pushed by the publishing houses of the churches must not be taken seriously as either art or gospel except that they are so popular and powerful in shaping the faith of undiscerning people. These romantic projections of maudlin sentimentality with all their attention to religious subject and all their pious persuasiveness can no more move us to the God of the gospel than a poster by Maxfield Parrish.

The Christian story concerns creation, the image of God, the fall, redemption, the coming of new life. These will be the categories of criticism. The nature of the God of this story is both hidden and revealed. This will make a difference in the way the artist handles his or her medium. The aim will not be obvious imitation nor even careful and detailed representation, but rather the suggestiveness and symbolism of revelation. Art will never directly communicate any more than the flesh of Jesus directly communicated the fact of his Messiahship. Art, like the Word itself, will be mediated immediacy, always pointing to the reality and leading to a faithful breakthrough but never robbing the viewer of his or her responsibility to contribute to the revelation. As Picasso said, "A picture lives its life like a living creature, undergoing the changes that daily life imposes upon us. That is natural, since a picture lives only through him who looks at it."

The creature is understood to be the glorious handiwork of God. None of this original goodness is lost, yet the whole image is turned upside down and no relic of purity remains. The whole creature is corrupted so that the world itself groans as in travail. Hence the artist must portray the pride, the lust, the greed which torment this world, and this will exhibit the quality of God's judgment. There must be restraint in the art work just as the law restrains and keeps order, but there must also be prophetic protest and exposure as the law leads us to a knowledge of our sin.

There will be the paradox of the perfection of imperfection, the restraint of the unfinished statement, and this will be true both because of the terrible turbulence of sin in the world and because of the yet-to-be-fulfilled wonder of salvation.

The great mystery the artist can and must proclaim is not that humans and earth can reach to God and heaven by the manipulation of a material medium, but rather that God has come down to earth, that the divine can be declared through the colors of clay! This will be difficult—for both artist and viewer. But why should art be easy? A work of art too easy to understand wears thin. It must have the mystery of new surprises each time it is viewed, touched, or heard. Van Gogh sharply retorted to Gauguin when Gauguin charged him with painting too fast, "You look too fast!"

The artistic statement will furthermore exhibit the quality of grace in all its splendor of freedom and renewal. The grace of redemption and new life will find expression in art insofar as the work shows surprise and risk and newness and even humor. Forgiveness is the gift of the ability to laugh at oneself. The comic relief of the grotesque gargoyles on the roof gutters of Notre Dame marvelously serves this function of holy humor as they laughingly proclaim that even the demons of hell must serve Christ. And what is so healing, what is so refreshing, as laughter over the incongruous, especially when it is the merriment of Michael and all angels rejoicing over a sinner that has been saved? Grace requires risk and surprise because it is free. This insures a future in art which will be constantly changing, bringing into play ever new and fresh experiments.

    Art must therefore be exciting without being bizarre, and also relevant without being banal. It must have all the adventure, the reach, the penetration of romance with none of the egoism and sentimentality. It must have all the protest and introspection of existentialism with none of the cynical despair and acceptance. It must have all the mystery and suggestiveness that points beyond the obvious but none of the obscurantism and mystical identity of the surrealists. Christianity will demand of art, as it does of culture and its own self, the judgment and grace of the Holy Spirit, for it is truly a fruit of the Spirit as it is used to communicate salvation.

8

Two Loves

Song of Songs 2:3-13

Like an apple tree
among the trees of the forest
so is my lover among the young men.
I delight to sit in his shade,
and his fruit is sweet to my taste.

He has taken me to the banquet hall,
and his banner over me is love.
Strengthen me with raisins,
for I am faint with love.

His left arm is under my head,
and his right arm embraces me.
Daughters of Jerusalem, I charge you
by the gazelles and by the does of the field:
Do not arouse or waken love
until it so desires.

The voice of my lover!
Look! He comes
leaping across the mountains,
bounding over the hills.
My lover is like a gazelle or a young stag.
Look! He stands behind our wall,
gazing through the windows,
peering through the lattice.
My lover spoke and said to me,
"Rise up, my darling, my beautiful one,
and come away with me.
See! The winter is past;
the rains are over and gone.
Flowers appear on the earth;
the season of singing has come,
the cooing of doves
is heard in our land.

The fig tree forms its early fruit;
the blossoming vines spread their fragrance.
Arise, come, my darling,
my beautiful one,
come away with me."

---

1 Corinthians 13

If I speak in the language of humans,
and even in the tongues of angels,
but have not love,
I am only a resounding gong,
or a tinkling cymbal.
If I have the gift of prophecy
and can fathom all mysteries
and all knowledge;
and if I have a faith that can move mountains,
but have not love,
I am nothing.
And if I give all my goods
to feed the poor,
and surrender my body to be burned,
but have not love,
I gain nothing.
Love is patient, love is kind,
does not envy, does not boast, does not vaunt itself.
Love does not behave unseemly,
nor does it seek itself.
Love is not easily provoked;
it keeps no record of wrongs;
it delights not in evil but rejoices in truth.
Always love protects, always trusts,
always hopes, always perseveres.
Love never fails.
Where there are prophecies
they will be abolished;
where there are tongues
they will cease;

where there is knowledge
it will vanish away.
We know in part and we prophesy in part,
but when perfection comes,
the partial disappears.
When I was a child I spoke as a child,
I understood as a child;
but when I became a man
I put away childish things.
For now we see but a poor reflection;
but then we shall see face to face.
Now I know in part;
then I shall fully know
even as I am fully known.
And now these three abide:
faith, hope, and love.
But the greatest of these is love.

Ephesians 5:15-33

Be very careful then how you live—
not as unwise but as wise,
making the most of every opportunity,
because the days are evil.
Therefore do not be foolish,
but understand what the Lord's will is.
Do not get drunk on wine which leads to debauchery.
Instead, be filled with the Spirit.
Speak to one another
with psalms, hymns, and spiritual songs.
Sing and make music in your heart to the Lord,
always giving thanks to God the Father
for everything in the name of our Lord Jesus Christ.

Submit to one another out of reverence for Christ.
Wives, submit to your husbands as to the Lord.
For the husband is the head of the wife
as Christ is the head of the Church, his body,
of which he is the Savior.

Now as the Church submits to Christ,
so also wives should submit to their husbands in everything.
Husbands love your wives,
just as Christ loved the Church
and gave himself up for her to make her holy,
cleansing her by the washing with water
through the word,
and to present her to himself as a radiant Church,
without stain or wrinkle or any other blemish,
but holy and blameless.
In this same way husbands ought to love their wives
as their own bodies.
He who loves his wife loves himself.
After all, no one ever hated his own body,
but he feeds and cares for it,
just as Christ does the Church—
for we are members of his body.
"For this reason a man will leave his father and mother
and be united to his wife,
and the two will become one flesh."
This is a profound mystery—
but I am talking about Christ and the Church.
However, each one of you also must love his wife
as he loves himself,
and the wife must respect her husband.

Love and Marriage

The Song of Solomon and Paul's letter to the Corinthians speak with the wisdom of the Church as it is moved by the Holy Spirit. Both speak of love but of radically different kinds. The first tells how the beloved is filled with delight and lifted to heights of ecstasy when her lover comes to her. She is surprised by joy. This is a love we all know. It comes naturally, needs no command. Indeed it would be absurd to exhort one to fall in love. This love knows neither law nor gospel; it belongs to the original goodness of God's creation. It makes us beautiful. In this love we are fulfilled. We go to sleep laughing and we wake with a smile. Will it last? No, but it can be renewed again and again; and if a marriage has lasting satisfaction it will be partly because we find ourselves unexpectedly falling in love over and over again. And then the bride will know what it means to be a queen, and the groom will be a king.

Natural human love is a glory to God, not a temptation. Its desire is as good as the desire for food or acceptance. Because of sin it can be abused as everything else. The "last temptation of Christ" was not to have sex with Mary Magdalene, as some critics mistakenly read Nikos Kazantzakis. It was for Jesus to be merely human and do only the good things that mere humans do, and not to do what his Father sent him to do. He only, because he is uniquely the Christ, was tempted to renounce the cup of the cross. Christ, who is God in human flesh, could be tempted to be not God. He was tempted to be merely human. We, who are not God but really and uniquely human, are tempted to be God, but we cannot be tempted to be human.

Paul speaks differently of love. Paul talks about a love that is not natural to us at all. Solomon's love is *eros*, the passionate love of the sexes. David's love for Jonathan is *philia*, the affectionate love of friends. Paul's love is *agape*, a gift of the Holy Spirit. *Agape* is unmerited grace whereby God turns sinners into saints. It is a gift that makes demands, and so we are commanded to love one another as Christ first loved us. As with creation, redeeming love cannot be understood by comparison with any human analogy. The use of resemblance will not bring us knowledge of, or relationship with, God and the gifts of God. The explosive power of revelation is needed. To be sure we have only human experience, human words, human analogies, but when God speaks to us he must take these analogies and blow them apart, pour new meaning into them, and recreate the metaphor so that it can carry us out of this old world of sin and death into a new world of righteousness and life. Human love—sexual, parental, filial, affectionate—will never reveal divine love. Jesus alone is the way to this love—and the Holy Spirit who always accompanies him.

Jesus' love not only excels all other loves but is radically different from all other loves. It is a love that also catches us by surprise, but wonderfully and strangely it does not fill us. It rather empties us and drains us with sacrifice and service. The lover feels moved by a demand to give himself totally to his beloved without expecting anything in return. This love commits us to faithful, long-suffering, yet cheerful, service, each for the other and both working for a destiny that cannot be enjoyed separately. With this love we make others beautiful.

A good marriage is a ballet. A good marriage is a *pas de deux* within a full blown ballet. That is why we have a public ceremony, because marriage is never a private matter between consenting adults. The whole community of friends and loved ones must give consent and support. But a *ménage à trois* is not choreographed. In a *pas de deux* the male dancer and the ballerina serve each other. The ballerina dances on her toes and she therefore needs support for her balance. She cannot go into her turns and spins and pirouettes without the help of her partner. She must therefore submit to him to do her part. And he must submit to her if he is to serve in the ballet.

Ballet is an art. So is marriage. It is creative beauty arising out of careful discipline. The male dancer must both serve and be served by the ballerina. Likewise the ballerina must serve and be served by her partner. Thus the author of Ephesians said we should submit to one another out of reverence for Christ, wives to husbands, husbands to wives. God made us different so we can complement each other, not compete. We are contrapuntal because there is need in a healthy body for relationships to be both hard and soft, firm and compliant, close and distant. Our binary nature gives us a rhythm to make music for the Lord. The wife serves him who serves her; the husband serves her who serves him. We submit to one another as Christ who loved the Church and gave himself for her. So then let us edify one another by singing and dancing to the Lord, for it is not we who make the difference in the full ballet; it is Christ. Christians in marriage experience both kinds of love, the warmth of human passion and the mystery of divine love through Christ.

Revelation turns everything inside out. We cannot know God or ourselves directly. There is always the imploding death of our human words and analogies and then the exploding resurrection of Divine Word giving us a surprising new meaning in place of the old. In addition to human love which is ambiguously good and evil, which is natural and therefore familiar, such that we fearfully cling to it to possess it, we receive from Christ and the Spirit a divine love that edifies by emptying, a love we never need to possess because it magnifies by giving itself up. Revelation tells us that when we truly love, whether in the created or redemptive order of things, we love because God first loves us. The crashing paradox has the same irony in every arena of life, in the relationships between the sexes, between parents and children or teachers and students, between rulers and subjects, between priests and devotees. In our natural sinful relationships we set up ideals or models which we think will serve us. But the ideal spouse, parent, teacher, ruler, priest becomes an idol that enslaves us. Revelation must crack these idols so that God can substitute for them all the living Christ. Only then can we know what it means to be the bride of Christ, to have a Father in heaven, to serve the King of kings, and to receive the intercession of the High Priest in heaven. We may all have a spouse, a father, a teacher, a king, a priest, but invariably we make them idols. Then we lose our freedom and the destiny God intended for us. Hence Jesus said, "And do not call anyone on earth 'father,' for you have one Father, and he is in heaven. Nor are you to be called 'teacher,' for you have one Teacher, the Christ" (Matthew 23:9-10). And to Pilate Jesus said, "My kingdom is not of this world" (John 18:36). The author of Hebrews designated Jesus our High Priest: "For this reason Christ is the mediator of a new covenant . . ." (Hebrews 9:15). And the Pauline writer said to Timothy: "For there is one God and one mediator between God and people, the man Christ Jesus . . ." (1 Timothy 2:5).

We have been speaking of two loves which embrace human relationships, one in the natural order of creation and the other in the gracious order of redemption. What shall we say about the love between God and humans? A grand tradition in the life of faith has expressed this love in terms of the metaphor of the Church as the bride of Christ. Surely this metaphor was never intended literally as a sexual union. Natural love in the created order may include companionate friendship as well as sexual bonding, but neither of these models pertain to our marriage with the Lamb.

Clarity in the use of metaphors in the language of revelation is needed. Above all we must recognize that Scripture uses words poetically, not univocally. Biblical language is actively forceful in creating many meanings on various levels of reality. Marriage to the Lamb literally is ludicrous, but when we speak these words as taught by the Spirit, we see that marriage with Christ includes a gracious relationship that does not involve sex.

Much confusion is currently rampant because many people are limiting words to single meanings. Usually this limitation has political motivation. The motivation may be legitimate or it may be downright illegitimate, but the resulting limitation of semantics is hurtful. This univocal literalism deprives God the Father the uniqueness of his infinitude. God is not Father as a male becomes a father when he procreates. In the Christian revelation God is not male, has no consort, is not female, does not give birth. It is a mistake to read Genesis 1:27 as a single verse, as if we were created male and female in the image of a God who is male and female. Plants and animals were created male and female, but they do not have the image of God. The image in which we were created refers to God's true nature as Father, Son, and Holy Spirit. Human beings alone among God's creatures have the Spirit breathed into them. This gives us the freedom to be either children of God or sinful slaves of the devil. The image in which we were created is not male nor female but the trinity. It is rank heresy to conceive of God as having either masculine or feminine traits. Humans alone have God's traits which are Trinitarian: uniqueness of the Father, intelligence of the Son, and freedom of the Spirit. Each human has the uniqueness of one's own name; each one of us is free to respond both positively and negatively. Our image of the Trinity is most awesome indeed; being male and female is only natural.

God is neither a big man nor an oversized woman. The psalmist, speaking of God, mocks this personification: "You thought I was altogether like you" (Psalm 50:21). Yet for centuries popular piety mistakenly conceived of God as a strong, wise old man who indulgently forgives. Now feminists want to make God a caring woman. To make things equal, we hear people praying to our Father-Mother. Others avoid masculine imagery by replacing the Trinitarian benediction with the triad: Creator, Redeemer, Sanctifier. They do not realize that these nouns are functions, not names. They do not describe God as Trinity.

A man is defined as male and a woman as female; and this definition marks our finitude. God has no such definition of finitude. The Father in the Trinity is said to beget a Son, but this begetting is from the beginning, not through sexual union with a consort. Just as there is no male in the Trinity there is no female. Christian revelation sharply differs from all human religions with their mythical imaginations that derive from our yearning to have a familiar, comfortable God.

But if God is neither male nor female why do we use language that makes God sound like a man? It must be understood that language has gender but no sex. Words in English may be masculine, feminine, or neuter; they are never male or female. We have three genders in English, some languages have no gender, others have six or more; but humans have only two sexes. The word for spirit in English is masculine because it comes from the Latin word (*spiritus*) which is masculine; but the Hebrew word is feminine (*ruach*), and the Greek (*pneuma*) is neuter. A masculine noun does not literally refer always to a male. Ships and countries are called by feminine names but they are not females. The name of God as Father does not make God male. The Son in the Trinity is not the male issue of sexual union. As we have said the Father has no consort.

It is not God's nature to become a father as a male creature becomes a father, but it is possible through divine grace for a human father to become like God. This is indeed God's promise for our destiny. But it is not possible for us to define God in our image, not male nor female nor any other dimension. To speak of God's feminine or masculine characteristics is idolatrous and does violence to both God and his creatures.

Why did Jesus name God Father rather than Mother? The prevailing religion in the Greco-Roman world at the time of Jesus was the worship of the *Magna Mater* (Great Mother). While feminine images were occasionally used in the Old Testament the metaphor of everlasting Father was commonly used in the Hebrew tradition. No doubt to reject the pagan imagery and to affirm the Hebrew revelation Jesus chose the name Father for the God in heaven who sent him to be the incarnate Lord and whose Spirit Jesus sends to give us life and holiness. The metaphor Father is appropriate because he initiates the active love that creates and redeems, as a father biologically is the giver and the woman is the receiver. Both males and females are the bride of Christ. Divine grace is active; human faith is receptive. This human metaphor may be difficult for anyone, male or female, who seeks independence, but then it is our original and persistent sin to reverse this direction. We should quit using our words as political weapons in sexual warfare and rather sing about God's infinite, mysterious, and magnificent holiness.

God's love is not like our love, which is always ambiguously good and bad; but by grace we can enter into a loving relationship which is uplifting, edifying, sanctifying, and everlasting. God's love begets in us the image of the Son through the power of the Holy Spirit. It is this transforming power of gracious love that makes all the difference.

If Christ is the Son of God it is because he was begotten from the beginning by the love of God. Jesus is not the Son of God because he was humanly born of Mary. Human birth is the product of human love, but the birth of Jesus was the result of pure divine love, sacrificial *agape*. Because Jesus is the Son of God, one with the Son in the Trinity, he was virgin born. He was certainly humanly born, seen with the mask of the flesh, but he was also virgin born. That this flesh was a mask is the point of revelation. Flesh alone does not reveal God; the Spirit must give us power to see the virgin birth by faith.

The Word of God became flesh and dwelled among us for a time. Two stories in Scripture say that the Word became flesh by way of a virgin birth, the stories in Matthew and Luke. Perhaps a narrative hermeneutic, based on the thesis that reality is fundamentally a story, will shed new light on the doctrine of the virgin birth. John, Paul, and Mark say nothing about it, nor is there mention of it anywhere else in the New Testament. Some passages speak of Jesus being born of a woman (Galatians 4:4) or of the seed of David according to the flesh (Romans 1:3), and there are the genealogies, but the early kenotic hymn of Philippians 2:6-11 ignores it and Paul says nothing about it in other references to the incarnation (Romans 8:3; 2 Corinthians 5:21; Galatians 3:13). But the early Church quickly included the teaching in its creedal confessions. Later pious legends said that Matthew and Luke got the story directly from Mary, but there is no evidence for this. It seems more likely that this is a narrative way of explaining a mysterious action of God.

The story of Jesus' miraculous birth is unique.[1] There are many stories in past cultures about gods and heroes being born of virgins, but these were always tales about gods or angels coming in human or animal form to have intercourse with mortal women. Usually the stories were mythical, not legendary, with the purpose of explaining the origin of some tradition or institution that arose out of the distant past. In Matthew and Luke the historical role of Mary is unique. Not only are the virgin birth stories of the New Testament lacking in any pagan parallelism but there is also no Old Testament background for the stories. Instead of other similar stories, we find prophecies in the Old Testament that were interpreted in the New Testament as being fulfilled by the birth of Jesus. God is described as doing what he had promised through his covenant. One example is where Isaiah 7:14 says a child will be born to a young woman and the child will save the world. Whether Isaiah had in mind a virgin birth the way Matthew did is

---

[1] Cf also Robert Paul Roth, *The Theater of God* (1985; reprinted, Eugene, Ore.: Wipf and Stock, 2005) 100–103.

not known. Discussion of the meaning of the words *almah* or *bethulah* and *parthenos*, whether they mean virgin or young woman, seems to be fruitless. It may not have occurred to Isaiah that this would be a "virgin" birth. The method of the birth is not the issue for him. What did occur to Isaiah was that God had spoken and promised to deliver Israel through a child whom God would send. This is a miracle in the true sense: divine power acting in a personal way on the stage of freedom. And the early Christians saw Jesus as the fulfillment of that promise.

Why then did the New Testament writers say the birth was virgin? Because they saw in Jesus not just a promised child but the holy God come to them. They did not read the story as Schleiermacher did. He understood Jesus to be unique in that he only among all human beings fulfilled perfect God-consciousness. Jesus was the elevation of one human being from natural humanity to divinity because he accomplished what is inherent in all of us. This is a story too. One might even tell it without Pelagian implications by saying it was God who raised Jesus to this holiness. But it is not the story told in the New Testament. Rather, joining the Isaiah prophecy with the virgin birth story requires us to say that Jesus is unique because God, the holy One, emptied himself of his holiness and came into the realm of sin, becoming sin with us, Immanuel. The virgin birth story is told to reveal that what was holy came into sinful flesh, the womb of Mary, not that God raised up something sinful and made it divine. God took what was divine and made it human, and not only creaturely human but also sinfully human (Romans 8:3; 2 Corinthians 5:21; Galatians 3:13). Thus for Irenaeus the virgin birth was testimony of Jesus' humanity in being the second Adam: true humanity. Luther has the same idea in his catechism when he says Jesus Christ is true God, begotten of the Father from eternity, and also true man, born of the Virgin Mary. It is theological error, therefore, to say that Jesus is divine because he was born of a virgin. It is the other way around. Jesus was born of a virgin because he was divine. It is theological error to say that Mary was immaculate. The point of this virgin birth story is that the holy God entered the sinful flesh of Mary, who was a sinner like the rest of us, and Jesus being born of Mary entered into our sin.

What then does account for Jesus' divinity in the story of his birth? The power of the Holy Spirit. The virgin birth is told in terms of the activity of the Holy Spirit bringing the new creation at this end-time, just as the Creator Spirit was active in the beginning. The virgin birth is comprehensible to us only as a mystery comparable in cosmic dimensions with the original creation. The coming of Christ is the new creature, and the new creature comes from God, as did the first creature. As the first creature came from the dust of the earth with the Holy Spirit breathing life into Adam, so the new Adam comes from the flesh of Mary and the Holy Spirit breathes life into Jesus.

What about the activity of Joseph in this story? As the story is told Joseph is angry when he finds that Mary is pregnant. He was not the father of her child. But on the other hand the story does not tell us that the Holy Spirit is the biological father of the child. We have said that the point of the story is not that a biological miracle guarantees the divinity of Christ. Instead of biological sequences described in the story we have narrative metaphor and language of mystery. It says in Luke 1:35 that the power of the Most High will overshadow Mary, *episkiasei*, the same word used in the transfiguration story for the cloud that overshadows the transfigured Christ and the disciples. Luke also says the Holy Spirit will come upon Mary, *epeleusetai*, and he uses the same verb in Acts 1:8 when the risen Lord promises the power of the Holy Spirit to come upon the disciples. The activity of God here is the mysterious presence of the Holy Spirit making all things new. This is the power of the Spirit in our baptism, our virgin birth.

What can we make of the fact that Joseph is rejected as father and Mary is affirmed as mother? Males at first will pout like Joseph and females will rejoice, but both would be wrong, for Joseph realized that this child was of God and Mary's heart was pierced with a sword. Joseph need not lament, because his rejection was not a rejection of human fatherhood or his male sexuality. His rejection in the story is representative of God's repudiation of human sin. It indicates the death of humankind in the process of salvation. And Mary's affirmation does not elevate virginity above marriage, as in Roman Catholic piety, but it indicates the acceptance of the creature as the object of God's love. This is not an affirmation of human motherhood or of Mary's female sexuality as such. The virgin birth tells a different story, not a story about biology and sexuality but a story about a new creation. The rejection of Joseph is a judgment on our sinfulness; the election of Mary is the affirmation of our creatureliness.

As part of the whole Christian story, the virgin birth story has had a remarkable role in shaping a new society, in creating a culture in which both patriarchal and matriarchal structures are replaced by the Church as our mother and God as our Father. This narrative explanation may be seen when we compare the virgin birth story with the classical drama of Orestes. Ancient cultures vacillated between matriarchal and patriarchal social structures. The Orestes story tells about the search for justice by affirming a shift from a matriarchal to a patriarchal system. It is quite realistic in telling how the sins of the fathers and mothers are visited upon the children. Orestes kills his mother, Clytemnestra, because she has killed his father, Agamemnon. Clytemnestra and her lover, Aegisthus, usurped the throne of Thebes from Agamemnon because he had sacrificed their daughter, Iphigenia, in order to get favorable winds from the gods on his way to Troy. Now Orestes is on trial for killing his mother. The Furies are the prosecuting attorneys. They charge that matricide is the worst crime because it is a blood crime, worse than Clytemnestra's crime because she only killed her husband, not a blood relative. Apollo is the defense attorney. He argues that matricide is not as serious as regicide, since the king is given his scepter by Zeus, the father of the gods. But moreover and chiefly, Orestes is not guilty of a blood crime because a mother is really no parent, only a workshop for the father's seed. Early religion was matriarchal and conception was thought to be by the wind. No father was needed. Later when the father was understood to be causal in conception, the phallus became a religious fetish and patriarchy the social structure. Some critics therefore see the judgment of the goddess Athena in favor of Orestes to be the narrative explanation for the advance in societal structure from matriarchy to patriarchy, and the conflict between the old law and the new is seen to be resolved as the Erinyes become the "Kindly Ones."

In contrast the virgin birth story in Christianity may be seen as a repudiation of both matriarchal and patriarchal societies and the affirmation of a new human relationship produced by the creative power of the Holy Spirit. This story in its fullness creates a culture free from the abuses of sexual fetishes of either gender and the tyrannies of both sexes. History has shown, however, that we have fallen far short of this in practice. Mary's song of praise still prods us to redress the wrongs perpetrated by the strong and the rich because God showered his favor on a poor and weak woman.

Stories exhibit the ambivalence that humanity entertains in our attempt through myth to explain the cosmic forces which both control us and are at our disposal. Throughout history there have been shifting inversions of the role of women. In the Sumerian myth of Inanna and Enki, Inanna, the goddess of Erech, gains by seduction the *mes* of civilization which are the rules of religious, social, and cosmic realities. A goddess thus becomes the patron of civilization. Enkidu in this Sumerian myth is also "civilized" by a temple prostitute, a representative of Ishtar (Inanna). Through intercourse with a woman man is tamed.

The same idea is prevalent with Pallas Athena, the goddess of Athens, who grew in myth out of a combination of the Minoan goddess of the city and the house (domestic wisdom) and the Dorian goddess of battle. Perhaps it was this martial quality in her genetic constitution that accounted for her "wisdom" in the Orestian decision which favored patriarchal society.

In Christianity Mary overcomes Eve. Eve also is associated with wisdom. In her seduction by the serpent Eve chooses to be wise rather than innocent, but in the biblical story this is a fall! Also in the Greek myth of Pandora, unlike that of Athena, woman becomes a curse. The early Church fathers pondered the inversion of the role of woman in salvation. For Irenaeus, not only does Mary counter Eve's disobedience but she becomes the "cause of salvation" (*Against Heresies* III, 22). Tertullian says, "What by that sex had gone into perdition by that same sex might be brought back to salvation. Eve had believed the serpent; Mary believed Gabriel; the fault which one committed by believing, the other by believing has blotted out" (*The Flesh of Christ*, 17).

Wisdom was feminine in Hebrew (*ḥokmah*) and was associated with Spirit (*ruaḥ*). This has led to speculation among some Christians about the plurality of personality in God, even the possibility of constructing a Trinity with a female member. However, it explicitly says in both Proverbs 8:22 and Sirach 24:9 that God created wisdom. It was this notion of a created wisdom that led Arius to insist that Christ as *logos* must also be created. Logically Arius was right, but his premise wrongly identified the original Word with created wisdom. It is interesting to see how in human mythmaking a Christological crisis was transferred to a Mariological exegesis as Mary became more and more exalted as the throne of God, holding Christ on her lap. As the mother of God, it was an easy step to say that Mary was immaculately conceived and bodily assumed. Next she becomes the co-redemptrix who is near to being worshipped as divine.

The historical, social damage that resulted from this misunderstanding of the story of Mary is manifest in the strongly entrenched institutions of celibacy for the clergy and the denial of ordination of women. Celibacy is affirmed as preventing one from loving God less because of the rivalry of a human love. But the love we give to God can never be rivaled by any kind of human love. Our love to God is what we give back to God in response to his love for us. God's love for us is *agape*, human love is either *eros* or *philia*; God's love is a sacrificial service, human love is romantic, biological, or friendly. Sexual love is always only between humans and never is directed to God; hence it can never rival love to God or inhibit God's love to us.

Limitation of ordination to males is likewise a perversion of our understanding of godly love. Since God loves us all equally there can be no hierarchical distinction between the sexes. The fact that the incarnation was in male form rather than female has only parabolic significance, just like the choice of Father for the name of God. This does not indicate a place of superiority in the economy of salvation for males. Indeed the history of a celibate, male clergy indicates that an economic reason for the practice may have been as influential in its establishment as the pressure of piety. In the Middle Ages, before the American invention of the corporate personality as a legal and economic institution, property was held in the name of the bishop. Since the bishop was the only one holding property in his person, not an impersonal corporation, it was essential that he be prevented from the temptation to hand over Church property to a wife or children. This originally may have been the real reason for the requirement of celibacy. The consequent elevation of celibacy to a holy estate higher than marriage has done untold damage to both clergy and laity. The expression of human love through sex is a blessing in the created order which has the highest sacramental significance. Far from being dirty or either a cause or the result of the fall, sexual love was written into the original creation as a natural gift for our mutual blessing.

Throughout this chapter we have been talking about various kinds of love which are distinguished in the Greek language by three different words: *eros*, *philia*, and *agape*. We translate all of them into the one English word love. Confusion arises when we do not recognize that our English word love has many meanings. We use it to speak of loving coffee, loving our dog, loving our country, loving our spouse, loving our friend, loving our brother, loving God. A story view of reality can embrace this multiplicity of meanings, but we must also recognize the differences. On the one side we have the merely human meanings which refer to our relationships with other creatures, whether human, animal, or inanimate. On the other side we have the unique relationship we have with God. The merely human relationships derive from our natural, creaturely capacity. The love we have for God comes to us from his love for us. Confusion has come from the failure to recognize the difference between *agape* and both *eros* and *philia*.

Throughout the history of the Church this confusion has been compounded by the attempt by theologians to interpret the Gospel in terms of the current philosophy and culture of the day. Origen tried to convey the Gospel through the idealism of Plato, Aquinas used Aristotle, Kant wrestled with rationalism, and today the University of Chicago school of process theology has found Whitehead to be the bride of Christ. All have failed because every human philosophical system reduces reality to a root metaphor that is inadequate to embrace what we all experience, both in all our creaturely relationships but also in our relationship with God through his revelation. The root metaphors of philosophy do not take into account such fundamentals as humor, chance, irony, paradox, contradiction, mystery. All of these are substantial ingredients of story. Story can embrace them because it does not try to reduce everything to a single universal category. Story rather rejoices in the multiplicity of reality, not only its many kinds of love but its infinite variety of surprises that come to us because of the passage of time with its possibility of freedom, and especially because of the grace of divine revelation.

9

God Calling Yet

Psalm 23

O Lord, my Lord, you are my shepherd.
You give me all I need.
You provide for me a resting place
in green pastures.
You lead me beside quiet springs.
You restore my spirit.
You guide me in paths of righteousness
for the sake of your name.
Even though I walk through the valley
of the shadow of death,
I will fear no evil,
for you are with me;
your rod and your staff, they comfort me.

You prepare for me a banquet
in the presence of my enemies.
You anoint my head with oil;
my cup overflows.
Surely goodness and mercy
will follow me
all the days of my life;
and I will dwell in your house, O Lord,
forever.

Isaiah 6:1-10

In the year that King Uzziah died
I saw the Lord seated on a throne,
high and exalted,
and the train of his robe filled the temple.
Above him were the seraphs,
each with six wings.
With two wings they covered their faces,

with two they covered their feet,
and with two they did fly.
And they called out to one another:
"Holy, holy, holy is the Lord God Almighty;
the whole earth is full of his glory."

At the sound of their voices
the doorposts and thresholds shook
and the temple was filled with smoke.
"Woe is me!" I cried.
"I am ruined!
I am a man of unclean lips,
I live among a people of unclean lips,
for my eyes have seen the king,
the Lord God Almighty."

Then one of the seraphs flew to me
with a live coal in his hand,
which he had taken with tongs
from the altar.
He laid it on my mouth and said,
"See, this has touched your lips;
your guilt is taken away
and your sin is atoned."

Then I heard the voice of the Lord saying:
"Whom shall I send?
Who will go for us?"
And I said, "Here am I. Send me!"
He said, "Go and tell this people:
'Be ever hearing but never understanding;
be ever seeing but never perceiving.'
make the heart of this people calloused;
make their ears dull,
and shut their eyes.
Otherwise they might see with their eyes,
hear with their ears,
understand with their hearts,
and turn and be healed."

Amos 5:4-15

This is what the Lord says to the house of Israel:

Seek me and live;
do not seek Bethel,
do not go to Gilgal,
Do not journey to Beersheba;
for Gilgal will surely go into exile,
and Bethel will be reduced to nothing.

Seek the Lord and live,
or he will sweep through the house of Joseph like a fire;
and the fire will devour;
Bethel will have no one to quench it.

He who made the Pleiades and Orion,
who turns blackness into dawn,
and darkens day into night,
who calls for the waters of the sea
and pours them out over the face of the land—
the Lord is his name—
he flashes destruction on the stronghold
and brings the fortified city to ruin.

You who turn justice into bitterness
and cast righteousness to the ground,
you hate the one who reproves in court
and despise him who tells the truth.
You trample on the poor
and force him to give you grain.
Therefore though you have built stone mansions,
you will not live in them;
though you have planted lush vineyards,
you will not drink their wine.
For I know how many are your offenses
and how great are your sins.

You oppress the righteous and take bribes
and you deprive the poor of justice in the courts.
Therefore the prudent man keeps quiet in such times,
for the times are evil.

Seek good, not evil,
that you may live.
Then the Lord God Almighty will be with you,
just as you say he is.
Hate evil, love good;
maintain justice in the courts.
Perhaps the Lord God Almighty will have mercy
on the remnant of Joseph.

Matthew 16:13-19

When Jesus came to the region of Caesarea Philippi,
he asked his disciples,
"Who do people say the Son of Man is?"
They replied, "Some say John the Baptist;
others say Elijah;
and still others Jeremiah or one of the prophets."
"But what about you," he asked.
"Who do you say I am?"
Simon Peter answered, "You are the Christ,
the Son of the living God."
Jesus replied, "Blessed are you, Simon, son of Jonah,
for this was not revealed to you by man,
but by my Father in heaven.
And I tell you that you are Peter,
and on this rock I will build my Church,
and the gates of hell will not overcome it.
I will give you the keys of the kingdom of heaven;
whatever you bind on earth
will be bound in heaven;
and whatever you loose on earth
will be loosed in heaven.

Mark 1:14-20

*After John was put in prison,
Jesus went into Galilee
proclaiming the good news of God.
"The time has come," he said,
"and the kingdom of God is at hand.
Repent and believe the good news!"*

*As Jesus walked by the Sea of Galilee,
he saw Simon and his brother Andrew
casting a net into the lake.
They were fishermen.
"Come, follow me," Jesus said,
and I will make you fishers of people."
At once they left their nets
and followed him.*

*When Jesus had gone a little further
he saw James the son of Zebedee
and his brother John
who were in a boat
preparing their nets.
Without delay he called them,
and they left their father Zebedee
in the boat with the hired men
and followed him.*

John 17:1-26

*After Jesus said this,
he looked toward heaven and prayed:
"Father, the time has come.
Glorify your Son,
that your Son may glorify you.
For you granted him authority over all people
that he might give eternal life
to all those you have given him.*

Now this is eternal life:
That they may know you, the only true God,
and Jesus Christ, whom you have sent.
I have brought you glory on earth
by completing the work you gave me to do.
And now, Father, glorify me in your presence
with the glory I had with you before the world began.

"I have revealed you
to those whom you gave me out of the world.
They were yours;
you gave them to me
and they have obeyed your word.
Now they know that everything you have given me
comes from you.
For I gave them the words you gave me
and they accepted them.
They knew with certainty that I came from you,
and they believed that you sent me.
I pray for them.
I am not praying for the world,
but for those you have given me,
for they are yours.
All I have is yours,
and all you have is mine.
And glory has come to me through them.
I will remain in the world no longer,
but they are still in the world,
and I am coming to you.
Holy Father, protect them
by the power of your name—
the name you gave me—
so that they may be one as we are one.
While I was with them,
I protected them and kept them safe
by that name you gave me.
None has been lost
except the one doomed to destruction
so that Scripture would be fulfilled.

"I am coming to you now,
but I say these things
while I am still in the world,
so that they may have the full measure
of my joy within them.
I have given them your word
and the world has hated them,
for they are not of the world
any more then I am of the world.
My prayer is not that you take them out of the world
but that you protect them from the evil one.
They are not of the world,
even as I am not of it.
Sanctify them by the truth;
your word is truth.
As you sent me into the world,
I have sent them into the world.
For them I sanctify myself,
that they may be truly sanctified.

"My prayer is not for them alone,
I pray also for those who will believe
in me through their message,
that all of them may be one, Father,
just as you are in me and I am in you.
May they also be in us
so that the world may believe
that you have sent me.
I have given them the glory that you gave me,
that they may be one as we are one:
I in them and you in me.
May they be brought to complete unity
to let the world know that you sent me
and have loved them even as you have loved me.

"Father, I want those you have given me
to be with me where I am,
and to see my glory,
the glory you have given me
because you loved me before the creation of the world.

Righteous Father, though the world does not know you,
I know you, and they know that you have sent me.
I have made you known to them,
and will continue to make you known
in order that the love you have for me
may be in them and that I myself may be in them."

Romans 12:1-8

I urge you therefore, brothers and sisters,
in view of God's mercy,
offer your bodies as living sacrifices,
holy and pleasing to God.
This is your spiritual act of worship.
Be not conformed to the pattern of this world,
but be transformed
by the renewing of your mind.
Then you will be able to discern
what is the good and pleasing
and perfect will of God.
For by the grace given me,
I say to every one of you:
do not think of yourself
more highly than you ought,
but rather think of yourself
with sober judgment
in accordance with the measure of faith
God has given you.
Just as each of us has one body
with many members,
and these members
do not all have the same function,
so in Christ we who are many
form one body,
and each member belongs to all the others.

*We have different gifts
according to the grace given us.
If it is prophecy
let us prophesy
in proportion to our faith.
If it is serving,
let us serve.
If it is teaching,
let us teach.
If it is encouraging,
let us encourage.
If it is contributing to the needs of others,
let us give generously.
If it is leadership,
let us govern diligently.
If it is showing mercy,
let us do it cheerfully.*

Vocation

The Bible is a grand saga with both cosmic sweep and interlacing stories about particular individuals and families and nations. All the stories of Holy Scripture may be seen from the perspective of God's call to various individuals and peoples for specific tasks in his design for the destiny of his creatures. In both of the creation stories in the book of Genesis God called our first parents, Adam and Eve, to have royal dominion over the fish of the sea, the birds of the air, and all the animals that crawl on the earth, and to till the soil and care for the garden of Eden. When, because of their sin, Adam and Eve were expelled from the garden, this divine calling was repeated, although the man now would have to work by the sweat of his brow and the woman would bear her children in pain. All people, therefore, have a calling from God to fulfill their vocations so that we can all live together, people and animals, birds and plants, water and air, mountains and plains, with mutual prosperity.

From the beginning, however, we have failed in that responsibility. So wicked did people become in the days of Noah that God called him and his family to build an ark to save a remnant of living things while the rest were destroyed by a terrible flood. We have seen how baptism is a great flood in which we share the death of Christ. But the biblical story tells us that God was not happy with what he did with the flood. He said he would never do that again, and he made a covenant with a rainbow to tell him, whenever a rainstorm occurred, that he should not destroy his creatures with rain.

Again we have seen in our discussion of baptism that the story of Jonah shows this reversal in God's design. Jonah was called by God to preach to the Ninevites, but he ran away from the call on a ship bound for Tashish. The ship was about to break in pieces because of a storm. According to pagan belief disasters of that kind were caused by the presence of evil people, hence they cast lots to find out who was guilty. The lot fell on Jonah, so they threw him overboard, one evil person to save many innocent. But God saved Jonah by having him swallowed by a great fish that spewed him forth on dry land. Jonah repented and went to Nineveh where both people and king turned from their evil ways. Thus one person called to bring good news saved many wicked people.

Abraham was called out of Ur of the Chaldees to be the father of a great nation. God made a covenant, sealed by circumcision, in which he called Abraham's descendants to be a light to the Gentiles. It is curious that invariably the people God called responded with reluctance and even resistance. Abraham and Sarah laughed in God's face when they heard of Isaac's birth in their old age. Moses protested that he was slow of speech and he feared the people would not believe him. Isaiah said he was a man of unclean lips dwelling among a people of unclean lips. Jeremiah said he was too young, only a child. They all had doubts about themselves and their congregations, but God knew them before they were formed in the womb, and they became leaders because God appointed them.

In the Old Testament there were three kinds of service: as prophets, priests, and kings. The prophets were specially called at a particular time for a specific purpose. They were gifted to meet a crisis. Their calls were always a surprise to themselves and to the people. Often they were rejected, but in the end their message prevailed. Never was popularity or attractive entertainment their motivation. Often they had to compete with false prophets who seemed to have greater success, but their truth could be discerned when people were set free and when peace was established with justice and unity.

While prophets were intermittent the priests were ongoing. They came from a single tribe of the Hebrews, the Levites, and they were respected for the authority of their office which brought continuity, stability, comfort, and redeeming renewal to the people of Israel. They circumcised the male children and offered sacrifices in the temple on the Day of Atonement. The prophets stirred the people from their wayward ways; the priests gave them solace in their grief and assurance that God would forgive them.

And after persistent requests from the people, God called Saul to be king over Israel. He and the kings that followed were admonished to rule with equity and compassion. When they failed, the crisis produced their downfall; but the office of king was needed to keep order and protect Israel from his enemies. Just as prophets spoke not for themselves but for God, and just as priests brought sacramental service from God, so likewise kings ruled not in their own right but as the called servants of God with responsibility for the people. Israel did not have a constitution of rights because all creation and especially their life together were seen to be the gift of God. Instead of laws protecting individual and community rights they had commandments which told them their obligations to their neighbors. Once obligations were fulfilled rights were no longer needed.

Jesus brought radical changes. He called his disciples away from their various vocations to learn for a time how to become apostles. A disciple is a learner; an apostle is one sent out to proclaim the gospel through preaching and the sacraments. Jesus ordained a special ministry which required unique education because the truth to be imparted is not just information or skills but the relationship that is nurtured among persons. Jesus said, "I am the way and the truth and the life."

Disciples become apostles when they are sent forth with authority to be ambassadors for Christ. They speak for him as he spoke for his Father in heaven. "As my Father sent me, so I send you." Their call is a summons from one who has authority to forgive sins. "Receive the Holy Spirit. If you forgive anyone's sins, they are forgiven; if you do not forgive them, they are not forgiven" (John 20:23). Pastors have authority which is delegated, and so they declare forgiveness; but they do not have power to forgive. God alone has power. God is unique in his power to create and redeem; we can do neither, and therefore God needs special servants to do for him on earth as his ambassadors what he alone can do. It is true that we must forgive one another when we have caused hurt to our neighbor. Luther calls this the consolation of brothers and sisters; but when our relationship with God is broken we need God's forgiveness. Pastors are called and ordained to bring this assurance.

Jesus brought an end to circumcision, Hebrew sacrifices in the temple, and the Levitical priesthood. Since he is our high priest who has made the supreme sacrifice on the cross there is no need for any other priest, and the sign of circumcision is replaced by baptism for females and males alike. Notice we are using the word priest, not pastor. A priest in this context is one who intercedes with God for the people. Priests offer sacrifices of atonement and thanksgiving to please God. Christ alone can offer the sacrifice of atonement and no other priest is needed; each of us can offer one's own thanksgiving in the Eucharist and again no priest is needed. Or to say it in another way as Luther did, in giving thanks to God there is a universal priesthood of all believers. Peter said this in his first letter: "You are the chosen race, the royal priesthood, the consecrated nation . . ." Here we have the glorious calling to the people of the Christian congregation to be living, active witnesses to the love of God in Christ. But pastors are shepherds who lead the flock and nurture them with responsibility to care for the multitude of their needs. Even though we commonly use the word priest for the leader of a congregation we do not give it the pagan or the Levitical meaning of a hieratical intercessor.

Pastoral care of a congregation and service in the ecumenical Church requires preaching the gospel, baptism, education, and confirmation of the young, continuing education of adults, the blessing of marriages, the comfort and healing of the sick and sorrowing, counseling the confused and despairing and unreconciled, support of the laity in their secular vocations, and burial of the dead with concomitant consolation of the bereaved. The whole gamut of life is served from birth to death through baptism, confession, teaching, preaching, eucharist, counseling, marriage, vocation, funerals. And moreover while performing all these services the pastor must supervise the business and polity of the congregation and promote all its programs of evangelism, stewardship, and social service. In the New Testament period of Church development another dimension of leadership arose which added the name of elder to the functional titles of shepherd, teacher, evangelist, deacon, bishop. The Greek word for elder is "*presbyteros*," from which by distortion we get our English word "priest." A presbyter is one who adjudicates and administers the affairs of a congregation. Obviously not everyone can be an elder; some must be younger. And finally and occasionally when the times call for it God raises up prophets to proclaim with warning and hope what the future demands.

During the Middle Ages the liberating light of the gospel was darkened by the fear that we must work for our salvation. Instead of trusting God's grace people tried to win God's favor by working at a legalized lifestyle. Ordinary Christians could be forgiven through the sacraments of the Church, but it was only a matter of indulgence, and their status before God was considered inferior to those who entered the priesthood and holy orders. Even among the specialized ministries of the Church there were levels of perfection. Women could not be ordained, priests could not marry. Priests who cared for congregations were called secular clergy, not so holy as those who entered monasteries and sequestered themselves from the cares of this world. Monks and nuns undertook vows of obedience, chastity, and poverty. These counsels of perfection gave them the highest status in the hierarchy of holiness. The most flagrant abuse resulting from this distortion of the gospel came with the sale of indulgences. Common people who did not devote their lives to the service of the Church could buy their way into heaven by the purchase of indulgences. The authority of the called ministry was abused when the clergy seized the power of God and commercialized the Church.

The Reformation corrected these abuses. Since Christ died for all alike there can be no hierarchy of holiness. Jew and Greek, bond and free, men and women, are all one in Christ. Our various vocations are equally acceptable to God, whether we are farmers or laborers, executives or professionals, pupils or teachers, artists or entertainers. Luther emphasized the sanctity of the secular calling. Whatever our station in life, since it is given by God, we contribute to the welfare of the community. Actually we all have at the same time several kinds of calling in our secular relationships. One may be a plumber, but also a father. Indeed we all have responsibilities in our family relationships. A woman's calling to be a mother has value before God and should be recognized in the world. A child is called to grow to maturity under the nurture and discipline of parents and teachers. The equality of value before God should tell us much about the need for equality in the distribution of wealth and the payment of wages and salaries. These liberating and equalizing forces are seeds of the gospel and they have been growing in history slowly but surely to establish peace and justice. Because of sin and Satan's deviltry, however, society constantly slips back into patterns of greed and exploitation; and therefore God must raise up prophetic leaders to correct these abuses. Pastors are specifically ordained to this task, and if they fail or if the congregations reject them, God will find ways to move history outside the Church, as he has done with civil rights. One thing is sure: his will on earth will be done sooner or later.

The story of Jesus Christ, revealed in the promise and preparation of the Old Testament and in the fulfillment of the New Testament, registers two types of calling, a general vocation for the various orders of secular society, and a special ordination for those chosen by God to carry out his mission to redeem sinners. The borders of distinction have always been blurred because of the failure of God's chosen servants of redemption to fulfill his will and because of the failure of people in the secular orders to fulfill their responsibility to establish peace and justice and unity. Hence both clergy and laity have responsibility for each other's agendas. But this does not mean that they do not have separate functions.

The functions of the Church are mission and stewardship. Mission is the propagation of the gospel so that all in the world may know the good news of God's grace. The spreading of this word will bring peace and unity to all who hear, and the Church will be built through this heralding of the faith as a sacramental, organic institution and a benevolent servant in society. The stewardship of the Church calls for financial support for its preaching, teaching, healing, and welfare ministries. It will also entail the prophetic claim of God for the care of the earth, for justice in society, and for peace and unity among the people.

The great scandal of the Church, in view of Jesus' pastoral prayer reported in John 17, is its continuing disunity. The division between Eastern

Orthodoxy and Roman Catholicism probably came because of cultural and political differences as much as the dogmatic schism over the procession in the Trinity. And ironically the Reformation did more to divide the Church than to reform it. Whatever the reasons for division, none can justify our sectarian separation. The quarrel over apostolic succession from Peter is a case of throwing the baby out with the bath water. Roman Catholics insist on an unbroken linear authority vested in the episcopacy; Protestants reject such apostolic succession because of the corruption of authority in the episcopacy. Catholics want authority to be delegated from Christ through his vicar in Rome; Protestants want authority to rise from the consent of the laity. Both should realize that when we are all one in Christ as Christ is one with the Father, then authority is one in both the episcopacy and in the laity. These two branches of the Church are not separate or independent but joined to the common stem of Christ. It is foolish to quarrel over whether the episcopacy is essential to the Church or whether authority should be centered in an office or in a person. Of course, episcopacy is essential, and there are no offices without persons. The office of the bishop functions only because a person occupies it who has the faithful consent of Christians who share the unifying life of the Church, the body of Christ.

The Church is an organic institution, and so its pastors will exhibit an authoritative, but not authoritarian, style of leadership. While the Church has polity, because it is a structure within the culture of this world, the Church should not be modeled after government, not after a monarchy, nor a dictatorship, nor a democracy. Since God never robs us of the freedom he gave us in his image the structure of the Church must never lack this freedom. It is true that we have popular votes in Church affairs but Christ is not our God by popular acclaim nor are truth and morality determined by majority opinion.

The Church is not the state. It has no power. It does not enforce the collection of taxes. It is supported by freewill offerings. Governments rule with a combination of patriotism at best and fear at worst. Patriotism is good so long as it does not prevent the welcome of strangers, but in the extreme it can substitute the state for God and become idolatrous, as has happened so often in history. The Church has no weapons; it lives only by the persuasive power of the Word.

Besides the structure of the Church as a physical organism it is also a mystical body. It has a charisma because of its mystery as the bride of Christ. This charisma can be twisted in secular fashion, however, and reduced to an attraction modeled after the excitement of entertainment. The Church is not the greatest show on earth, neither a circus nor a television extravaganza. In the Middle Ages people bought indulgences from ecclesiastical hucksters because they feared hell and wanted heaven. Today people crave instant salvation with tangible material comforts, healing and wealth, but the Church does not sell nor entertain.

Nor should the Church be modeled after business. The Church does not produce a product nor sell a commodity or a service. Sacraments, counseling, all programs of the Church are free. But since the Church is in this world it must conform to the structures of this world, and therefore it must conduct its affairs in accord with good business practices. It will not, however, learn from the advertising techniques of Madison Avenue which create wants and exploit desires.

The models which best describe the nature of the Church and its ministry are the metaphors used in Scripture: shepherd and sheep, body with head and members, family with Father and children. In every case the leader in these metaphors is Christ or God. Christ is the good shepherd, Christ is the head of his body the Church, and God is the Father of his family on earth. The concern to avoid the tyranny of a corrupt or freedom-robbing leadership in the Church is genuine and must be satisfied by a responsible sharing of power.

The other calling, the vocation of the laity, involves two kinds of service: the priesthood of all believers, and the sanctity of the secular calling. According to the priesthood of all believers every Christian is called to bear witness to his or her faith in every way that is edifying to the Church, by word of mouth and by lives of thanksgiving to God and service to one's neighbor. According to the sanctity of the secular calling every Christian is called to use one's talents to edify the secular community, by contributing to the welfare and prosperity of all who are within reach.

This will involve, as the saying goes, being in the world but not of the world. It means that Christians are called to serve in the world in every way that will bring health and wealth and prosperity to the secular community. Farming, manufacturing, commerce, construction, design, art, entertainment, health care, legal service, teaching, governing, homemaking, parenting, protecting—all the walks of life which are necessary for a stable, peaceful, just, and prosperous society are holy in God's sight insofar as they enhance the welfare of God's children.

Throughout history tensions have arisen among various forms of government and various forms of business as well as between government and business. Is the best form of government a monarchy, a dictatorship, a democracy, and if democracy should it be constitutional or parliamentary? Is there a divine right of kings? Is there a historical imperative that calls for the necessity of temporary dictatorship in order to establish the utopian society? Should the citizenry have a voice and vote to determine their own governance? Perhaps because societal conditions vary in time and place different systems of government are proper for different conditions. We are observing the collapse of communism in Russia and its radical modification in China, with the destabilizing effect of the introduction of capitalism in Russia and the burgeoning success of its introduction in China. Is there any light from revelation that will help us to answer these questions?

I do not think there is a simple word of the Lord to tell us how to govern society or how to conduct its business. What we can do is apply ethical criteria to both the public sector and the private. A farmer has to decide whether to accept money from the government in a soil bank program that makes him curtail production in order to boost prices while people in other countries are starving. The American Catholic Bishops have issued a report in which they say Christians and the Church cannot tolerate an economic system in which poverty is rampant, and therefore some kind of correction must be made by government intervention. Liberation theology says that a revolution is needed to liberate people who are locked into a political and economic system that denies human dignity. The development of third world countries to help them catch up with richer capitalist nations will not solve the problem because that would imitate the model that is the cause of the problem.

It is important to recognize that the language used in discussing economics and government is often equivocating and confusing. Words are weasels. People sometimes use the same words with different meanings. Both economists and theologians talk about the old-time religion; both economists and psychiatrists talk about depression. Thus people often identify Christianity with capitalism and the American way of life. But Christianity says people do not live by bread alone; what shall it profit a man if he gains the whole world and loses his soul? The principles or economics which economists call the old-time religion are 1) the profit motive, 2) the protection of private property, 3) a free market with no control of prices or wages, and 4) a particularistic development of science for business exploitation in which specialization is pursued without regard for the whole. The same word, religion, is used to label capitalistic society and the kingdom of God, yet they are radically different. Private greed is supported in this capitalistic religion because it is successful. Then must we say that the most successful people in our society are so because they are the most greedy? Some economists have thought that self-seeking is only temporary because universal prosperity is possible in the long run. Thus the great Lord Maynard Keynes said in 1930:

> For at least another hundred years we must pretend to ourselves and to everyone that fair is foul and foul is fair; for foul is useful and fair is not. Avarice and usury and precaution must be our gods for a little longer still, for only they can lead us out of the tunnel of economic necessity into daylight.

But I submit that we can no longer afford our idolatry to the god of greed. We need to make a quantum leap which will interject the Christian vision into all we do. Economics without Christianity will soon prove to be uneconomical, politics without Christianity will not produce justice and peace, education without Christianity will not give us wisdom, science without Christianity will rob us of our humanity. What we need as a society of human beings is health, beauty, and permanence. What we have today is a society hellbent for its own destruction because it lacks vision, because it is looking in the wrong place for its fulfillment. We look only where it is bright and easy for the short term gain. We have not the courage to look in the dark, but it is precisely the dark sides of both capitalism and democracy that make them the best systems of governing and service to our society. Neither can be identified with the kingdom of God, but both have the possibility of self-correction. It is the failure to exercise self-correction that turns both systems into an idol. Both systems, like scientific method, are experimental. In a democracy bad laws, bad legislators, bad executives, bad judges all can be removed. In business unprofitable policies can be corrected when the pressures of the market demand it. These changes always entail the risk of trying something in the dark that was not seen before. In this respect faith is the guiding force in secular vocations as it is in our relationship to God. Repentance and forgiveness and the faith that risks one's life for here and hereafter operate in the world of science and business and government just as they do in the community of the Church. This is why the secular calling may be called holy.

Christian ethical principles for our vocation in life require freedom and equality (John 8:36; Galatians 3:28). Always, however, both freedom and equality must be exercised within the parameters of justice and mercy. Both justice and mercy can be abused; justice can become tyrannical egalitarianism and mercy can become sentimental indulgence. But freedom requires the constraint of responsibility and equality requires the flexibility of need. The kingdom of God is not a democracy, nor is its economy capitalist, although on this side of history a good case can be made for the development of democracy and capitalism out of the Christian revelation of freedom and equality. Tribalism, feudalism, fascism, and communism allow for neither freedom nor equality.

The Christian revelation proclaims the judgment of sin and the promise of forgiveness (Psalm 14; Psalm 130; Romans 7:19; Colossians 3:13). Because of God's mercy we can receive the gift of repentance and the consequence of forgiveness which then prompts us to bear fruits of service to others. This progression of repentance and forgiveness is the foundation for democratic and economic progress. It is also productive of scientific method and personal relationships because science builds on experiments that give us a second chance when we recognize failure, and persons can build community when they acknowledge one another's deficiencies. First we must admit our mistakes and then turn to a new start. Thus we experiment in politics, business and science just as we do in personal relations. And we judge our behavior by the consequences (Matthew 7:16).

In government, business, and family finances "the love of money is the root of all evils" (1 Timothy 6:10). Therefore the freedom to acquire money, and all it can buy, must be restrained with the proper balance of equality and need. When Jesus was asked, "Teacher, tell my brother to divide the inheritance with me," he said, "Watch out! Be on your guard against all kinds of greed; a man's life does not consist in the abundance of his possessions" (Luke 12:13).

The guiding principle for the distribution of wealth—and this must shape our taxes, our prices, and our inheritance—Jesus taught us in Luke 12:48: "From everyone who has been given much, much will be asked." Thus the early Christians naively practiced communal sharing: ". . . those who owned lands or houses sold them, brought the money from the sales and put it at the apostles' feet, and it was distributed to anyone as he had need" (Acts 4:32-35). This kind of communal sharing has never worked as evidenced by experimental sects down through time, but the principles of freedom, equality, responsibility and need should nevertheless guide us in all our ethical decisions. Karl Marx picked up this principle of communal sharing with his manifesto: "From each according to one's ability; to each according to one's need." But obviously the communists did not practice this. They did not take into consideration the universal propensity for sinners to fall into corruption. Christian vocation recognizes that in time we must progress through stages of development involving repentance of sinful behavior so that we can turn with forgiveness to a sanctified life of service and love.

10

Ad Futurum et Mysterium

Daniel 7:1-14

In the first year of Belshazzar king of Babylon,
Daniel had a dream,
and visions passed through his mind
as he was lying on his bed.
He wrote down the substance of his dream:
In my vision at night I looked,
and there before me were the four winds of heaven
churning up the great sea.
Four great beasts, each different from the others
came up out of the sea.

The first was like a lion,
and it had the wings of an eagle.
I watched until its wings were torn off
and it was lifted from the ground
so that it stood on two feet like a human,
and the heart of a human was given to it.

And there before me was a second beast,
which looked like a bear.
It was raised up on one of its sides,
and it had three ribs in its mouth between its teeth.
It was told, "Get up and eat your fill of flesh!"

After that I looked, and there before me was another beast,
one that looked like a leopard.
And on its back it had four wings like those of a bird.
This beast had four heads and it was given authority to rule.

After that, in my vision at night I looked,
and there before me was a fourth beast—
terrifying and frightening and very powerful.
It had large iron teeth; it crushed and devoured its victims
and trampled under foot whatever was left.
It was different from all the former beasts,
and it had ten horns.

While I was thinking about the horns,
there before me was another horn, a little one,
which came up among them;
and three of the first horns were uprooted before it.
This horn had eyes like the eyes of a human
and a mouth that spoke boastfully.

As I looked,
   thrones were set in place,
       and the Ancient of Days took his seat.
His clothing was as white as snow;
       the hair of his head was white like wool.
his throne was flaming with fire,
       and its wheels were all ablaze.
A river of fire was flowing,
       coming out from before him.
Thousands upon thousands attended him;
       ten thousand times ten thousand stood before him.
The court was seated,
       and the books were opened.

Then I continued to watch because of the boastful words
the horn was speaking.
I kept looking until the beast was slain
and its body destroyed and thrown into the blazing fire.
(The other beasts had been stripped of their authority,
but were allowed to live for a period of time.)

In my vision at night I looked,
and there before me was one like a son of man,
coming with the clouds of heaven.
He approached the Ancient of Days
and was led into his presence.
He was given authority, glory, and sovereign power;
People of every nation and language worshipped him.
His dominion is an everlasting dominion
that will not pass away,
and his kingdom is one that will never be destroyed.

John 6:28-40

At Capernaum Jesus was asked:
"What must I do
to do what God requires?"
Jesus answered, "The work of God is this:
to believe in the one he has sent."
So they asked him,
"What miraculous sign will you give
that we may see and believe you?
What work will you show us?
Our forebears ate manna in the desert;
as it is written:
'He gave them bread from heaven to eat.'"

Jesus said to them,
"Truly, truly, I say to you,
it was not Moses who gave you bread from heaven,
but my Father gives you the true bread from heaven.
For the bread of God
is he who comes down from heaven
and gives life to the world."

Then they said to him,
"Lord, give us evermore this bread."

Then Jesus declared:
"I am the bread of life.
He who comes to me will never hunger,
and he who believes in me will never thirst.
But as I told you,
you have seen me, and still you do not believe.
All that the Father gives me
will come to me,
and whoever comes to me
I will never drive away.
For I came down from heaven
not to do my will
but to do the will of him who sent me.

And this is the will of him who sent me,
that I shall not lose one of all he has given me,
but I shall raise them up at the last day.
For my Father's will
is that everyone who looks to the Son
and believes in him
shall have eternal life,
and I will raise him up at the last day."

Revelation 7:9-17

After this I looked
and there before me was a great multitude
that no one could count,
from all nations and kindreds,
and people and tongues,
standing before the throne
and in front of the Lamb.
They were clothed in white robes,
and they held palm branches in their hands.
And they cried out in a loud voice:
"Salvation belongs to our God,
who sits on the throne,
and to the Lamb."

And all the angels
stood round about the throne,
and about the elders and the four beasts,
and fell before the throne on their faces,
and worshipped God,
saying,
"Blessing and glory and wisdom
and thanksgiving and honor
and power and might
be to our God forever and ever.
Amen!"

Ad Futurum et Mysterium

Then one of the elders asked me,
"Who are these arrayed in white robes,
and where did they come from?"
I answered, "Sir, you know."
And he said, "These are they
who have come out of great tribulation.
They have washed their robes
and made them white
in the blood of the Lamb.
Therefore
they are before the throne of God.
They serve him day and night
in his temple;
and he who sits on the throne
will dwell among them.
Never again will they hunger;
never again will they thirst.
The sun will not scorch them,
nor any searing heat.
For the Lamb at the center of the throne
will be their shepherd;
he will lead them to springs
of living water.
And God will wipe away all tears
from their eyes."

The Real Presence in Holy Communion

THE LITURGY for Holy Communion has been fashioned by the drama of salvation. It is staged, choreographed, and enacted to present the story of Christ's life, death, and resurrection. It also embraces the human participants as grateful recipients of the grace of salvation. The drama begins with the declaration of this grace. The rhythm is contrapuntal: divine gift and human response. Thus the announcement of the grace of Christ, the love of God, and the communion of the Holy Spirit is followed by the penitent prayer of the *kyrie*. We then sing the song of praise in which the Christmas angel announces God's peace to his people on earth. Our response extols God the Father, our heavenly king, God the Son who takes away the sin of the world, and God the Holy Spirit in the glory of the most high. Our prayer is followed by God's word to us in Scripture which is expounded in the sermon. We respond with the confession of our faith in the Nicene or the Apostles' Creed and in prayers of petition and thanksgiving. God's peace is then announced and shared, with the response of the offering which is brought to the altar. The Great Thanksgiving is a story within the greater story of the liturgy. It brings the climax of the presence of Christ in the bread and wine, for which we signal our anticipation as did the disciples in the *sanctus* and the *benedictus*, and our thanksgiving with the Lord's prayer. The singing of the *agnus dei* and other hymns during the distribution of the elements is followed by a final prayer of thanksgiving, and the liturgy concludes after the benediction with a triumphant charge to go in peace and serve the Lord.

This final charge declares that liturgy is not only where God comes to the faithful in the Church, but it is also where people of the Church meet people of the world. Worship has a double motif of incarnation and resurrection producing a double climax, once at the distribution of the elements and again at the dismissal of the people. The action of Christ's passion, which we receive by meeting him in bread and wine, is then carried into the world where we offer ourselves as living sacrifices, holy and pleasing to God—our spiritual worship.

Christian liturgy is the action of the people in petition for and in grateful response to the gracious action of God in Jesus Christ. Liturgy is sacramental. Sacraments are outward signs of inward grace. They communicate mysteriously through visible elements the hidden reality of God's saving activity. They realize for us in the present a token of what will come in glory in the future. They are more than communicators or revealers; they are effective means or realizers of God's grace. In them God really comes to us and gives us life out of death. Sacraments are God's means by which he puts us in his service, not our means by which we appropriate divine favor. It is grace that uses sinners in the service of God, not we who use grace in our own service.

The sacrament of holy communion is so rich in meaning it is impossible to embrace its mystery in words. Its many names tell the many dimensions of meaning. This liturgy is a *breaking of bread* or *Lord's supper* because we partake of food which gives us life. It is a *holy communion* in which the Holy Spirit calls and gathers the congregation to participate in the living body of Christ. It is the celebration of the *real presence* of Christ because the risen Lord comes to be with us in a holy relationship as he promised. It is the *sacrament of the altar* because God in Christ has sacrificed himself to bring forgiveness and new life to sinners, and as a sacrament it anticipates the *Messianic banquet* in the fulfilled kingdom of heaven. It is the *eucharist* because we give thanks for God's gracious gift. It is a *memorial* because we remember in celebration the passion and resurrection of Jesus. It is the *mass* because from it we are dismissed to serve in the world; it is truly our *service of worship* that we carry to our neighbors.

What was the origin of our rite? Most likely holy communion had its origin in the resurrection appearances of the Lord at the meals of the disciples between Easter and Jesus' ascension. This means it did not have its origin in the common meals of Jesus with his disciples during his ministry. This would have shaped our worship as human fellowship, and it would be difficult to distinguish between the providence of Christ as he is present at breakfast and the redemption of Christ as he is present at the eucharist. Nor were there two types of eucharist, as some scholars argue—an earlier Jerusalem meal of joyful thanksgiving and a later Pauline meal of sad sacrificial remembrance.

In all accounts from the beginning we detect both joy and sadness. There was realized joy in the presence of the risen Lord as well as hopeful, expectant joy in his coming at the last day. There was also solemn remembrance of the death of Jesus with its terrifying significance, and the deep sorrow for the great weight of sin. The presence of the living Word of Christ together with the guidance of the Holy Spirit brought the early Christians away from their worship in the temple and established a new worship centered in the risen Lord.

The victorious presence of Christ at mealtime instructed the disciples concerning the meaning of the last meal Jesus enjoyed with them at the approach of the Passover season. His words and actions were recalled in light of his death and resurrection. They now recognized that his death was a sacrifice for them. When he took bread and broke it he dramatically foretold the breaking of his body. When he poured wine he foretold the shedding of his blood.

The sacrifice is once for all, yet, as he broke bread once and fed 5,000, so he gave us bread to distribute to many in all generations. The broken bits of bread join with the flesh of each believer and are taken up into our life, becoming a guarantee of the restoration of our real self with the presence of the real Christ.

The flesh and blood of Jesus in his incarnation conveyed the living Word to his contemporaries. This was the function of the flesh. Now we do not have the incarnate Jesus but we have the bread and wine of communion. They function for us as did his flesh and blood for his contemporaries. We do not have the baby in the manger, but for us Christ is born in the cradle of our hands when the communion bread is placed there.

Jesus could therefore say, "This is my body . . . this is my blood . . . you have seen me in the flesh but now I am going away and you will no longer see me, but I will leave you this sacrament. You will see the bread and the wine as you see me. They will do for you what I have done, but as flesh and blood do not reveal this grace so also the Spirit must come with the bread and the wine."

In this conception of communion there is no need for speculation on the change of bread to the substance of Christ's body. The concern is to proclaim what God has done, is doing, and will do in the sacrament, not to give us a rational explanation of the mystery.

Also in this view, action really occurs and continues to occur, and therefore we cannot reduce the doctrine of the eucharist to a mere memorial. This might falsely stress what *we* do and not what God does. The memorial, if it speaks of God's act at all, does so only as a remembered act in the past. But the sacrament involves not only a past act but the present and future service of God. In a Christian view of the sacrament we cannot stress enough the reality of time—past, present, and future.

It is true for holy communion, as it is true for the sermon and the other sacraments, that God effectively works his grace unconditioned by the officiant or the receiver. In the medieval view this grace was conceived as spiritual substance which when infused into believers gives them merit to journey into the presence of the faraway God.

The biblical view tells another story about God coming in the presence of Christ the Word who becomes known to us by intercession of the Holy Spirit. Instead of grace taking the sinner to God, God brings himself in grace to the sinner. Hence a new covenant is established in which Christ gives himself to us in the seal of his death. We receive this guarantee in bread and wine which function as the visible reality of his presence for us just as his flesh and blood did for his disciples. Hence he re-presents to us the sacrifice which he gave once on Golgotha, and which he continually presents to the Father in heaven (Romans 8:34).

This is not a magical operation that automatically saves. It is a sign revealing the hidden mystery of God. It must, therefore, like the signs in the sermon and the other sacraments, be received in faith. Consequently when it is not received in faith it works condemnation. As the Word is a two-edged sword, the sacrament can cure or curse. All depends on discernment in faith by the Holy Spirit. It should be clear that this discernment comes by testing in the Spirit and not by cognitive exercise. The significant words used by Paul in this connection are "examine" and "recognize" (1 Corinthians 11:28-29). Neither can be construed in any intellectual sense without making the sacrament an exclusive esoteric rite limited to those who have the right knowledge. Nor can they be construed in a moral sense without taking away the very grace of forgiveness the sacrament offers.

The sacrament is a visible vessel for showing the Lord's death and resurrection before the world. It is not a secret ritual but an open proclamation. The sacrament is not offered promiscuously, but it is openly declared that here the crucified Lord is victoriously present. The Lord is blessed life for those who believe but terrifying death for those who reject the gift of the Spirit. Receiving Christ worthily does not mean in good behavior or right cognition but in Spirit-led faith. Such reception brings forgiveness and with it healing and victory over death. Unworthy or faithless reception brings the separation of sin and its consequent sickness unto death.

Therefore, the sacrament of holy communion should not exclude Christians from each other's altars, but should be the sign to all of us that Christ and the Holy Spirit are binding us together in the bond of peace by building us into a holy priesthood so that we can bear one another's burdens and serve each other's needs. Lutherans and Roman Catholics and Episcopalians and Presbyterians and Orthodox and Reformed and Methodists and all in the various grand traditions in the Christian family actually celebrate the gracious presence of the same living Christ. Even if we have diverse understandings of what the sacrament means there is no cause for exclusion. We can learn from each other, adding to our treasury of insights without fear of losing our heritage. If there is any error among us we can help to correct each other by our very coming together. As the author of Hebrews said, "therefore, since we are surrounded by such a great cloud of witnesses, let us throw off everything that hinders and the sin that so easily entangles, and let us run with perseverance the race marked out for us. Let us fix our eyes on Jesus, the author and perfecter of our faith who for the joy set before him endured the cross, scorning its shame, and sat down at the right hand of the throne of God" (Hebrews 12:1-2).

We have said that there is both sadness and joy in the eucharist. The sadness reflects the sacrifice God made in the incarnation with its culmination of Jesus on the cross. The enormity of our sin in the light of this sacrifice elicits sorrow beyond measure. The joy reflects the resurrection of Jesus conquering sin and death. Our sanctified lives sing to the glory of God as we serve our neighbor.

What is the meaning of God's sacrifice? Why was sacrifice the means for atonement for sin and death? Sacrifice is an offering of something to a deity for the purpose of making the devotee holy and pleasing the deity. Sacrifice of one kind or another may be found in all religions including the religion of the Old Testament. We must distinguish religious offerings from the revealed sacrifice of Jesus Christ.

Søren Kierkegaard in *Fear and Trembling* uses the sacrifices of Iphigenia, Jephthah's daughter, and Abraham's son to make these distinctions. Agamemnon and Jephthah make their sacrifices for a reason: Agamemnon vows to offer his daughter to gain a favorable wind on his way to Troy; Jephthah vows to provide a thank offering of whoever comes to meet him from his door if God will grant him victory over the Ammonites. Abraham has no reason whatsoever that may be justified ethically. He simply prepares to sacrifice Isaac in obedience to the Lord. What was done by Agamemnon was a supreme human effort to control the gods; what was done by Jephthah was a valiant human attempt to preserve the integrity of the heart. Both have the ambiguity of noble religion and sinful selfishness. Abraham alone accepted the intercessory work of God by offering whatever God provided, whether it be his only beloved son or a ram caught in a bush.

Sacrifice in religion provides both points of contact and points of contrast to the sacrifice which God gives through revelation. In religious sacrifice it is recognized that a broken relationship with God must be healed. Something must be done and that involves a cost. The Christian story of the cross tells of this cost. But the contrast in the story is that the cross does not appease an angry God. Nor is the cross a sop to Satan. And the cross is

Jesus' work, not ours, and so it does not offer to God our holiness. The cross is what God lets happen to him in the free exercise of our sin.

The revealed concept of intercession has its roots in the priestly sacrifices of the Old Testament. God was at work in the family of Israel, providing sacrifices which were acceptable for atonement before the once-for-all sacrifice of Jesus. No doubt other tribes and cultures have their Old Testament too. In the Old Testament revelation Aaron was instructed to come once a year to the holy place with a bull, a ram, and a goat, sacrificing them with the laying on of hands and sprinkling the blood of the bull and the goat on the mercy seat and offering the ram as a burnt offering (Leviticus 16:3-19). A second goat was driven into the wilderness with the laying on of hands and the confession of the sins of the people. This system of sacrifices hearkened back to the experience of Abraham in which God provided a ram as a substitute for Isaac, and it projected forward to Christ in the anticipation of the Suffering Servant of Isaiah on whom was laid the iniquity of us all (Genesis 22:8; Isaiah 53:6).

The significant thrust throughout the history of Old Testament sacrifice is therefore not human offering but the intercession of God. It is God who provides the sacrifice from the ram of Abraham to Jesus, the Lamb of God, who was also caught on the branches of a tree. Precisely here is the difference between the revealed biblical understanding of sacrifice on the one hand and both pagan and perverted Jewish notions on the other. In pagan sacrifice a gift is offered by humans in hope of gaining favor from the god. Thus humans try to work a change upon the god through the offering. In the practice of Judaism a work is done by humans in the hope of changing human hearts, cleansing us so as to render us acceptable to God. But the Christian revelation in both Testaments teaches that God intercedes, providing the sacrifice which changes the wrath of God into mercy and the sinner into a saint.

When, according to the history of salvation, the right time had come, God's Messiah interceded by means of his sacrifice, in order to reconcile helpless and rebellious sinners with the Father. Thus, as in the Old Testament the priest represented humanity and offered a sacrifice to God, so now Christ Jesus as man offers himself as a "fragrant offering and sacrifice to God" (Ephesians 5:2). "For our sake he (God) made him (Christ) to be sin who knew no sin, so that in him we might become the righteousness of God" (2 Corinthians 5:21). "Therefore he had to be made like his brethren in every respect, so that he might become a merciful and faithful high priest in the service of God, to make expiation for the sins of the people" (Hebrews 2:17).

The second motif in holy communion, in addition to the sadness we feel for the death of Jesus and our sin, is the joy we share in Jesus' resurrection and our new life in Christ. Jesus' work is not ended with his death on the cross. It is finished in the sense of being completely done and satisfying to God, but it continues through the intercessory pleading of the risen Lord in heaven. Sacrifice we found to be the basic meaning of Christ's intercession, since through it God is glorified magnificently over his enemies, and his rebellious creatures are reconciled. This is an atonement of victory. But in the Old Testament, the central moment of sacrifice was not in the slaying of the victim but in what was done with the blood when it was released. Blood was understood to mean the *life* of the victim. When blood was shed it signified the pouring out of the victim's life. On the Day of Atonement the ritual sacrifice brought the priest into the holy of holies behind the veil of the temple, where he sprinkled the mercy seat with the life blood of the sacrificial animal. This religious ritual prepared the way for the revelation of the once and for all sacrifice of Jesus, but the moment of the cross has significance for all moments because the ascended Jesus presents this sacrifice to the Father in heaven. Paul gives this emphasis to the heavenly intercession when he says, "Is it Christ who died, yes, who was raised from the dead, who is at the right hand of God, who indeed intercedes for us?" (Romans 8:34). And the author of Hebrews, who is so careful to guard the once-for-all character of the sacrificial death on Golgotha, is no less concerned to declare the continuing intercession in heaven: "Consequently he is able for all time to save those who draw near to God through him, since he always lives to make intercession for them" (Hebrews 7:25).

The concluding application in the eucharist of Christ's intercessory work concerns our share in this intercession. The suffering of Christ is proclaimed in the liturgy as God's glory. Inasmuch as this work is done on our behalf the Spirit calls and gathers us into the worshipping community which we call the Church. Thus the author of Hebrews says: "Therefore, brethren, since we have confidence to enter the sanctuary by the blood of Jesus . . . let us draw near with a true heart . . . and let us consider how to stir up one another to love and good works, not neglecting to meet together. . . ." (Hebrews 10:19-24). The shape of our response to Christ's intercessory work is the sacrifice of thanksgiving, in which we offer ourselves as living sacrifices. Thus Paul says to the Colossians: "Now I rejoice in my sufferings for your sake, and in my flesh I complete what is lacking in Christ's affliction for the sake of his body, that is the Church. . . ." (Colossians 1:24).

Luther makes the distinction between the sacrifice of atonement and the sacrifice of thanksgiving. Christ's sacrifice is once-for-all, the all-sufficient sacrifice of atonement. Our share in this intercession is our thankful participation of response, the Eucharistic worship commemorating Christ's atoning sacrifice, in which we repeatedly plead Christ's work before the Father and thus provide the context in which the Church offers itself in union with Christ's own sacrifice to God. The offering of the Church is the grateful stewardship of enacting the truth, of suffering and sacrificing and serving in the world on behalf of the neighbor. This is the true meaning of the doctrine of the priesthood of all believers. The universal priesthood has nothing to do with a polemic on Church polity, but it has everything to do with our share in Christ's intercession. It means that every person in Christ becomes a priest to his neighbor. It is not that every person is one's own priest in any sense of individualism, but that through Eucharistic oblation in the Church every person is able and must be exhorted to become a little Christ (i.e., a Christian) to one's neighbor. Neighbor love requires the implementation of justice, the equalization of wealth, the establishment of safety in society, the removal of fear and anxiety, the deliverance of health and welfare to all in need, the guarantee of peace and unity, the sharing of all things beautiful and edifying, the offering of help from the strong to the weak and from the wealthy to the poor—all the values that make up the coming kingdom of God.

It should be clear, in conclusion, that the biblical proclamation of Christ's intercessory work teaches that the glorious suffering of Christ draws us into a participating fellowship, in which peace is made with God through our glorious suffering. New life is given to God's fallen creatures so that they in turn may glorify God through their joyful suffering in this world. As John says in his first letter: "My little children, I am writing this to you so that you may not sin; but if anyone does sin, we have an advocate with the Father, Jesus Christ the righteous" (1 John 2:1). In his Gospel John uses the same word, advocate (*paracletos*), to designate the function of the Holy Spirit in guiding us to truth here on earth. Thus, whether the work is seen to be oriented to God in heaven or to people on earth, the gracious love of God is always all-sufficient for our needs. We are assured that we have an advocate, one who is called alongside to help us, whether we are strong in our works of love or weak in our failures of sin. Jesus Christ is our comforting, interceding friend whose suffering love is for us and the world.

Sorrowful for sin, joyful for forgiveness, we go forth with faith, love, hope, confidence, and Spirit-led imagination, sharing in the edification of the coming kingdom of God.

Eucharist and Eschaton

Our future is a mystery not solved but celebrated. We are engaged in a story which moves from a mysterious beginning to a more mysterious end, and its climax is the cross of Christ. The story we have to tell on Good Friday is about a man who was executed for treason and blasphemy. Yet he is the man we Christians worship as the God who created and redeemed us. This man from his cross said some strange things. He asked forgiveness for the people who killed him. He promised paradise to the thief next to him. This man spoke as if he were God. Who but God can promise paradise? Then he spoke as a man, with compassion and care for his mother, with anguish and pain from thirst, with horror and mystification for being forsaken by God. And finally he finished his work with a word of triumphant trust in his Father in heaven.

This drama reveals to us that Jesus is the Christ. God and Jesus are one and the same. This blessed contradiction, that Jesus is both true God and true man, is mind-boggling for theology but refreshing for faith. The story of Jesus' birth announces the holiness of this good earth. Therefore we are saved not by escaping to some timeless realm of immaterial spirit but we are saved in the midst of our suffering and serving here in our homes and schools and farms and factories. The coming of God as Jesus affirms the original creation. The wonder and infinite variety of events and things are all to the glory of God. Homer's rosy-fingered dawn and wine-dark sea praise the Creator as much as the psalmist when he sings: "Praise the Lord from the earth, you great sea creatures and all ocean depths, lightning and hail, snow and clouds, stormy winds that do his bidding." This resounding affirmation admonishes us to care for the precious and fragile creation with the consummate love that fathers and mothers have for their children. So Jesus the God-man, even when he was dying, cared for his mother and for all creation.

And Jesus' death propels us from this mortal earth into the joy of heaven. The cross conquers the spoliation of sin. The human cry of dereliction, "Why have you forsaken me?" becomes a triumphant, godly declaration of grace. "All is finished, the victory over sin and death is won, Satan has fallen like lightning from heaven." Our future has been fashioned for heaven with a glory that outshines the sun.

In the meantime, however, the revelation from the cross has produced the joyful celebration of Christian worship. It has many names and many meanings. Those who are bored with it or do not like it will be bored with heaven and will choose to stay away. We call our worship the breaking of bread, the Lord's Supper, the holy communion, the eucharist, the mass, the sacrament of the altar, the liturgy, the service of worship. It means the real presence of Christ giving us forgiveness and renewal through his victory over sin, death, and the devil. It means the sacrifice of atonement whereby God suffers for our iniquity and the sacrifice of thanksgiving whereby we offer our sin and death in a happy exchange for God's holiness and life. It means holy communion in which we receive unity of spirit with peace and justice for all. It means a memorial and proclamation of good news in which we placard before the world the scandal of the cross which paradoxically hallows and heals. And it means sacramental anticipation of the Messianic banquet at the Eschaton as we proclaim the Lord's death until he comes.

What is distinctive about Christian worship is the action of God in it. We are recipients of God's grace, and we do not offer anything to God to gain his favor. He does not need to be pleased because it has already pleased God to suffer on our behalf. In contrast, natural religion imagines God to be either hungry or angry.

Hungry gods must be propitiated by gifts which represent life. They crave the destruction of living things because the rhythm in nature is the drumbeat of life and death. Death is thought to bring new life. Without death constantly making room for new life the gods grow weak because death is the object of life and thus its food. The pulse-beat of eating and sacrificing, living and dying, is the cadence of nature. In pagan religion nature, gods, and devotees are physically and metaphysically one. So the bush people of Africa and the Indians of the Americas ate their gods to achieve divine communion. In the extreme form this became human sacrifices and ritual cannibalistic feasts. They could imagine they were eating the god because their gods were the forces of nature and the highest form of nature was the human form. The Aztecs danced in the skins of their sacrificial victims.

Angry gods must be mollified by ritual and moral performance in which the devotees work to expiate their sin so that they can offer themselves and their holiness to God for divine approval and thereby win rewards of prosperity on earth and happiness in heaven. This has manifested itself in legalism which has perverted the piety of all great religions. When people seek divine approval for behavior they arrogate to themselves a chosen status. Thus it is always an error to think that God's election of Israel, as a blessing to the Gentiles, means obedience to the law of Moses. The election is rather to be a witness to the promise of the Gospel (Genesis 12:30).

But Christian revelation tells us that the sacrifice which saves is not ours, not even the offering of thanksgiving which, of course, is our response to God's saving grace. Salvation is won for us by the atoning work of Jesus on the cross. He is the bread of life. He offers bread to us. His sacrament of bread and wine replaces all our frenetic offerings because he alone can give life. Pagan sacrifice offers life to God, whether in the simple wheat cakes and honey of Hindu *puja* or the catastrophic cannibalism of New Guinea bush people. The object is to win God's favor. The work is done by humans; an attempt is made to change God. Jews and Muslims say they attempt to offer a pure heart and a life of ritual and moral rectitude. Again the object is to win God's favor. Again the work is done by humans, but the attempt is to change us, not God, to make us acceptable to God. By contrast, in Christian worship the work is done by God. He makes the change in us. Liturgy is response to God's grace which comes before we ask. Thus we are free from the anxiety and labor of pleasing God. Salvation on earth and in heaven is beyond our power to achieve. This is God's work. Our work is to establish community. We may not fully realize a peaceable community in this life, but it *is* our work and we must use all our wit and wisdom to accomplish it. So in thanksgiving we present our bodies as living sacrifices. Not having to work at religion we are free to work for peace and justice.

Religion generally seeks to preserve the goodness of creation. Life is sought and its triumph over death has various shapes. Hope springs eternal, from the Hindu notion of re-incarnation to the *houri* paradise of Islam. Miraculous births, wonder-working gods, dying and rising deities, gods who bring wrath, gods who bring peace—these are the events and characters in the stories of natural religions around the world. The Christian story is different. Its climax is the cross with a sacrifice performed by God as his gracious gift to us. The unique revelation of Jesus is not a biological wonder of nature; it is a new creation. The cross of Jesus is not the defeat of a good man; it is God's victory over Satan. And the resurrection of Jesus is not a miraculous resuscitation but the first fruits of a new heaven and a new earth. Lazarus came forth from the tomb to die again. Jesus came forth to ascend to his Father in heaven, and, behold, all things shall become new. This is not the eternal return in the cycle of nature but the eschatological eucatastrophe which brings hope for the future.

The Father of our Lord Jesus Christ is neither hungry nor angry. He prevails with suffering love. His grief over Satan's rebellion and our complicity is the story of the cross. He joined himself to our sinful, mortal dust so that when he rose again from the dead he could liberate us from death's captivity and raise us in glory to his victorious heavenly throne. Satan has fallen like lightning from heaven, the great Beast is beaten, the original Worm can work no harm. We are free. We are clean. We have nothing to fear. Our future is secure in the embrace of Christ who died that we might live. What all this means we cannot begin to imagine. "No eye has seen, no ear has heard, no mind has conceived what God has prepared for those who love him" (1 Corinthians 2:9).

An old Danish fable tells about a spider that slides down a single thread from the lofty rafters of a barn. Spiders attach a thread from above and then ride down that thread until they reach the floor or a rafter below. This spider found a good location for her web and prospered there for some time. One day she was wandering about her premises and she saw the thread stretching up into the dark unseen above her. "What's that for," she said, and snapped off the thread. At once the whole web collapsed, because everything in her home depended on this attachment to the rafter above.

There is a tie of faith that binds our life to the unseen above us. Our web of life includes our homes, our government, our schools, our businesses, our farms, our legal structures, our church; and all this depends on the tie to the unseen above us and ahead of us, for the unseen God is the source of all life and goodness. Break that tie and there is collapse and ruin. Keep the tie of faith and everything in life will be secure because it rests in God.

When Jesus came preaching to people on earth he demanded a personal faith in himself because he was that thread, that tie, which we have with the unseen; and this unseen God not only lifts us upward in the present but he also pulls us forward into the future. Jesus is the link we have with our Father in heaven. Jesus said: "He who has seen me has seen the Father. Let not your hearts be troubled; you believe in God, believe also in me. I am the way, the truth, and the life. No one comes unto the Father but by me." Because Jesus died on the cross we can endure the fiercest onslaught of the devil. In our present sorrow and fright Jesus raises us in hope and carries us into a future destiny that is rich in mystery and overflowing with eternal happiness.

Amen. Come, Lord Jesus.

Revelation and Eschatology

The language of the Bible which deals with eschatology, the last things, is invariably poetic and metaphorical. Images are portrayed graphically with the intent to stir us to feel with intensity and to act on our feeling with hopeful courage and faithful conviction. The story of God's destiny for his creatures moves to a triumphant conclusion, the mystery of which is beyond our comprehension but totally satisfying for those whose trust is in the Lord. The end time cannot be literally defined or described, any more than the beginning time, and hence everything is veiled in suggestion.

Much of prophetic writing in Scripture was politically motivated. The politics of the Israelites, however, had more than a horizontal dimension. All community relationships were understood to be shaped by Yahweh, the God who had called them to establish his Lordship among all nations. Yahweh would therefore rescue Israel from his enemies so that Israel could be a light to the Gentiles. Most of this biblical literature is exhortation to preserve the integrity of Israel as a nation. The trials of establishing a cohesive community in the land of Canaan among the Edomites, Moabites, and Ammonites were perceived as directed by Yahweh for their historical destiny. This belief in God's care for his chosen people continued and was intensified in Israel's later history during the division of the kingdoms of Samaria and Judah, and during the Babylonian exile. All this is historical and penultimate, not eschatolgocial.

The vertical dimension of God's intervention on Israel's behalf, however, led to the projection of visions of intimacy that went beyond the vicissitudes of history. The problem of human sin was seen to be so great that a radical renewal was called for to correct it. Daniel's vision is directed to the "time of the end." The pictures of beasts with horns are allegorical, much like political cartoons about national tensions and divisions on the editorial pages of a newspaper today. They represent the kings and nations of the time struggling for supremacy. The purpose of the vision is to inspire hope and courage in the face of menacing enemies that assail the Israelites from all sides. But beyond the instruction to be vigilant and to keep pure and faithful there is the intimation that the final solution to all human trouble must transcend this "bank and shoal of time."

The last book of the Bible likewise deals with the last things, not the end of time but the time of the end. The language is again metaphorical and graphic. Weird pictures are drawn with wild stories about a red dragon with seven heads and ten horns and another beast with "two horns like a lamb but he spoke like a dragon." It is folly to try to make intellectual sense of these images. They should simply be enjoyed for their powerful, colorful, stimulating impact upon our sensibilities. The tapestry by Jan Lurcat in the apse of the chapel at Assy in France tells in dramatic design and color the vision of John of the woman who was clothed with the sun with her feet on the moon. The story told in this vision is the mythical portrayal of the same story told in historical form by the Gospels. We need not theologize about it or reduce it to abstract concepts. We should rather let it speak to us and move us heartfully to confidence and courage in the midst of our fears and doubts and desperation.

Eschatological visions and images probe heights and depths in our present consciousness, but they also project hope for the future in a final sense. They are intended to tell us that history is penultimate, that we have a destiny that reaches into a time beyond this era of our exile from Eden. While history does not repeat itself, the mistakes of the past are often repeated because people do not learn from them, and this leads to a cynicism in which we give up hope. Revelation about the future Eschaton restores hope and gives us courage to live in the present.

It is this thrust of ultimacy that brings together the eschaton and the eucharist. The sacrament of bread and wine is a prolepsis of the Messianic banquet in the age that is to come. Jesus referred to this at the last Passover meal he had with his disciples before he was crucified: "For I tell you I will not drink again of the fruit of the vine until the kingdom of God comes" (Luke 22:18).

The significance of the eucharist in which we celebrate the real presence of Christ marvelously includes the anticipation of the future fulfillment of the kingdom of God. The beginning of the kingdom is already here in the presence of Jesus, but this presence is veiled in the flesh. The disciples saw only a human person like themselves, not the glorified Son of the holy Trinity. We see bread and wine, again not the glorified Son of the holy Trinity. But the Son of the holy Trinity came into the flesh of Jesus by the power of the holy Spirit, and the Son comes into the bread and the wine by the same power for us all. This mystery we cannot fathom, but our faith celebrates it. And because of the earthly presence of the eternal heavenly Son we can be sure that in the future, according to God's appointment of time, the same Son who is present to us now will be revealed in glory to us then.

We must clearly distinguish the passages in Scripture which refer to signs of historical events from passages that refer to the time of the end. The struggles of Israel and their kings, the slavery in Egypt, the exile in Babylon, the oppression of the Roman Empire are all penultimate concerns. They should be instructive to us in our historical tensions and tribulations, but they should not be taken allegorically nor literally as predictions for the present. Jesus spoke of nation rising against nation, of fearful events and great signs from heaven, of Jerusalem being surrounded by armies. He said the people in Judea should flee to the mountains, and those in the city should get out, and those in the country should not enter the city. Obviously he was referring to the impending destruction of Jerusalem under Roman oppression, not the final end of this age, not the Eschaton.

But when Jesus spoke at the last supper with his disciples about eating again at the fulfillment of the kingdom of God, he was clearly referring to the Eschaton. Paul made the same reference to this transcending hope in his hymn of love in the first letter to the Corinthians: "For we know in part and we prophesy in part, but when perfection comes, the imperfect disappears."

Both the great weight of sin and the magnificent grace of God call for a new heaven and a new earth. This world in which we now live is too fraught with ambiguity, division, destruction, and death to be the place or the time for our final reconciliation with God. Nothing short of a new creation will bring us, not back, but forward to meet our Creator and Redeemer face to face. We live now by faith, but then we shall see reality as it is; we shall look into the eyes of Jesus and see through his tears and his smile the grace and glory of God.

Unfortunately the story of the human search for salvation tells us that we do not want to live by faith. We want to grasp certainty about the future from the signs of the times. Whenever times produce tensions that are severe people project their fears to a cosmic solution which can be seen in the world-shaking events that are causing their fears. Both catastrophes caused by human origins and natural upheavals such as earthquakes and tsunamis prompt people to read into them a sign of divine retribution.

The error is a repeated failure to understand the development of revelation, which is a progression from the earliest accounts of God as an instrument of wrath, as in the flood, to God as a Father of mercy, as in the incarnation of Jesus. In spite of the good news of salvation by the sacrifice of Jesus, from time to time, because of terrible tribulations, people seek comfort in a cataclysmic intervention by God to set things right. The Civil War, World War I, the rise of Hitler, Communism, the threat of nuclear weapons all have been taken to be signs of the end, even though Jesus specifically said this kind of worldly disturbance does not predict the time of the end (Luke 21:9). Yet people are duped by such predictions. Popular apocalypticism, with a complete misreading of Scripture, invents a blueprint for the end times which feeds on the fears of millions.

Because the world has run amok it is assumed God will straighten things out with a plan that is as precise as it is fanciful. Supposedly we are now in the era of the Christian Church, a time when we can look for the signs of approaching doom when a sudden "rapture" will occur. The chosen living Christians will be lifted up to heaven along with deceased Christians of former times. The wicked unbelievers will be "left behind," and the chosen ones will be united with Christ in heaven as his holy bride. Those who are "left behind" will suffer tribulation under the terrible tyranny of the devil who will rule for a time until the Second Coming of Christ who will vanquish his enemy in the battle of Armageddon. Jesus will reign then for a thousand years, after which Satan will be released and then destroyed. The resurrection of judgment follows and those whose names are not written in the Book of Life are cast into the lake of fire.

This scheme is especially attractive because it presents details which give it the appearance of authenticity, and it claims revelatory support. There is no justification for this religious speculation, certainly not in Scripture nor in the life of the Church. While Scripture and the history of the Church clearly affirm a cosmic struggle between God and his adversary, and our creeds proclaim belief in the final resurrection of the dead, there is no justification for millennial apocalypticism with the threat of a rapture. We simply cannot write God's story for him. He, and he alone, is its author, and we must wait for him to give us our lines. Moreover, there is no need for us to know the precise plan of God for the end times. It is sufficient for us, and indeed altogether proper for us, to know and rejoice in the gospel of forgiveness and resurrection, which frees us to concentrate our energies on immediate opportunities to serve in this world. The author of the book of Revelation warns his readers not to add anything to his words of prophecy. Let us therefore rest with the wonderful promise that Jesus will come. Amen! Come, Lord Jesus.

A Eucharistic Prayer

Our gracious Father in heaven,
We shudder in awe
At your glory and mercy.
We thank you, thank you, thank you.
Your silence in beginning
Punctuates our lives.
Singing from your imagination
Has brought us into the beauty of being.
Sweet breath from your Spirit
Surprises us into life.
Snowy owl and swirling nebula
Witness to your majesty.

Divine Disclosure

Ancient loon and whelping whale
Ride waves of roiling wind.
You turn the tumult, still the storm.
Kyrie eleison.

The garden you gave us to tend with joy
We spoiled by believing the devil's lie.
Expelled now we build in an alien land
A city both wondrous and doomed to decay.
Kyrie eleison.

The waters once drowned the nubile earth,
And buoyed up the Ark;
A rainbow replaced your wrath.
With promise you made from nothing
A people gifted with light.
Delivered from Egypt,
Returned from Babylon,
With law and temple they endured.
Your Word and Spirit returned not void,
A fire of warning, a cooling hope.
But no one believed,
And all went astray;
You delivered them up to go their own way.
Kyrie eleison.

Then mercy prevailed.
Christ came as a child,
Son of God, son of Mary.
Gentle Jesus, King and Lord,
With pierced side and blood outpoured,
He suffered death and gives us life.
Grant all wassail for Christ we hail!
Christe eleison.

Christ has died, Christ is risen, Christ will come again.

Now bread he gives and wine to all,
As on the night when Judas fell.
Christ's presence real in earthly fruits
We celebrate with heavenly joy,
Invoking his Word, recalling his life.

Ad Futurum et Mysterium

His Word creates, his life redeems.
"Given for you
In remembrance of me,
This is my body, this my blood."

Amen. Come, Lord Jesus.

Your Church, a leaven in the world,
Cries out for ferment, freedom, right.
Send down upon our darkness light;
Renew us with your Spirit bright.

Amen, Come, Holy Spirit.

Sanctify these gifts and us.
Straightly steer our course to thee;
Forgive us when we list to starboard or port.
The future you give in mystery;
Its freedom frightens
And beckons in time of the end,
Not the end of time
But the beginning of all things new.
Kyrie eleison.

With all the hosts of heaven and earth
We join our praise in glory,
And thank you, thank you, thank you,
Creator Holy Spirit.
Domine, dona nobis pacem.
Kyrie eleison.

Amen. Gracious Father, come.

www.ingramcontent.com/pod-product-compliance
Lightning Source LLC
Chambersburg PA
CBHW050350230426
43663CB00010B/2064